Selected Correspondence of Bernard Shaw

Bernard Shaw and H.G. Wells

Selected Correspondence of Bernard Shaw

Bernard Shaw and H.G. Wells

Edited by J. Percy Smith

UNIVERSITY OF TORONTO PRESS

Toronto Buffalo London

Published by University of Toronto Press Incorporated

Toronto Buffalo London
Printed in Canada
Reprinted in 2018
ISBN 0-8020-3001-7
ISBN 978-1-4875-7214-3 (paper)

Printed on acid-free paper

Canadian Cataloguing in Publication Data

Shaw, Bernard, 1856–1950
Selected correspondence of Bernard Shaw

Includes bibliographical references and index.
Contents: v. 2. Bernard Shaw and H.G. Wells.
ISBN 0-8020-3001-7 (v. 2)

1. Shaw, Bernard, 1856–1950 – Correspondence.
I. Smith, J. Percy. II. Title.

PR5366.A48 1995 826'.912 C95-930151-8

University of Toronto Press acknowledges the financial assistance to its publishing program of the Canada Council and the Ontario Arts Council.

The Press also acknowledges a generous subvention from Mr John Wardrop. We also thank the Academy of the Shaw Festival and the University of Guelph for their support.

Contents

for M.K.

'a Bright Particular Star'

General Editor's Note

What is astonishing about Bernard Shaw's correspondence is not its sheer abundance. That a professional author with wide interests should in the course of a long life write a great many letters – even into the thousands – is not remarkable. That one should do so in unfailingly athletic prose, invariably directing at his correspondent a fund of detailed knowledge and a combination of forthrightness, penetrative argument, teasing wit, and good humour – in short, invariably projecting the persona of the author – is extraordinary indeed. These qualities appear when Shaw is writing to friends and adversaries, public personages, and private citizens, from the world of theatre, of letters, of political affairs.

Obviously, any item in Shaw's correspondence projects one voice in a dialogue that might be long-continued, involving another voice often capable of responding to Shaw in terms as forthright and downright as his own – if seldom as witty. The volumes in the present series are intended to make available some of the longer dialogues that GBS had with particular friends and colleagues in various fields: fellow workers in literature or socialism, translators of his plays, the film producer Gabriel Pascal, the illustrator John Farleigh, and so on. Other volumes will comprise letters written exclusively by Shaw to a large number of individuals focusing on particular aspects of his career, such as the theatre and publishing.

The Selected Correspondence of Bernard Shaw series has been planned by an editorial advisory board made up of senior Shavian scholars. The aim of these volumes is to present accurate texts of letters almost all of which are previously unpublished and situate them in the context of Bernard Shaw's life and career.

J. Percy Smith

Introduction

Whatever subsequent history may have to say of them, Bernard Shaw and H.G. Wells were among the best-known figures of the twentieth century: their words were read, their voices heard, their figures and faces seen everywhere in the world. Both were zestful heretics, vigorous and outspoken, rebelliously critical of the social and political, familial and sexual conventions and structures of their time, and determined that they must be changed. Both wrote professionally, voluminously, compulsively. 'GBS and H.G. Wells cannot stop writing,'[1] Beatrice Webb noted in her diary in 1943; 'they will die with an unfinished book on their desk.' She might as aptly have spoken of an unfinished letter; for the two men were obsessive composers of letters – to their friends, their enemies, the world, and each other.

There existed between them strength of opinion and readiness of wit, and also – too often unrecognized – a richness of feeling more worthy of them than the antagonisms that have at times divided their respective followers. 'The idea must not get about that the Wellsians and Shavians have any differences,' Shaw wrote in his eighty-fifth year. 'They are in fact the same body.'[2] On the next day Wells, who had just seen the film *Major Barbara*,[3] wrote to GBS, 'Our minds move in sympathy.' And he concluded, 'Whatever happens now we have had a pretty good time.' That they debated vigorously and sometimes quarrelled ferociously will be obvious to any reader of this volume. They argued insultingly in their private correspondence and outrageously in the press, at least once reaching a point at which reconciliation seemed impossible. They provided what Vincent Brome called a 'study in quarrelling.'[4]

They first met in January 1895 as they emerged from the St James's Theatre after watching the notorious first performance of Henry James's *Guy Domville*. They walked northward together to their respective dwellings, the first of many such walks. Four decades later, remembering that occasion and Shaw's talking 'like an elder brother to me in that agreeable Dublin accent of his,' Wells reflected, 'I liked him with a liking that has lasted a lifetime.'[5] At almost the same time Shaw commented reflectively, '[Wells and I] are old friends; and we like oneanother as well as any two mortal men can.'[6]

Quite aside from their native genius, verbal fluency, and ebullient high spirits, the two had much in common. Each was a product of a marriage in which the husband was ineffectual as breadwinner and parent, the wife much the stronger personality. Each had known the miserable frustrations of bad early schooling. Each had had to struggle through a series of vocational false starts: when they met they were scarcely past the beginning of their ultimately illustrious careers. They shared, too, rebellious and unpopular views of society and its mores, held strong opinions about liberty of thought and opinion, the wrongs of capitalism, the rights of the working classes, sexual freedom, Christianity and its errors, the rights of women, the tyranny of the family: in short, both were radicals and socialists. Shaw, whose love affair with Jennie Patterson was ten years in the past and had been succeeded by others less tempestuous, would in two years begin his long, quiet marriage with the green-eyed millionairess Charlotte Payne-Townshend. Wells's first marriage, of four years, had ended, and soon he would marry Catherine Robbins, with whom he had been living for many months. He had not yet begun his notorious and numerous exercises of his belief in sexual freedom. The roles of both Charlotte Shaw and Catherine (soon to be known universally as 'Jane') Wells in the careers of their husbands, as well as in their personal relationships, were crucial.

The differences between the two men – and they were emphatic – arose in part from disparities in age, education, and experience. The Irishman Shaw was born in 1856 – virtually a decade before the Englishman Wells. Moreover, the Shaws – however 'downstart,' as GBS liked to call them – had aristocratic connections, upper-middle-class tastes and manners, even if they could not afford them. Shaw's father had been engaged in 'trade' (in which he was a failure), but it was 'wholesale' and therefore not quite unbecoming to one of his class connections. Wells's father was first employed as a gardener, became briefly a professional cricketer, and was then forced by bad luck into shopkeeping (in which he too was a failure). HGW himself, having had two years of oppressive experience as apprentice to a draper, escaped through his combined grit and genius. Physically, Shaw was tall, erect, lean, impressive in appearance, with a strong, clear voice. Wells was short and slight when young, later inclined to be pudgy, with a soft voice liable under stress to become squeaky. Inevitably both men were conscious of these differences; not surprisingly, Shaw was never entirely above reminding Wells of them – in however teasing a manner – knowing that they combined to give him a psychological advantage, not merely a physical one, and that the reminders were for Wells irritatingly unpleasant. Sometimes they goaded him to fury, providing Shaw with the delight of a verbal victory that he may not have deserved, as in the case of Wells's second visit to Stalin. In his *New Statesman* comment on that visit,[7] Shaw's impish choice of the verb 'trotted' to describe Wells's entry into the Kremlin was enough to provoke a furious retort that could only reduce the impact of Wells's account – just as GBS intended.

Other distinctions were of greater importance. At the time of that first meeting, Shaw was thirty-nine years old, Wells twenty-nine. The chronological difference in itself mattered little; the difference in the range and nature of their experience mattered a great deal. In particular, one aspect of Shaw's development is crucial to our understanding of the relationship. It had a dual nature, combining development of the skills of the orator, the debater, the platform artist, with the knowledge, quick perceptiveness, humour, and sharp analytical judgment of one who had read widely in the literature of social and economic theory, thought deeply about it, and discussed it interminably in public and private for a decade and a half with economists, politicians, Marxists and other socialists, republicans, and anarchists: political thinkers of every stripe. In November 1887 Shaw had participated in the march and demonstration by the unemployed that was forcibly broken up by mounted police in Trafalgar Square on what came to be called 'Bloody Sunday'; and the object lesson of that day was not lost on him. Of what is commonly called success he had had scarcely a taste. Yet he had become well enough known to have received two invitations from Liberal constituencies in London to stand for nomination in the election held in the spring of 1889 and accepted one of them – though he was not in fact chosen as the candidate, essentially because he could not afford to pay his election expenses.

By then Shaw had been for long an avowed socialist, and a member of the Fabian Society, that little group of intellectuals dedicated to social betterment, virtually since its inception in 1884. His long, self-imposed apprenticeship had not only equipped him with the skills of a debater and a politician. It had brought him – whatever his youthful attitudes may have been – to a view of human nature that combined mistrust, often amounting to hatred, of existing political and social institutions, with an equally strong conviction that the way to betterment meant much more of patient toil than of exciting drama: hence the value of laughter. He never ceased to work – lecturing, campaigning, pamphleteering, serving on countless committees – for the cause of socialism. Yet even while doing so, he early recognized that the mass of humanity for whom his message was intended would not be reached for a very long time, much less moved to effective action, by what he and his like had to say. So in the *Fabian Election Manifesto 1892* that he wrote for the Fabian Society, even while arguing the case for an Independent Labour Party he remarked: 'The same workman who pleads want of education and opportunity as an excuse for not understanding party politics is at no loss when the subject is football, or racing, or pigeon-flying, or any subject, however complicated, that he really wants to understand.'[8] A year later, as one of five Fabian Society members in a delegation of some sixty-five British socialists at an International Socialist Workers Congress in Zurich, Shaw was just slightly less acerbic: 'The average English worker ... does not yet believe in the capacity of his class for governing and will not give himself any serious trouble about politics. But he has the invaluable quality of never being satisfied. He is the worst Socialist and the best Grumbler in Europe.'[9]

While Shaw's artistic genius was at last to find its home in the theatre, his proclaimed commitment to socialism and the human freedom that it implied ended only with his death. The last of Wells's letters to him, in 1944, has to do with Shaw's nonagenarian final book of socio-political analysis and propaganda. Long before that, in September 1924, Shaw had summed up the effect of his experience in a lecture at Kingsway

Hall: 'Socialists [he said, according to his draft notes now in the British Library] usually begin with no experience and great expectations. They mature with great experience and no expectations.' Yet he went on to argue that 'the Fabian who had become a pessimist wakes up and becomes a hopeful and vigilant opportunist.'[10]

In short, Shaw was a passionate socialist and an experienced campaigner who had learned the principle of the inevitability of gradualness well before he joined the Fabian Society. When he and Wells met he had had almost two decades of working at socialism, intellectually and practically. As his playwriting and theatrical career occupied more and more of his time, he found – not surprisingly – that he had become tired of Fabian work, felt indeed that younger people with fresh ideas should take up its leadership; but his loyalty to its principles and spirit, and to his early Fabian friends, did not end. A year or two before Wells in his autobiography expressed, not for the first time, his contempt for Fabianism,[11] Shaw was asserting that the need for it was greater than ever – in part because the constitutional methods that it insisted on offered the only apparent alternative to the emergence of dictatorships.[12]

Despite the similarities of background that have been mentioned, the case of Wells was in fact sharply different. If Shaw could say in later life, jocularly but not altogether truthfully, 'I did not throw myself into the struggle for life; I threw my mother into it,'[13] Wells did not need to make such an admission. Very soon after he became, under his mother's pietistic influence (for Wells testifies that her belief in drapers was almost as unquestioning as her faith in God) an apprentice in a draper's shop, he recognized not only that he could never live a life restricted by pins and measured by tapes, but that if he wanted to rise to something better he would have to free himself entirely from parental authority and make his own way. That Wells did so – with not a few false starts and steps – testifies to his imagination, his courage, his determination, his essential high spirits. For a long, long time he had to fight not only grim poverty in an unsympathetic world, but physical illness and hunger, loneliness, emotional deprivation. Shaw's description of him as 'a spoiled child,' in the piece that he wrote in 1909 for *The Christian Commonwealth*, and later included in the volume called *Pen Portraits and Reviews* (1931), is less than fair, however teasingly intended.

Thus, when Shaw was educating himself in socialism and political activity, Wells was making his way – sometimes with brilliance, sometimes not – up the ladder of more formal schooling and incidental employment. He succeeded in enrolling at the Normal School of Science, having the burning excitement of science and its possibilities roused in him by T.H. Huxley's lectures, and almost having it dissipated by duller teachers who nevertheless could not extinguish the flame of interest, especially in biology, that Huxley had lit. Gradually he was to discover his role to be not in the practice of teaching science but in the exploration through the medium of fiction of some directions it might take, some imagined possibilities.

Wells too was learning socialism. His response to the harsh realities that he had experienced, which might have caused a lesser spirit to look for a refuge, made him only hostile to things as they were and restless to change them. He read Henry George's *Progress and Poverty* and other economic treatises. He began attending socialist meetings such as the Sunday evening gatherings at William Morris's house in Hammersmith (where he watched and listened to the young Shaw, though he did not then meet him). He became active in the Debating Society at the Normal School, and at least one member found him unequalled as a speaker – witty and brilliant.[14] But it was after he had reached success as a writer that Wells joined the Fabian Society. That was in 1903, and one of his two sponsors was Shaw.

The letters (with their head- and end-notes) tell the remainder of the story; but one is bound to ask a crucial question: why, if Shaw and Wells so liked each other and their minds moved in sympathy, did they so often bash each other about, publicly and in private? A partial explanation of course is that they enjoyed the exercise: Shaw as a young man had had some training as a boxer, and had loved the ring. Wells was less an athlete, yet had a passion for games – indeed, invented them and became famous for them. That such a pair should become sparring partners, exercising their skills to the full, for the most part good-naturedly, in contests of ideas and wits, is unsurprising.

Yet the matter goes deeper. There were subjects about which the two had profound intellectual differences. For example, some of their most interesting and amusing exchanges deal with the nature of science and the philosophical, ethical, and religious problems posed by it, in particular by biology and evolutionary theory: interesting because of the seriousness of the subject-matter, amusing because of the exuberance and good nature of the sparring. Wells felt secure on the ground explored by Darwin and his followers; Shaw, rejecting outright the notion of life and consciousness as purposeless accidents, developed his hypothesis of Creative Evolution, made it his religion, and was equally secure in it. On such matters the two could argue vehemently with the greatest good will. That does not at all mean that Wells turned his back on the deepest religious questions: his autobiography makes that clear, as do several of his books. Indeed, as the Second World War darkened over them, the minds of the two friends seem almost to have met in a common desperate notion: that the process of evolution (or the Life Force working through it) might indeed be abandoning *homo sapiens* as an evolutionary mistake. Mind having reached the end of its tether, Man will finally be replaced by another Lord of Creation, Wells affirmed in 1945 – a year before his own death.[15] 'Mankind is an experiment in godhead, so far not a successful one,' Shaw wrote in 1946. 'But the Life Force will no doubt try again.'[16]

In any case, readers of the letters will recognize that not all the exchanges were good-natured sparring, that the tone of some is not an invitation to laughter. They are the expression not merely of intellectual differences, but of profound convictions about human nature, conduct, values, modes of behaviour – passionately held, passionately stated.

The most obvious differences of conviction had to do with the nature, and more especially the methods, of science. As to the former, Shaw wrote in 1901, 'These doctors all think that science is knowledge, instead of being the very opposite of knowledge: to wit, speculation.'[17] 'Science,' Wells replied, 'is neither knowledge nor speculation. It is criticism ending in wisdom.'[18] Shaw did not retort directly. He had for many months been at work on *Man and Superman*, with its eventual subtitle 'A Comedy and a Philosophy,' finding dramatic form for what he knew of speculation, criticism, and wisdom. His sense of the significance of metaphysics was to be fully expressed in the Preface to *Back to Methuselah* (1921). He and Wells had none the less a common concern for what Matthew Arnold called the application of ideas to life.[19]

Their sparring over the issues arising from that concern might be gloveless and fierce. It tended to centre on two questions, especially in relation to biology: whether life, as evolved and evolving, has a purpose;

and whether there are moral considerations that must govern the ways in which humanity, as the most highly evolved form of life, deals with the other forms. For Shaw, to deny the first question was stupid and unimaginative; to deny the second was a diabolical betrayal of humanity itself. For Wells, the first was unsupported by anything in science, the other was secondary to the claims of scientific investigation. The flash-point for the two different views was most frequently the practice of vivisection: Wells admiring the courage and imagination of Pavlov, for example, and Shaw stirred to Swiftian rage by the arrogant cruelty involved in experiments on animals. These were more often the subjects of debates in the press than in their personal correspondence; yet on occasion they appear here also.

In spite of such deeply held differences, Wells and Shaw retained – with vicissitudes that the reader of this volume will note – their closeness of friendly relationship through more than forty years. The fact is even more surprising when one recognizes that, mixed with their genuine mutual admiration and esteem and the qualities that lay behind them, there were temperamental differences that at times brought the relationship close to breaking. The most obvious example is the earliest.

When Wells joined the Fabian Society, filled with enthusiasm for the cause of social changes of many sorts, and attracting to it many a younger enthusiast inspired by his energy and charm as well as his genius, he joined a group of people as desirous as he for social change. Yet those of Shaw's generation had come to believe deeply in the necessity of basing action on analysis; of constitutionalism; of educating politicians regardless of party; of mistrust of violent or dramatic methods. None of which suited Wells in the least, as to either temper or program. That he and his followers should clash with the 'Old Gang' – Shaw, Sidney and Beatrice Webb, Hubert Bland, and so on – was inevitable.

The clash and its outcome are sufficiently dealt with in the letters and their accompanying annotations. One may conclude that Wells was on the wrong side in the quarrel, or simply that he handled the affair badly; but despite (perhaps in part because of) the laughter that accompanied Shaw's merciless destruction of him, it is easy to see why Beatrice Webb found the whole business 'altogether horrid.' The fact that before long the two men had resumed their friendship on a basis of greater candour says much for their essential mutual regard.

Aspects of Shaw's temperament could indeed be irritating and at times deeply hurtful to Wells. Shaw's readiness to assume a pose of Olympian authority (as in the Fabian affair), and to lecture Wells as if he were a schoolboy (as in the aftermath), was not always or necessarily amusing to his subject. Potentially far more hurtful and complex was Shaw's difficulty, which he himself recognized, in dealing with the idea of useless and unaccountable physical suffering and untimely death. His letters to Wells and to Dorothy Cheston Bennett at the time of Jane Wells's fatal illness are tactless to the point of being bizarre, though that very quality is an indication of the pain that he himself felt; for he was deeply fond of Jane. Perhaps the other side of his own pain is to be seen in his consistent refusal to comment on Wells's sexual adventurousness.

In one of the later letters, Shaw does comment on an aspect of Wells's temperament with which he had to learn to deal. Perhaps it was HGW's exuberant energy, too much for his slight frame, or some directly physiological imbalance that at times caused him to break into ungovernable anger, or periods of the kind of sulky rage that, as Shaw said, used to be called 'the spleen.' The most notorious of the resulting quarrels – which could destroy friendships totally – involved Wells with Henry James. The best example provided in the Shaw/Wells correspondence is the one that eventually involved the Society of Authors, in which GBS played – not without difficulty – the role of advisor to HGW. Although on that occasion he intervened, Shaw had learned through observation and experience that in such times of brooding anger it was best to leave Wells alone. A free discussion of this perplexing aspect of HGW's personality that is sympathetic and candid, but never demeaning or lacking in warmth, is provided in Vincent Brome's biography, called simply *Wells*.[20]

Doubtless Shaw's self-esteem as well as his humour, and what Frank Harris called 'his exasperating patience,'[21] protected him from the shafts that Wells directed at him. Certainly the letters collected here tell of the long friendship of two writers of genius, whose mutual liking overcame and outlasted their temperamental and other differences. Reflecting on them, one may regret that Wells did not devise a working model of his Time Machine that would enable us now to overhear him conversing with GBS, ferociously or not, in whatever Utopian world they may now be arranging to rearrange.

NOTES

1 The Diary of Beatrice Webb, ed. Norman and Jeanne MacKenzie, vol. 4 (Cambridge: Belknap Press of Harvard University Press 1985), 485
2 See p. 190, below.
3 See p. 191, below.
4 Vincent Brome, *Six Studies in Quarrelling* (London: Cresset 1958)
5 H.G. Wells, *Experiment in Autobiography* (London: Macmillan 1934), 455
6 Bernard Shaw, *Collected Letters 1926–1950*, vol. 4, ed. Dan H. Laurence (London: Max Reinhardt 1988), 393
7 *New Statesman and Nation*, 24 November 1934
8 *Fabian Election Manifesto 1892*, Fabian Tract no. 40 (London: Fabian Society 1892), 9
9 BL 50680 f 40
10 BL 50557, f 269
11 *Experiment*, 201ff. and elsewhere
12 'Preface to the 1931 Reprint,' in *Fabian Essays in Socialism* (London: George Allen & Unwin 1931)
13 *The Irrational Knot*, 'Preface to American Edition of 1905' (New York: Brentano's 1905), xx
14 Elizabeth Healey, quoted in Norman and Jeanne MacKenzie, *The Time Traveller* (London: Weidenfeld & Nicolson 1973), 61
15 *Mind at the End of Its Tether* (New York: Didier 1946), 19
16 Letter to *The Freethinker*, 30 June 1946, published in *Bernard Shaw, Agitations: Letters to the Press 1875–1950*, ed. Dan H. Laurence and James Rambeau (New York: Frederick Ungar 1985), 339
17 See p. 8, below.
18 See p. 10, below.
19 'The Study of Poetry,' in *Essays in Criticism, Second Series* (London: Macmillan 1888)
20 Vincent Brome, *Wells* (London: Longmans, Green 1951)
21 Frank Harris, *Bernard Shaw* (London: Gollancz 1931), 263

Editor's Note

The letters in this volume are almost exclusively the personal correspondence of Bernard Shaw and H.G. Wells. A few by other hands are included, in whole or part, to assist the reader's understanding of events in which the two men were concerned. Most of these were written by Shaw's wife, Charlotte F. Shaw. No attempt has been made to include the large number of letters written to newspapers. Those exchanges – fascinating and still timely as many of them are – were in essence vigorous public debates on a wide range of topics, and not infrequently drew in other writers. Their inclusion here would both double the size of this volume and to some extent divert it from its purpose. For the particular intention is to provide insight into two remarkable personalities in a relationship closer than that offered by records of public debates, even when the participants are incomparably unabashed self-publicists. A very few exceptions have been made for 'public' letters that had also a private intention.

The gaps in time that occur in the correspondence, some of them several years in length, may be attributed to various causes. Over a long period the Shaws and Wellses met socially with some regularity, as the diaries of both Jane Wells and Charlotte Shaw testify – not to mention references in the letters themselves – making much letter-writing superfluous. They had common interests in music and the theatre, and indeed shared dramatic occasions that needed no theatre: the copyright performance of Granville Barker's *Waste*, for example, or (earlier) Shaw's *Man and Superman*, a copy of which Shaw gave to the Wellses with the inscription,

Read, for the very first time in its life,
To H.G. Wells and Jane his wife

Moreover, for a time they were meeting in Fabian Society gatherings, committees, and the like.

Not all the gaps had similar causes. Shaw and Wells were extremely busy professional writers and eminent public figures, much in demand for a wide variety of causes. Finally, it must be added that both travelled a great deal – and that Wells in particular spent long periods of time on the Continent, especially during the course of his liaison with Odette Keun. Other causes are referred to in the letters themselves. All things considered, it is surprising that so many survived – a fact that, as David C. Smith has pointed out, is largely due to the diligence of Wells's daughter-in-law, Marjorie Craig Wells, who after his death 'bundled up much of the personal correspondence in his files and posted letters back to their recipients' (*H.G. WELLS Desperately Mortal* [New Haven: Yale University Press], 363). As Smith goes on to say, that fact does not preclude the possibility of further letters eventually coming to light.

Her efforts may, however, explain why of the more than 150 letters in the correspondence, about two-thirds were written by Shaw. Of these a score are contained in Dan Laurence's four-volume collection: Bernard Shaw *Collected Letters*. Virtually all the others are here published for the first time, as is true also of the letters of Wells. A few of the latter have appeared, in whole or in part, in biographies and other works; unfortunately no published general collection of Wells's letters exists. This fact, as well as the preponderance of Shaw's letters, may be partly due to the Wellsian impetuosity, which – although it has a certain charm – is reflected in his breathtaking penmanship, as also in his frequent omission of addresses and dates, matters in which GBS was almost unfailingly scrupulous.

In presenting the correspondence a good deal of bridging material has been necessary, for which there are two reasons. First, the letters span four and a half eventful decades; and while some of the 'events' – the First World War, for example – need virtually no comment, some others, from the Fabian Society tempest to Wells's quarrel involving the Society of Authors, require that the circumstances be outlined. Second, it is simple fact that Shaw and Wells were among the most allusive of writers, and their letters are at times thick with passing references: a matter especially true of Shaw, who once remarked that classical literature consists largely of allusions.

Material sufficient to place each letter in its context is provided in the form of a headnote preceding the letter. Annotative matter follows the letter, the subject of each annotation being in boldface type. This arrangement enables the reader to be provided with relevant contextual information before proceeding to a letter, and to read without the irritating interruption of numbers pointing to footnotes that he or she may not require.

As in the other volumes of the series, the persistent idiosyncracies in Shaw's spelling and punctuation have been preserved. Rather than introducing cycles of *sics*, however, occasional obvious errors in spelling and the like have been silently corrected. Necessary editorial interruptions – where, for example, a word or phrase must be either conjectured or acknowledged as illegible or missing – are placed in square brackets, with conjectured text in regular type and editorial matter italicized. Square brackets are in fact used throughout the volume to identify editorial material. Certain physical elements of the letters, such as the placement of heading information (addresses, dates) and closings, as well as the form of addresses and dates (e.g., '12th May 1924') in the headings, have been standardized.

Acknowledgments

All quotations from the letters of Charlotte Shaw are reprinted by kind permission of the Trustees of the Will of Mrs Bernard Shaw. The excerpt in Letter 82 from a letter of Virginia Woolf is reprinted by permission of the Estate of Virginia Woolf and The Hogarth Press. I wish to express here my thanks for aid and encouragement first to Dan H. Laurence, for whose industry and generosity every Shaw scholar of our time is indebted. To him and to Professor Leonard Conolly I owe my involvement in this volume and in the project of which it is a part, and my thanks for vital assistance. I owe special thanks also to Mrs Catherine Stoye, granddaughter of H.G. Wells, for generous help and counsel, and to her cousin Dr Martin Wells of Cambridge; to Dr R.C. Anderson, Professor of Zoology in the University of Guelph; to Dr

Margaret Belcher; to Dr Sylvia Hardy, Secretary of the H.G. Wells Society; to Dr Barbara McLean; to Mr W.B. McMurray, Headmaster of Oundle School in Northamptonshire and Mr Dennis H. Ford, the school's archivist; to Professor Patrick Parrinder, of the University of Reading; to Suzanne Rancourt of University of Toronto Press – editor with a sense of humour; to the Master, Fellows, and officers of Robinson College, Cambridge, for hospitality generously provided; to Mrs Nancy Sadek and her staff in the Archival and Special Collections section of the University of Guelph Library; and to Roma Woodnutt, of the Society of Authors, in particular for making certain of the Society's records available to me. I thank also the Research Advisory Board of the University of Guelph for a helpful travel grant. Finally, my deepest thanks are signalled by the dedication of this volume.

The largest portion of the letters in this volume are found among the papers in the great H.G. Wells archives of the Rare Book and Special Collections Library in the University of Illinois at Urbana-Champaign. In acknowledging my indebtedness to that university for permission to publish material from the archives, I wish to thank especially Mr Gene Rinkel and the staff of the Rare Book and Special Collections Library for their cordial and generous support.

I wish to extend grateful acknowledgment also to the following institutions for permission to publish materials held by them, and to the officers of those institutions for their valued assistance. The institutions are briefly identified in connection with each relevant letter.

Boston University: Mugar Memorial Library. Margaret R. Goostray, Assistant Director, Special Collections

British Library (BL): Department of Manuscripts. Miss C.M. Hall, Higher Executive Officer

Colgate University: Case Library, Special Collections Department, Richard S. Weiner Collection of George Bernard Shaw. Melissa McAfee, Special Collections Librarian

Cornell University: Carl A. Kroch Library, Bernard F. Burgunder Shaw Collection. Dr James Tyler, Curator, Burgunder Shaw Collection

University of Delaware: University of Delaware Library. L. Rebecca Johnson Melvin, Senior Assistant Librarian, Special Collections

Hofstra University: Department of Special Collections, Hofstra University Library, Hempstead, NY. Barbara M. Kelly, Curator, Special Collections

New York Public Library (NYPL): Berg Collection. Francis O. Mattson, Curator

Harry Ransom Humanities Research Center (HRC): The University of Texas at Austin

Yale University Library: Beinecke Rare Book and Manuscript Library. Vincent Giroud, Curator of Modern Books and Manuscripts

Abbreviations

ALS	Autograph letter or letter-card signed
ALU	Autograph letter or letter-card unsigned
ANS	Autograph note on 'compliments' card
APCS	Autograph postcard signed
(c)	Carbon copy
CL	*Collected Letters* of Bernard Shaw (see Editor's Note for full reference)
HLU	Holograph letter unsigned
HLS	Holograph letter signed
TDU	Typed draft unsigned
TLS	Typed letter signed
TLU	Typed letter unsigned

Letters

1 / To G. Bernard Shaw

Hotel Metropole
St Margherita Ligure
Italy
Friday
[*c.* 25 January 1901]

[ALS: BL 50552 ff 3–4]

At an early stage in their relationship, Wells and Shaw began the practice, which was to be lifelong, of sending each other copies of their new books as they appeared. Three Plays for Puritans *was published 15 January 1901 (a Tuesday), when Wells was vacationing in Italy.*

My dear Shaw,

I have just finished reading the Three Plays. I am in a room filled mainly with an English clergyman & the family he has thrown off, there is a bitter cold wind outside & what will happen when I have done this letter God only knows. So the chances are the letter will run long. I have read the book right through with vast entertainment & all that sort of thing. I need not expand. Of the three plays I certainly prefer Caesar & Cleopatra, though I don't for a moment feel the fighting in the lighthouse scene in Act III & consequently there's no sense of urgency & the scene as a whole misses fire. That's very probably my fault. (Fat little man with gold spectacles & a voice like a watchman's rattle going slowly, has entered the room, dived into the very midst of the clergyman's domestic exudations & swims there in a seething froth of commotion. I gather Mrs. Humphry Ward proposes to visit this hotel. I resume but without complete possession of my faculties.) I find Caesar a fine & sympathetic character (curiously reminiscent at moments in tone & manner of Sidney Low) and the whole creation that constitutes the play admirably conceived. The weakest point is certainly Caesar's speech to the Sphinx. It's not fine spouting and it goes so far out of the intimacy of frank self-communion that I think it ought to be. Ftatateeta with her throat cut is a gorgeous effect to *read* anyhow. God & possibly a few persons he has gifted know what could be done with it on the stage. (God damn that little man with the gold spectacles! God bitterly & everlastingly damn him!) And the end of Caesar & Cleopatra is good. Now the end of Cap'n Brassbound is not good. P. 300

impresses me Sir as being relatively – all through I speak relatively, we being dwellers on a High Plain of Intelligence – a damned nuisance. I don't believe you knew what you were up to. If you did you haven't got it, which is really very much the same thing. You got those two people together there and the machine jammed. The line:

Brassbound 'But you will'

might have been written by Barrie. I believe you ended the play at first *à la Barrie.* Then you saw *that* wouldn't do anyhow – or you may have reread your very sane & proper criticism of the 'Little Minister' (& I strongly recommend your own criticisms to your careful study for they are full of good things that will be of use to you) and you chucked that end & stuck in ['my pictures' ?] & touched up the end righter but not nearly right. The last line gets me as quite the right last line (Lady Cicely's 'How glorious! how glorious! And what an escape!') coming after a starchy provisional version of what was going to be, and now will probably never be, an amazingly glorious piece of comedy. *Your* play of course, not mine, but why couldn't she have kept her head to the end & played Brassbound off the stage with a fine mutual renunciation scene? And incidentally why do you not learn to use the quadrupled period? That last sentence should be, I submit,

'How glorious! how glorious! .... And what an escape!'

Concerning 'The Devil's Disciple,' with all its volumes of entertainment & dramatic effect, I have to complain of the same flaw of an ineffective curtain. But there I trace it quite back into the structure of the play. Anderson goes wrong. He becomes explicit just when a man is not explicit. In the moment when his character rises up & prevails over his beautiful little scheme of home life & all the rest of it, – he vanishes as a man. I perceive him, flat & painted & through the hole in the canvas that replaces his hitherto fleshly lips, speaks the voice of the Eminent Vegetarian. The first time is a moment & he says, 'You don't know the man you're married to!' That's awful! And the second time is the speech on page 79 – G.B.S. – fresh preface. That's all I think. You are, now that Wilde is dead, the one living playwright in my esteem.

Concerning The War of the Worlds (p.xvii) it is a fact that the hero of that story for all practical purposes absolutely forgets his wife & certainly is 'inspired' to do nothing on her account, all through the stress of the war. Finally he is 'inspired' to snivel. You just look up that point, because you have done me a grave injustice.

With very many thanks for your book again

I am, my dear Shaw
very faithfully yrs,
H.G. Wells

Wells was habitually careless about noting dates of his letters, sometimes mentioning (as here) the day of the week, often ignoring the matter entirely. Mrs. Humphry **Ward** (1851–1920) – novelist, woman of letters, and social worker whose defense of Victorian moral values was anathema to Wells – was wintering near Genoa. Sidney (later Sir Sidney) **Low** was a barrister, historian, and journalist. *The Little Minister*, a novel by J.M. **Barrie** (1860–1937), was adapted for the stage in 1897. Shaw's criticism of the play is in *Our Theatres in the Nineties* (vol. 3: 241–9). His comments on Wells's novel ***The War of the Worlds*** occur in the Preface to *Three Plays for Puritans*, in its first edition (1901), p. xvii. The point to which Wells refers is that at the end of the Martian invasion, the hero of the story 'felt a wave of emotion that was near akin to tears,' not first because of the loss of his wife, but because of the hope that came suddenly to him as he looked over the wreckage of London, 'this dear vast city of mine,' and envisaged its renewal.

2 / To H.G. Wells

10 Adelphi Terrace WC
12th December 1901

[TLS: Illinois]

Wells had sent Shaw Anticipations of the Reaction of Mechanical and Scientific Progress upon Human Life and Thought. *His 'anticipations' included the establishment of a world state: a 'new republic.' Arthur Conway Dobbs (b. 1874) had written Wells a letter from Ireland about currency reform, which Wells had evidently given to Shaw for comment. On 11 October 1922, by then an official in the government at Calcutta, Dobbs was to write Wells again, thanking him for advising him twenty years earlier to 'read up-to-date books on Economics & criticize them.' He enclosed a paper evidently repeating what Shaw called 'Dobbsism,' arguing that gold is not an appropriate basis for currency because gold is capital; that the appropriate base for currency must be found in income; and that the best solution to the problem (as his earlier letter seems to have proposed) would be a currency based on energy.*

Wells, my boy

On the threshold of all new Republics lies a fell beast called the Currency Crank, whose object it is to prove that as the Guernsey Market was built for nothing on a basis of inconvertible paper, which the Channel Islanders took in with one another's washing, so can we take short cuts to the Millennium by a suitable modification of our standard of value. I have myself conversed with a man who came to a colony in America in the course of an afternoon's walk; did twenty minutes work; got a banknote for twenty minutes; and bought a dinner with the banknote. I have by me old volumes of Owen's journals of his New Moral World, with records of the Labor Exchanges in the Grays Inn Road and other places, where you exposed the product of your labor marked in minutes and hours; that is, in Energy measured by Time. I grieve to say that these anticipations of Dobbsism have left so violent a prejudice against Currency projects in the minds of all experienced New Republicans that they dare not touch the best considered scheme for fear of being branded with Laputanism.

The letters sent me by Guest refer to previous correspondence, and leave me in the dark as to what Arthur C. Dobbs is exactly driving at. Guest himself calls it a token coinage representing units of energy. Now if, as appears to be the case, he means potential energy, every tramp can say, 'Fill me with a shilling's worth of food and I will sell you half a crown's worth of potential energy; and you can stop the shilling out of the price.' One foresees an attractive chapter on The Tramp as the Kinetic Man. But that sort of Kinetic Man, being a tramp, would not wash. On the other hand, if the energy is expended energy, it must take the form of a manufactured product. If it is stored energy, it must take the form of an accumulator, or a cylinder of compressed gas, or a connection with a generating station. In the three last cases, there is no special currency problem involved: the products of accumulators or connection can be paid for in money of the present type; and the problem of the New Republic need not be complicated by the technical question of establishing new media of currency or standards of value.

You may reply, however, that the New Republic is not a problem, but simply the totality of a series of technical reforms of just this currency type. But that be blowed! Your business is the preaching of the synthesis, not the execution of its constituents. What can be done for Dobbs is to put him off the track of currency reform, and make him take up the question of energy straightforwardly. Ruskin long ago rubbed in the fallacy of measuring national wealth by exchangeable products: you may remember his illustration of the immoveable Tintoretto ceiling and the two-francs-fifty obscene Parisian lithograph. What needs rubbing in now is that English prosperity has hitherto depended on her contiguous heaps of coal and iron: that is, on her early exploitation of these stores of energy. We are now getting cut out because other nations are developing not only their coal and iron stores, but their waterfalls. Now we dont develop anything. Nature has given us tides which exist hardly anywhere else in the world, and has provided a current in the Pentland Firth which would, if used, mop up Niagara. But we sit staring at the tides and sketching them in water colors. If Dobbs will only hammer away at that, using his currency suggestion merely as an illustration to bring out how poorer we shall be than the energy-exploiting nations even when the country is covered with American millionaires paying a vast Income Tax, he will do some good. Let him work out, if he can, a tabular index founded on our output of energy, for that founded on staple commodities in The Economist; but keep him off the notion that currency reform is any use by itself, or that the exploitation of Pentland Firth will be of no use without currency reform. That way madness lies, and exasperation on the part of the readers, and a premature end in bathostic ridicule for the New Republic.

This is what occurs to me at the first glance. I purposely shoot it down before there is time to reflect, because what my first impression is will be that of others also. I shall not exactly *mention* the matter to Webb; but I shall break it to him and see how he takes it. I dont think the London School would be quite so eager to harbor a new currency scheme as they would be to set up a smallpox ward – for the memories of Bimetallism are recent and bitter – but still the London School pulse can be felt in a casual manner. I see by the Academy that Webb has placed Anticipations among his books of the year. As it was I who shoved it on to him, I consider that I have rolled your log in return for your noble recognitions of the profundity of Plays for Puritans.

As it happens, I had been reading Reid on Alcoholism. But though he thinks with a certain vigour, science has induced in him an abject credulity which makes one despair of any good coming out of it at all. The step from a mild belief in the efficacy of baptism to a frantic and persecuting conviction of the absolute necessity of Vaccination is so appallingly retrograde, and so characteristic of the whole scientific movement, that it indicates a decay of the human intellect. Besides, this turning from the simple truth of Lamarckism to the mechanical rationalism of Natural Selection is very unpromising. A man who cannot see that the fundamental way for a camelopard to lengthen his neck is to want it longer, and to want it hard enough, and who explains the camelopard by a farfetched fiction of an accidentally longnecked Romeo of the herd meeting an accidentally longnecked Juliet, and browsing on foliage which the other Montagues and Capulets could not reach, ought really to be locked up! Tell Reid to read Samuel Butler's Luck or Cunning, and to bear in mind that the difference, so far, between the Pentateuch and the scriptures of the scientific materialism of the sixties, is the difference between shrewd nonsense and DAMNED nonsense. I am accustomed to hear all that side of things from the Anarchists, who shew the necessity of dynamite exactly as the Horsley sort of idiot shews the necessity of vivisection and all the other modern means of bringing 'research' within the means of the lowest capacity.

Some of what Reid says needs saying; but this dream of a community rendered Immune from everything by giving up preventive and defensive measures and substituting Temptation in the Wilderness would scandalize the Inquisition, and revolt the builders of the Tower of Jezreel. These doctors all think that science is knowledge, instead of being the very opposite of knowledge: to wit, speculation.

In haste, ever
G. Bernard Shaw

Robert **Owen** (1771–1858), pioneer in the socialist co-operative movement, first published his *New View of Society* in 1814. **Laputa** is the flying island in *Gulliver's Travels*, where Swift places his foolish 'scientists' and immortal Struldbrugs. **Guest**, to whom Shaw refers, was to be listed in *Who's Who* as Leslie Haden Haden-Guest (1877–1960), providing an explanation of the variations in his name as it appears in this volume: in subsequent notes he will be referred to as Haden-Guest. A physician, he was one of the young Fabians who supported Wells in his efforts to revolutionize the Fabian Society, and served twice on the Executive. He became a Labour MP, and in 1950 was created Baron Haden-Guest.

John **Ruskin** (1819–1900) was greatly admired by Shaw for his art criticism, in which he vigorously defended the Pre-Raphaelites, and for his energetic attacks on social injustice. Shaw's reference here has to do with Ruskin's attack on John Stuart Mill, in the opening paragraphs of *Munera Pulveris*, for apparently failing to distinguish between price and value. The London newspaper **The Economist** was founded in 1843. The **Pentland Firth** is the body of water separating the Orkney Islands from the mainland of Scotland, notorious for its strong tides and rough seas. The **London School of Economics**, founded in 1895, had for some time close links with the Fabians. In economic theory, **Bimetallism** is a system of currency based on two commodities (usually gold and silver) instead of one (usually gold). G. Archdall **Reid** (1860–1929) was a medical scientist and writer whose article 'The Rationale of Vaccination' in the *Monthly Review*, January 1902, may have helped in prompting Shaw to write *The Doctor's Dilemma*. **Lamarckism** was the pre-Darwinian theory of evolution propounded by the French naturalist Jean Baptiste Pierre Lamarck (1744–1829), who held that the evolution of species was a continuous and gradual process, occurring through the inheritance of characteristics acquired in response to environmental demands. *Luck or Cunning as the Main Means of Organic Modification?*, by Samuel **Butler** (1835–1902), was published in 1887. Shaw read and reviewed it in that year. With its attack on 'natural selection' as an explanation of evolution, and its proposal of an alternative theory, Butler's book was crucially important in Shaw's development of his hypothesis of Creative Evolution. Sir Victor **Horsley** (1857–1916) was a surgeon, neurologist, and endocrinologist. In the biblical narrative, it was from the tower of **Jezreel** that Jehu was seen approaching on his mission to kill Jezebel (*2 Kings* 9).

3 / To G. Bernard Shaw

[*no address*]
13th December 1901

[ALS: BL 50552 ff 1&2]

Honoured Sir:

Dobbs is no currency crank & I'm going to make it beautifully clear to you what a good thing he has in hand. But for that – speech. I am coming up to London Jan 6 & then I will fire it all into you. Dobbs has a new attitude towards values – a new phrasing of certain fundamental means of expression that will be very illuminating by the time it is worked out. He's solid and sober. He is not going to be associated with the N. Republic in nothin'. Guest's explanation (of a token coinage) is simply the statement of a passing illustration of a fine fertilising general idea. Dobbs won't affect currency at all. But I will tell you all about it when I see you.

You are very unsound on Reid – very. Your reproduction of Salisbury's B. Association remarks astonishes me. There again I feel the need of unlimited talk. Cannot I find a house for you in Sandgate. A month or so of steady walking and talking about here would improve a lot of nonsense out of existence – I am civil enough to say – for both of us.

Yours ever
H.G. Wells

Science is neither knowledge nor speculation. It is criticism ending in Wisdom.
[*The initial letters of 'Wells' and 'Wisdom' are encircled, the circles being connected by a straight line.*]

The Marquess of **Salisbury**, President of the British Association for the Advancement of Science, had addressed the Association in 1894 on the subject *Evolution: A Retrospect*, referring to Darwin with admiring acceptance, rejecting Weismann on *natural* selection, and finally quoting Kelvin in favour of the notion of *design*, for which he saw 'overpoweringly strong proofs.' Wells's principal residence was at **Sandgate** for about a decade.

4 / To H.G. Wells

10 Adelphi Terrace WC
26th January 1902

[ALS: Illinois]

Wells lectured at the Royal Institution on 2 January, on The Discovery of the Future. *The lecture, which Wells's biographer David C. Smith calls 'one of the key items to an understanding of Wells's thought,' was published by Fisher Unwin.*

I have just found Dobbs's letter lying about among my papers. Here it is in case you want to keep it.

My missus gave me an astonishingly complete report of your lecture at the R.I. from a few very scanty notes; so you must have impressed her considerably. Why not give it to the Fabian? – a live audience is better than a stuffed one.

Samuel Butler was here on Friday. He declared with great energy that Darwin had banished mind from the universe.

Pease attributes to the weakness of your stomach the fact that the king disagrees with you. I share your sensibility on this point.

Reid has an article in the Monthly Review which certainly proves that Darwin has banished mind from *him*.

G.B.S.

As already noted, Samuel **Butler** had a profound influence on Shaw, whose account of him is in *Pen Portraits and Reviews* (1931). Butler had for some time a furious dislike for GBS because of his Shakespearian criticism, his enthusiasm for Wagner, and so on. They met in November 1889, and some time later began visiting each other occasionally. Butler died on 18 June, and the visit referred to here by Shaw may well have been his last. Edward R.

Pease (1857–1955) was a founding member of the Fabian Society, and its paid secretary from 1890 to 1913.

5 / To G. Bernard Shaw

[*no address*]
27th January 1902

[ALS: BL 50552 f 6]

My Dear Shaw:

God forbid I should ever read that paper into a Blank again but I *would* read it to the Fabian *if* I could be sure of six effectual complete criticisms in the subsequent debate. I will read Reid's last. Why not get *him* to give a paper to the Fabian & afterwards tear him to pieces & run all about the meeting with the bleeding bits. So far from Darwin having banished mind from the Universe, I am an umble follower of Darwin. I suppose Samuel Butler means there wasn't any room for his thundering old God. *I* don't care. You seem to find scope for yourself & I find scope for myself.

Yours ever
H.G. Wells

6 / To G. Bernard Shaw

[*no address*]
29th January 1902

[ALS: BL 50552 f 7]

My Dear Shaw,

It weighs on my conscience that I said something in my last about reading that *Disc[overy] of the Future* paper to the Fabians. Which the fact is I can't. Unaccustomed as I am to public affairs of that sort they totally disorganize me for days before & after. For ten months I have dissipated my mind in relation to *Anticipations* & the thing has to stop & all this business of speeches at dinners, press cutting packings, R.I. lectures, comments, congratulations, notes to newspapers has to end. Feb 1st and forward I am in retreat, with an egotism grown large & painful & a mind in bleeding rags. I return to the roomy solitudes from which I came – to heal.

Yours ever,
H.G.

7 / To H.G. Wells

Mayberry Knoll, Woking
10th November 1903

[ALS: Illinois]

My dear Wells

You really might have the common decency to write and thank Henry Arthur Jones (38 Portland Place W) for sending you Metchnikoff's *Études sur la Nature Humaine* last spring. I feel personally concerned about it, because he sent you the book through me. It is true that I did not pass it on; but as Jones does not know this, you can hardly expect him to excuse you on that account. He must think it devilish rude of you; and I must say I think he is right.

When he gave it to me for you he was in bed with influenza; and I thought I would wait for it to disinfect itself before I sent it to Sandgate. Besides, on looking into it I found old Metch such a captivatingly intelligent specimen of the most stupendous variety of Pasteurite scientific gull that I resolved to read him myself first – a course expressly sanctioned by Jones. I read a couple of chapters and then got overtaken by a rush of work, & never thought of Metchnikoff again until your review in the *Speaker* was sent to me because it contained the monstrous statement that I – I! the chief insister on the need of the Life Force for a mind's eye to stop its blundering – am an XVIII century believer in the perfection & infallibility of Nature. Where do you expect to go to when you die?

Henry Arthur & his wife lunch with us at Adelphi Terrace on Friday next at 1.30. Will you be up in town then by any chance?

I should explain that Jones improves his mind sedulously with the best literature of the day, including yours. On learning that I knew you he handed over the Études, which he had just finished, and remarked, with a fine eye for your credulous side, that he thought you would like to read them, and would I give them to you from him. Which I shall, some day.

By the way, did I send you a Superman? I have got quite muddled as to who I supplied & who I didn't. Mankind in the Making was sent to me; but I have no patience with it: half of it is a righteous exposure of that impostor & quack, the schoolmaster, and the other half is a demand for more schoolmaster. Do you call this good sense? I much prefer your stories, which I bought on Saturday – four & six laid on the altar of friendship.

Do you know whether Conrad has seen the Superman, & if not, whether he would like to.

GBS

Henry Arthur **Jones** (1851–1929) was a leading author of plays and other works at the turn of the century. Élie **Metchnikoff** (1845–1916) was a Russian biologist who had become deputy director of the Pasteur Institute in Paris. His studies of immunity led him to discover the macrophage and the phenomenon of phagocytosis. In the Preface to *The Doctor's Dilemma*, which Shaw was to begin writing in 1906, he refers to Metchnikoff's 'suggestive biological romances' and links his name with that of Sir Almroth Wright, on whom the character of Sir Colenso Ridgeon was supposedly based. Metchnikoff was awarded the Nobel Prize for Medicine, with Ehrlich, in 1908. Wells's ***Mankind in the Making*** had appeared in 1903. Joseph **Conrad** lived within easy cycling distance of Wells at this time, and for some years they shared a strong literary friendship.

8 / To H.G. Wells

10 Adelphi Terrace WC
26th March 1904

[TLS: Illinois. Typescript to 'asinine' (in fourth paragraph), remainder in Shaw's handwriting along l.h. and top margins. Signature in large caps.]

Shaw's The Common Sense of Municipal Trading *was published in February 1904. Wells, having joined the Fabian Society in February 1903, resigned a year later in protest against the tract* Fabianism and the Fiscal Question, *written by Shaw in an effort to circumvent Fabian differences over the question of tariffs. After various gestures of appeasement by the Shaws and the Webbs, and appeals from Pease, he withdrew his resignation.*

Dear Wells

What is all this in your last letter about the financial part of my Municipal Trading book being wrong? I want to get the plates corrected for a second edition; and if you have anything useful to say, out with it. Nothing can be more improbable than that I am wrong: still, even I am not absolutely infallible; and as you are an interesting youth, I may as well hear what babble you may have to offer.

Your dastardly resignation has created the greatest indignation on the Fabian Executive. What the dickens is the matter with you? The tariff tract was submitted to you as well as to everybody else. It cost me months of work to fit it to the greatest common measure of all the members. Every idiot had his little go at it, and his little correction made to please him. Macrosty, who objects strenuously to anything but uncompromising free trade, nevertheless helped me nobly with it and stayed away from the final meeting to save trouble. It represents enormous sacrifices on my part, and does not, even at that, express the views of any individual on the executive or in the society. You never helped us in our agony: among the piles of letters I had to wade through, adjusting the tract to any grains of sound wheat that grew amid their tares, I looked in vain for anything from you. Lots of members with about a fiftieth part of your ability managed to be really helpful in all sorts of ways, from spotting a misprint to hitting out a new light; but you did nothing; and now, because the job is not exquisitely to your liking, you resign. What do you mean by it? Have you any sense of shame? This is a nice outcome of your blessed new Republicanism. Nothing but the Nonconformist conscience after all, awkwardly put on by a lazy literary mugwump. I am ashamed of you. I blush for my age and my profession. I dont believe you have any views on Free Trade or any other subject. I believe you are so spoiled by living in a world of your own invention, peopled by your own puppets, that you have become incapable of tolerating the activity or opinions or even the phrases of independent individuals. Since you have had live infants to play with you have become worse than ever. Jane is greatly to blame. She spoils you in a perfectly disgusting manner. If she had married *me* there would be some excuse for her: *I* really do deserve some petting after my daily struggle hand to hand with the Philistines. But you live in a Pearson's Paradise, swelling your head with kloophorbia and other products of the laboratory, and discharging your Fabian gardeners because they have sent you crumpled rose leaves.

But a day will come. Those two infants will grow up, not your way, but their own. To them the ancient Fabians will be great men; and you will only be the governor. They will not read Anticipations; and they will punch the heads of boys who mention Mankind in the Making with evident designs to chaff them about it. And Jane will take their part against you, very properly.

However, let me have your objections, however asinine, to Municipal Trading; and if you still feel that you cant stand the Fabian, try a couple of years of the Social Democratic Federation, a stalwart Liberal body only a century out of date, and – consequently – manned exclusively by pioneers who despise the Fabian Society and all its works.

Give my love to Jane. Observe, *my love.* I mean it. I will not have her affections starved in Sandgate with nobody but you to cherish her.

yours,
SHAW

The **last letter** referred to has not been found. Henry W. **Macrosty**, a civil servant, was a member of the Fabian Executive, 1895–1907. Edwin **Pearson**, a bookseller, published '*A relic of Old London before the Great Fire. Paradise transplanted and restored in a most artful and lively representation of the several creatures, plants, flowers and other vegetables ... Written by J.H. Gent., London, June 23, 1642*. Reprinted for the curious by E.P. 1871.' A book by Rev. John N. **Pearson** called *The Days in Paradise*, published in London in 1854, went through several editions. It is probable that Shaw is referring to the former volume. The Wellses now had two sons (**infants**): George Philip ('Gip' – persistently spelled 'Gyp' by Shaw), born in 1901, and Frank Richard, in 1903. The **Social Democratic Federation** was founded in 1881, initially as The Democratic Federation, by Henry Mayers Hyndman (1842–1921), a journalist and apostle of Marxism. Shaw attended some of its early meetings, as did William Morris.

9 / To H.G. Wells

10 Adelphi Terrace WC
29th March 1904

[ALS: Illinois. Handwriting Shaw's, but lower l.h. portion of first page has been cut away, also lower r.h. portion of second page, and signature. Five lines are affected. Possible wording of first three gaps is shown in square brackets.]

Wells's reply to the previous letter is missing.

My dear H.G.W.

I breathe again. Your criticisms are ingenuous errors; and the chapter is sound from end to end. 'From each according to his ability' is a perfectly solid canon of taxation. There is no confusion whatever between house owner and ground landlord: the distinction is quite irrelevant in this place. In fact it is the terms house owner & ground landlord that are vague, as there is probably not a single case in existence in which the man called the ground landlord is getting the exact site value and the house owner getting the exact interest on the cost of the building. As likely as not, when the tenant is a tenement holder, his rent is divided between the house owner, two or three intermediate leaseholders, a mortgagee or so, and the so-called ground landlord. Next door the occupier may be himself the [leaseholder?] with the house mortgaged from the first floor to the roof, or quite [the opposite as the?] case may be. My term 'the landlord' is not a confusion, but a general term covering the whole morphology. You might as well say that 'cavalry' is a confusion of horse & man, sword & saddle. The idle shareholder is a phenomenon alterable, no doubt, by complete Socialism – who deniges of it, Betsy? – but it is perfectly independent of the permanence of this or that particular investment. The stage coach always lasts until the railway comes. You were quite right to emphasize the peculiarity of the modern capitalist class – Cobbett's 'funding system' – in *Anticipations*; and I am quite right in pilfering from that work intelligently. There is nothing bountiful whatever in a proposition to exempt incomes under a certain figure from rating. That is a delusion of the home made political economy of the Robinson Crusoe order. You really dont understand the operation of rent & interest in wealth distribution, or you would not confuse redistributive devices with sentimental charity. Finally, the comparison of real responsible landlords with Sir Gorgius Midas is intentional & appropriate. The point is that the landlord is an ascertainable, responsible person, whereas the capitalist is nameless, irresponsible, unidentifiable except as a fictitious type.

Now sit down & rewrite the chapter yourself, and see [if you can make something] different out of it. I really must see some more of you: you [*words missing*] this rate [*cut away with signature*]

'Who deniges of [*denies*] it, Betsy?' is the question asked three times of Mrs Prig by Mrs Gamp in Dickens's *Martin Chuzzlewit* (chap. 49). William **Cobbett** (1762–1835), writer and social reformer, recognized that the land-owning class controlled Parliament simply by funding the candidates it chose to support. Sir Gorgius Midas seems in part a Shavian invention. In Greek mythology, Gordius was a Phrygian peasant who travelled to the city by oxcart, and in conformity with the pronouncement of an oracle was made king. He became the father of Midas – of the golden touch and the ass's ears. The oracle had prophesied also that the man who succeeded in untying the knot by which Gordius had bound the pole of his wagon to the yoke would rule all Asia. Shaw, though he – whimsically, perhaps – misspells the name of Gordius and makes him a knight, seems to be arguing that under capitalism, with private ownership of the means of wealth, riches and poverty are tied together by a Gordian knot that only an Alexander (or a Lenin – or an Undershaft?) could ever undo. Shaw is probably also making a punning reference to Gorgias, the rhetorician and sophist after whom one of Plato's dialogues is named.

10 / To H.G. Wells

Maybury Knoll, Woking
5th April 1904

[APCS: Illinois]

Although Wells's reply – or retort – to Shaw has vanished, its nature may be deduced from Shaw's postcard that follows. The Shaws had given up their rented cottage at Woking. Charlotte's diary for 1905 (a year after Shaw wrote the following note) records that they spent the early days of April with the Wellses at Sandgate, and on April 6 went 'to see site for house in afternoon.' But it was not until November 1906 that they moved into the rectory at Ayot St Laurence, the house that was to be their country home for the remainder of their lives.

Et tu, Sardanapale!

Luxury & indolence indeed!

Well, write the next tract yourself, and be blowed. *I* shant resign: I shall chuckle.

We are in the agonies of house hunting. Now is the time to produce an eligible residence, if you have one handy.

GBS

Sardanapalus, a legendary figure of unknown origin, was mistakenly identified by the Greek historian Ctisias with the last of the Assyrian emperors, Assurbanipal. Sardanapalus supposedly lived, with his court, a life of inordinate 'luxury & indolence.' In the end, his capital Nineveh was captured by the Medes and he set fire to his palace, destroying his court and himself. A version of Byron's tragedy on the subject, ending with the spectacular burning of Nineveh, was performed in the 1870s under the direction of Charles Calvert (1828–79). As a young man in Dublin, Shaw had seen the production when it was on tour.

11 / To H.G. Wells

The Marine Hotel
North Berwick
29th September 1904

[ALS: Illinois]

The Shaws spent most of August and all of September in Scotland. This letter may well be a response to a comment or suggestion made by Wells in conversation. After completing his novel Kipps, *in May 1904, Wells was ill from exhaustion. He was troubled also by financial worries, and told Arnold Bennett that he contemplated writing 'a couple or so of plays that would possibly bring in a fortune'* (The Journals of Arnold Bennett, Vol. 1 *[1932], 189). The idea was not new: Wells had written a dramatic adaptation of his novel* The Wheels of Chance *under the title* Hoopdriver's Holiday, *but it had not been produced. His biographers Norman and Jeanne MacKenzie report that he 'put the same idea to Shaw.' Shaw, for all his theatrical experience and knowledge, was just entering the period of his success as a playwright.*

Dear H.G.W.

Just a word about your Haymarket suggestion, as you may easily mistake the situation.

If you imagine that you have so artfully concealed your brains that Cyril Maude (compared to whom in point of intellectual appetite Welch is a Goethe) or Frederick Harrison (who is a man of reasonable culture) will accept you unsuspiciously as a disciple of Jerome K. Jerome, you err most prodigiously. In the west end theatrical world *The War of the Worlds* seems as abstruse as Newton's *Principia*; and *Anticipations* & *Mankind [in the Making]* have given away the rest of the show. And this is so much the better, because the successes of Barrie, whose mighty brain staggers the Strand, and the current suspicions that there has been some mistake about me, have now set the managers hankering after intellectual superiority, and even Stage-Societyness, if only it can be combined with popularity. If you could once demonstrate that your stuff would get over the footlights, and not involve giants and Martians & suchlike games, you would not have as much trouble as the regular old stagers.

One thing that is almost beyond conception is the ignorance of the theatrical people of every world besides their own, however contiguous. When Forbes Robertson – one of our 'scholarly' actors – said of R.L. Stephenson 'Oh, I thought it (*Macaire*) was by THE Stephenson' (meaning B.C. of that ilk, who perpetrated the libretto of 'Dorothy'), he *placed* himself and his whole profession exactly, as far as knowledge of current literature and its reputations goes. If you get a play produced by the Stage Society or any other enterprise that can secure the regulation notices, those notices, with their allusions to your literary fame, will be your first introduction to nine tenths of 'the profession.' And the superstitious awe with which they will regard you then will be a product of the dense ignorance in which they live now concerning you. The other tenth will have accidentally read your books and will know too much about you to be at the mercy of conventional inferences from an S.S. performance.

But as a matter of fact, it is waste of time to trouble about these considerations. Until you actually write the play, you don't know what it will be like. The chances are that it will not be a play for 100,000 Hoopdriver's colleagues, male and female, but for a smaller number of better people. Now at the Stage Society there is one blessing: you can't fail. There is no means of ascertaining failure. Your audience is bagged beforehand; and the number of performances cannot be exceeded or fallen short of. If the audience is pleased, the play is none the worse: *Op o' my Thumb* went up like a shot at the St James's; and other plays that we have done – commonplace ones enough – are now getting played on the strength of their London notices in the provinces & colonies. The suspicion that S.S. plays mean clever plays has been most effectually dissipated by poignant experiences, in spite of my masterpieces.

You must also consider that a dramatist wants rehearsal experience, a part of his apprenticeship that is worth a good deal of solid gold to him. By jumping at all my chances I have rehearsed for public performance nine of my plays, with the result that I am as much an expert behind the scenes as Pinero, and am not sent to the stalls to see my work botched by idiots who havnt read it and wouldnt know what it is about if they did. You cant trust anybody to handle your play; and yet it is only by practice that you can make your company accept your direction as a matter of course. The author is the only person who really wants everybody to be a success, and who can get rehearsals through without friction amid general devotion and hallucination as to being on the brink of a great event. And the most heaven born author-stage-manager cannot do this the first time he goes behind the curtain. Your £20,000 will be all the surer if, by the time it is rehearsed, you have learnt exactly how much of the thousand blunders of the first rehearsal will correct themselves later on without your interference, and how many of the rest you may safely correct at one rehearsal without wrecking the nerves of the company.

There are heaps of things to learn even if you start with the fullest knowledge of what is to be done.

Another point for you to consider is this. A £20,000 success is all very well; but the repertory play like *Hamlet* is still better. The popular play blazes and dies, whilst a thing like *Everyman* goes dragging round the world for ever. I cannot say that I have made much by playwriting – less than £5,000 probably, from first to last (ten years); but only three or four of my 14 plays have been exploited, and these with two exceptions (in New York) not seriously exploited, whilst in the meantime I have had to make the running for the eternal 'new' drama. If the hardy pioneer can make nearly £500 a year average in his first ten years, and still have a whole fistful of virgin plays which will hereafter bring him in lots of money, the game is not such a bad one – not bad enough to justify any first rate man in doing second rate work on the plea of – but this is moral babble, as Comus says. The main point is that the Stage Society game is by no means to be despised, and if the people who scorned the old Independent Theatre had written for it all they could, several of them would have been expert dramatists now.

Finally, I would urge that if you are going to write plays, the 20,000 pounder will only be one of them. You can easily give another, not necessarily to the S.S., but to the Court or some other venture of the kind. I scribble all this to knock the thing straight into your head, as the career of a dramatist is not to be entered on without careful consideration, and the great game in it cannot be won without an apparently reckless preliminary expenditure of genius on all sorts of side shows.

GBS

Cyril **Maude** (1862–1951) and Frederick **Harrison** (1854–1926) managed the Haymarket Theatre from 1896 to 1905. James **Welch** (1865–1917), actor, appeared in several of Shaw's early plays. Jerome K. **Jerome** (1859–1927) was a novelist and playwright, remembered chiefly in the theatre for *The Passing of the Third Floor Back* (1908). (Sir) Johnston Forbes-**Robertson** (1853–1937) had a notable career as actor-manager from 1874 to 1913. ***Macaire*** is a three-act farce by W.E. Henley and Robert Louis Stevenson. **B.C. Stephenson** (1839–1906) was a writer and librettist who collaborated with Alfred Cellier (1844–91) in the operetta ***Dorothy***, in which Shaw's sister Lucy sang and acted for some five years, and which GBS reviewed for *The Star* in September 1889. The **Stage Society** was founded in 1889 to enable the production of plays unacceptable to commercial managers. Its first production was Shaw's *You Never Can Tell*. It produced ***'Op o' Me Thumb***, a one-act play by Frederick

Fenn and Richard Pryce, at the Royal Court Theatre, 13 March 1904. **Comus**, a minor Roman god of revelry, was a central figure in John Milton's poetic masque, *Comus*, produced in 1634 at Ludlow Castle.

12 / To H.G. Wells

North Berwick
2nd October 1904

[APCS: Illinois]

Never heard of Ella Hale. I gave up all idea of corresponding with Guest because he wrote his letters on horseback apparently; at any rate I couldn't read them. Two unsuccessful attempts were made to read his letters to the Fabian Executive, and since then he has been banned. The cablegrams look serious, and it seems hardly a case for consulting his wife, unless *she* is Ella Hale.

We return to London on Tuesday.

G.B.S.

Ella Hale remains unidentified, as do the cablegrams. In the *Who's Who* entry previously referred to (p. 8), one of Haden-Guest's listed recreations is riding. David C. Smith states that Haden-Guest's wife appears to have been one of the women with whom Wells was sexually involved in his Fabian days (*H.G. WELLS Desperately Mortal*, p. 209).

13 / To H.G. Wells

10 Adelphi Terrace WC
17th October 1904

[ALS: Illinois]

My dear Wells

Are you in England? There is a young American here who implores me to make you let him photograph you. Name, Coburn, a representative of 'the American invasion' in photography. He has operated on me to a frightful extent, having the good taste to regard me as a deserving buffer whose efforts have helped to bring about the golden age of Wells, Kipling, Chesterton & other heroes, all, in his opinion, inferior to Wells as a force. In case he writes to you to ask for a sitting I testify that he is good at his trade, 23 years of age, looks 17, and is a nice, soothing, pleasant, amiable, intelligent lad, whose visits are not in the least unbearable.

The only subject on which he is harassing is you: he has bothered me into writing this letter.

He is insatiable as a photographer; so Jane had better interfere and rescue you after the sixth plate; but in all other ways he is unexacting & positively quieting – an excellent thing in an American.

Yours ever
G. Bernard Shaw

P.S. What about that play? We must make up our program soon. I've got one from Hewlett which would cost about £6,000 to mount & requires a choir of angels to play it.

Coburn (1882–1966) was an American photographer who had photographed Shaw in early August (See *CL*, Vol. 2, p. 435). In *Alvin Langdon Coburn, Photographer: An Autobiography* (1966), he refers to the many occasions when Shaw helped him, and quotes a note he received from GBS dated 1 November 1905. As a result of it he and Shaw travelled to Folkestone the next morning, spent the day at Sandgate, and returned to London on the morning of the 3rd: a memorable experience for Coburn: 'in the dusk we three went for a walk. I remember how proud I was to have the opportunity of knowing two of the keenest minds in Britain,' he wrote. He and Wells were to have a long friendship.

When Shaw wrote this letter he was deeply engaged with the beginning of the Vedrenne-Barker management of the Royal Court Theatre and with finding new plays for it. *John Bull's Other Island* was to open on 1 November. Maurice Henry **Hewlett** (1861–1923) was a civil servant, historical novelist, and playwright.

14 / To G. Bernard Shaw

Spade House
Sandgate
5th November 1905

[ALS: Illinois]

John Bull's Other Island, *having had a highly successful run at the Royal Court in May 1905, was given a second run – also successful – in the late autumn. Wells attended a performance at which he noted the presence of the Prince of Wales (later King George V), although the actual date is unknown. Wells had been greatly impressed, as the following letter shows. Presumably the play was a subject of discussion when the Shaws dined at Sandgate on 6 December, for on 24 December Charlotte wrote Wells from Shropshire: 'I was dreadfully penitent when I suddenly remembered this morning that I had promised you those extracts from "John Bull" ... Fortunately I have the play with me here where I am staying for Christmas, so I was able to send them for you. Best love to you both. G.B.S. is blooming after a week in this country. He came down a wreck.' She enclosed a copy that she had hand-written of two short passages from the play. Wells jotted the following marginalia on them: 'Shaw in many respects much the greatest figure – Not like my great fig he has a vice – he does not it is true smoke or drink or swear – in most vicious directions he displays not so much self-control as a lack of appetite ... Shaw has a devil of laughter.' (Some additional words are illegible, as are some words in his letter.)*

My dear Shaw:

In spite of your disgraceful caricature of me in Broadbent – even my slight tendency to embonpoint was brought in – I enjoyed John Bull's Other Island. There was something very dramatic in the P.o.W., a well-meaning person I'm told, peeping at it. Perhaps he learn't something – perhaps he was deeply impressed.

But really you know I don't want to [*illegible*] everywhere. The play has some really gorgeous rhetoric, beautiful effects, much more serious Shaw than ever before, & I'd rather see it again than see anyone else's new play. All the same there's dreadful things in it. A fine speech by the daft priest for example is quite spoilt by the old Butlerism about the hellish cruelty of teaching children to read. And the dreadful pulling of the girl's character was due to sheer laziness on your part; you might go over her again. Then of course the contrast of English & Irish is just late Victorian sham – all the balderdash about the soil you people & so on. As a matter of fact Larry is just as much English as Irish. I can't distinguish him from Hamlet. And Broadbent looks like Redmond & behaves most like an Anglicized Dutch Jew of any people *I* ever met. None the less it's an admirable play and a picture of a politico-social system better than I thought could be done on the stage. The [final act] is [jolly].

Your [*sic*] a great swell Shaw really – with something in your blood that ever & again breaks out in little blemishes of perversity. You have every element of greatness except a certain independence of your own intellectual excitability. You can't control your own wit & your love of larking. You ought to dull yourself with meat & then you'd be vast!

Yours ever,
H.G.W.

John Edward **Redmond** (1856–1918), Irish nationalist leader and Member of Parliament, was a member of the Commission that dealt with the Irish Land Question in 1903 – the year preceding the one in which Shaw wrote *John Bull's Other Island.*

15 / To H.G. Wells

10 Adelphi Terrace WC
14th February 1906

[APCS: Illinois]

1905 had become a year of unrest for the Fabian Society, partly as a result of the strong presence of Wells, in particular his forceful appeal to the younger, more radical members. By the month of June he was being urged to reform the Society; a little later he wrote of 'throwing it into the dustbin.' By December dissension was coming to a head. Shaw had been promoting socialism since before the Fabian Society was founded – when the young Wells was at the beginning of his education in science – and after years of lecturing and leadership he was becoming doubtful about the Society's continued effectiveness and aware of its need for fresh blood and ideas. He called for a report on the results of its work. Wells, much more impatient, launched an attack on the established leadership – the so-called 'Old Gang' – especially through two papers (the second called Faults of the Fabian*) that he read in the early weeks of 1906. Eventually the executive agreed that a special committee be established, with Wells as convener, to inquire into the structure and operations of the Society.*

The composition of the committee was a contentious matter. The minutes of an executive meeting on 9 February record, under the heading The Wells Agitation, *that the secretary was 'ordered to write Wells (a) that the Executive Committee desire all to be members of the proposed Committee; (b) that we will put on any members he nominates within reason as to numbers ...' It appears that Wells discussed the question with Charlotte Shaw, herself a member of the executive, for on 13 February she wrote him a 'confidential' note:*

'Here are some suggestions for the membership of our Committee ... I do not *advise Dr. Haden Guest ... but of course I will work with him to the very best of my ability if you [appoint him].*

'I think it will be a grave mistake if you dont have Mr. [E.R.] Pease on as ex officio or secretary ... A committee is a more difficult thing to work than I believe you realize!' On one matter GBS disagreed. Eventually, on 28 February, the committee elected Sydney Olivier its chairman and Jane Wells its secretary; it continued to be referred to as 'the Wells Committee.'

I advise you to make a Royal Commission of that committee of yours. Do not ask Pease to act as secretary: how could he, when you want to discuss him? Appoint a secretary and ask for power to examine witnesses. Then you can call Pease & examine him. You can also examine me, Webb, & Bland *separately*, and compare our stories & views. The discrepancies will provide all the levity you want in your report. This form of procedure is by far the best for all your purposes.

By the way your facts are all pure romance; so do not press for publication of your paper *by itself*, as we should be understood to assent to it and to throw over E.R.P.

G.B.S.

Sydney Olivier (1859–1943), later Baron Olivier, who served on the executive from 1887 to 1899, was to have a distinguished diplomatic and parliamentary career. Sidney **Webb** (1859–1947) and Hubert **Bland** (1856–1914) were, like Shaw, members of the current executive – and of the Old Gang. The paper referred to here is *Faults of the Fabian*, read to the Society on 9 February.

16 / To H.G. Wells

10 Adelphi Terrace
17th February 1906

[ALS: Illinois]

On 16 February Charlotte recorded in her diary that Wells lunched with the Shaws and they had a 'long talk.' It is safe to assume that a principal topic was the affairs of the Fabian Society, in particular the composition of the special committee. The date of the 'private conference' referred to in the letter that follows is not stated.

Dear H.G.W.

On considering this confounded committee of yours at a private conference with Bland & Webb, we have come to the conclusion that the only way to fix up the business satisfactorily is to withdraw your four executive members – Charlotte, Chesterton, Headlam & Standring – and keep your committee outside the executive completely, whilst giving you the run of it by my plan of inviting you to summon any of us and get what you want out of us.

The reasons for this are obvious – or would be if you had any sense. Your position is that the executive is a stick-in-the-mud body and the secretary a duffer. Now you cant reasonably make an unrepresentative minority of the executive a party to an inquiry which has primarily to establish that fact. They would be in a ridiculous position when the executive came to consider your report. You must either make the executive a party to the inquiry by having the whole 15 on chock-a-block, which would mean a large committee tremendously dominated by the old gang, or else keep them off it altogether. Chesterton promptly refused to serve when he realized the situation; Charlotte sees that political adultery, however publicly gloried in by a brazen co-respondent, should be conducted with at least a show of fidelity to the executive; Standring will not throw his old pals over; and Headlam would not serve alone. Therefore you must be prepared next Friday with four substitutes for your executive selection (unless we can find them for you unofficially)*. When you meet, you must appoint an honorary secretary. If you want to consult Pease, you can have him up for examination; if you want me, ditto; Webb, ditto; Bland, ditto; Charlotte, ditto; &c &c &c &c &c. Thus you will have the run of the whole place without any risk of being bulldozed or outvoted by the old gang. Finally you will make a report; and the executive will consider it and either adopt it or criticize it or make alternative proposals or deal with it in some way or other before it goes to the society. We may confer with your committee on it. Anyhow, that is the routine as we see it.

We cannot afford to quarrel with you because we want to get tracts out of you; and in any case you will see that we are not hostile, as we let you have an absolutely free run at the meeting. Your paper was full of small misapprehensions which could easily have been seized on to secure an easy debating triumph; but we felt that they really didnt matter, whereas the general drift of the thing was to the good. But the affair, however friendly, must be in clear form. You must not go about amiably disclaiming any intention of attacking us, or trying to shape the proceedings on that assumption. You can be of no use unless you attack us and meet our defence. The society will say 'if you are not attacking the old gang, then what the devil are you wasting our time for, and where does our fun come in?' And on the other hand, when we treat your onslaught *as* an onslaught, and hold the fort against you, dont suppose that we are in a huff. It is only by placing ideas in clear opposition that any issue can be created. It is our business & yours to create an issue; and if you consider your feelings or ours in the matter you are simply unfit for public life and will be crushed like a trodden daisy.

In haste – G.B.S.

* Or you may simply omit the four. A committee of six would be quite sufficient. However if you want ten, ten can no doubt be found.

Rev. Stewart Duckworth **Headlam** (1847–1914) was founder of the Guild of St Matthew, a prominent socialist, and a member of the Fabian executive. Cecil E. **Chesterton** (1879–1918), a brother of G.K. Chesterton, was a journalist and editor, also at this time on the executive, as was the journalist George **Standring** (1855–1924).

17 / To H.G. Wells

10 Adelphi Terrace WC
24th March 1906

[ALS: Illinois]

On 18 February Charlotte, as a member of the Fabian executive, wrote Wells as follows – probably after conferring with her husband:

'Dear Mr. Wells
This decision of the Conference of the old gang is rather a blow! Of course I cant go against their opinion – & of course members of the Executive would be in a rather awkward position when they had to consider the report of a Committee which had sat – to a certain extent – in judgment upon themselves!

I dont think this need make very much difference to you. You lose me & Mr. Headlam, Standring & perhaps someone else off your committee, but you can invite us to attend and help whenever you want us, & you can either leave our places empty & have a smaller committee; or you can, I am sure, *find other good, useful people to fill them. The whole business is a little ticklish & difficult to* start *& wants diplomacy; but I feel sure once we are under way things will get easier. If we get splits & quarrels we shall lose a lot of useful work that we may rope in by care & patience. Mr. Bland is in a very obstreperous mood, & I strongly advise his being ménagé just a little!*

I went down to the office on Friday evening, after we had been talking, & discussed the printing of your paper in the news "in extenso". I told the Committee that you would like it to be printed, but there was only one opinion: "it couldn't possibly be done". The argument was that it could not be printed without correc-

tions of matters of fact, & an answer from the Executive to follow it, & the proper time for the answer is not now, but later on when the new Committee has reported.

Shall you be up in Town, & can we have another chat?

Yours ever,
C.F. Shaw'

On the following day she recorded in her diary 'another long talk' with Wells. Indeed, in the next few weeks references to him and to the committee are frequent; at times both the tone of the talks and the efforts at maintaining friendliness are suggested (e.g., 'Sun.25 – Came up to Town. Talk! – Mr. Wells. He withdrew publishing his paper himself. He stayed to luncheon.') Charlotte nonetheless remained a member of the committee as finally constituted, and of the executive.

Wells had for some time (with a good deal of support, especially among the younger members) held that the 'Basis,' the document stating the socialist aims and basic principles of the Fabian Society, needed virtually complete revision. He therefore drafted a 'Proposed Revised Basis' to be discussed by his committee and the executive at the 23 March meeting of the latter body. The executive minutes record that 'a long discussion ensued. No resolution was proposed or adopted.' Wells was about to go on an extended visit to the United States.

Dear H.G.W.

Do not forget to call on Brentano, Union Square, New York. They are expecting you. They have treated me very well, and are very satisfactory people to deal with, as they began, not as literary amateurs with a capacity for doing nothing and a taste for talking to authors, but as newsboys in the street. Arthur Brentano, the one who called on me here, is quite a decent human being. They write to say that they will appreciate a visit from you enormously. They also have views about your works & the American public which they will no doubt intimate with due regard to your susceptibilities – most complimentary to you and most uncomplimentary to the A.P.

During your absence I will write the report of your committee, probably, and get it adopted through Charlotte. Your intellectual vivacity and sense of humour have certain disadvantages – among them an inordinate delight in pure impish cheek. Your basis is of course obviously much better than the existing basis; but as I told you, anybody who was the least bit of a literary workman could have produced a better basis any time these 20 years. But he couldnt have produced one that would have conciliated Lawson Dodd and Headlam and Webb and Pease and Macrosty and all the sections they represent. To get anything through a corporate body, you must say the same thing over again in different ways. You must stick on absurd excrescences in the nature of china eggs to make the hen lay. You must get round differences of meaning between members by saying something that neither disputant means or that means nothing. And you finally never get anything more artistic out of them than an average King's speech. Now it is no use imagining that the conciliations of 20 years ago are out of date. I assure you they are not. Either you have the very same men to deal with – Headlam, Pease, Webb, Bland &c, or you have *abler* successors to the departed ones – Stanton Coit, Dodd, [Cecil] Chesterton. Your one chance is to show a perfect appreciation of and sympathy with the exigencies which imposed on us the obvious blemishes in the basis, and to appeal for an attempt to get a more attractive one through by a concentration of our prestige & authority sufficient to silence the guerrilla leaders in the society – though when I think of Aylmer Maude, Victor Fisher, Isaac Mitchell, Marson &c &c &c &c I dare not hold out any hopes of that proving possible. But that is your best chance. Instead of which, you amuse yourself by treating us to several pages of cheek to the effect that the imperfections of the basis are the result of our own folly and literary clumsiness. This doesnt irritate me, nor Bland, nor Webb (*much*), nor any of the old birds with a spice of your own impishness in them; but it does irritate Macrosty and some of the others. None of them, old or young, enjoy a sally at their own expense as much as a sally at yours; and as the game is one which both sides can play at, it is not a helpful one. Standring's lampoon, for instance, is a very harmless stuffed bludgeon compared to your thrusts; but you probably found that it did not conduce to cordial co-operation on your side with George. Your tactics would be admirable if you wanted to force a fight. But you dont; so you had better drop them. You may say that you are making superhuman efforts to be amiable. No doubt you are; but you are not amiable enough, in spite of your efforts. And you are too reckless of etiquette. You really mustnt poach on our departments. You had no more right to report that debate than you had to write our cheques; and that is just one of the things that the human animal will not stand. If, instead of making unscientific, obsolete and untenable distinctions between habits and instincts, you would *préciser* the distinction between the terms of your committee's reference and the duties of the executive, you would have none of these difficulties. Even if your report had been approximately accurate instead of a blaze of wanton mendacity from beginning to end (I go this length because I told you myself viva voce that you must not claim more than that your resolutions had been carried nem. con.; and you agreed), still the committee – *any* human committee – would have jibbed at having its account of its own action dictated to it. You must study people's corns when you go clog dancing.

Generally speaking, you must identify yourself frankly with us, and not play the critical outsider and the satirist. We are all very clever; and long ago we have come to understand that we must not play our cleverness off against one another for the mere fun of it. The whole business is a ridiculous one for us. It is a case of Songs of Innocence and Experience. Your innocence is stupendous in some ways. Our experience has humbled us until we are morbidly afraid of playing off our experience against you, and willing to allow you to teach your grandmother to milk ducks to any extent on the chance of getting a workable idea here & there, and, at all events, a fresh impulse. But there are limits to our powers of enduring humiliations that are totally undeserved. You havnt told us anything yet that we dont know – havnt pointed out any error in our ways that is not the work of Natural Selection. You havnt discovered the real difficulties of democratic work; and you assume that our own folly and ill will account for their results.

If you want to persuade us to throw the basis into the melting pot, you will have either to convince us that it is excluding desirable recruits on a serious scale, or else to add something to it – say a proposal for a set of observances of the Samurai order. An expansion of the basis is always a thing to keep open for. But a change on what I call academic grounds is too risky: the more perfect your draft is when it goes in, the more grotesque it is likely to be when it comes out of the general butchery.

Give my love to Jane, that well-behaved woman. Why she married you (I being single at the time) the Life Force only knows.

G.B.S.

PS I have just had a talk with Olivier, and suggested to him a means by which we might possibly get the new basis through unaltered by adding to it a lot of Samurai order regulations which would draw all the debate and, though not surviving it themselves, secure an undisturbed passage for the rest. It would be very interesting besides: Webb & I, for instance, are far keener on pushing notions of this sort than on academic discussions about rent & interest & so forth. Olivier also is of the same mind.

Brentano had become Shaw's American publisher. Frederick Lawson **Dodd** (1868–1962), a dentist, was a member of the Fabian executive; Shaw goes on to mention other society members *en passant*: Rev. Stanton **Coit**, of the Ethical Church; Aylmer **Maude**, author and translator; Frederick Victor **Fisher** (1870–1954), writer and editor, who joined the society in 1899 but nine years later left it to join the Social Democratic Federation; H. Isaac **Mitchell**, alderman and labour union leader; Rev. Charles L. **Marson**. George **Standring's lampoon** was a humorous satirical attack on Wells based on Aesop's fable of the ambitious frog. Shaw's mention of **Songs of Innocence and Experience** refers to the best-known poems of William Blake (1757–1827), first published as *Songs of Innocence* (1789) and *Songs of Experience* (1793). The two volumes were brought together as *Songs of Innocence and of Experience* in 1794. Wells had given the name **'Samurai'** – the title of the Japanese military order of knighthood – to the group of self-selecting wise professionals who would rule the world, in his novel *A Modern Utopia* (1905).

18 / To G. Bernard Shaw

Spade House
Sandgate
26th March 1906

[HLU: BL 50552 ff 9–10]

Dear G.B.S.

You leave my Committee alone while I'm in America.

If I'm to identify myself with 'us', who's us? I'm not going to identify myself with your damned executive nohow, but I'm always open to a deal that will give results.

About 'Natural selection' & all that you ought to read Mark Baldwin. He has something to tell you.

Jane will forward letters, poor dear!

I've got five names now of people excluded by the Basis, & more will no doubt turn up.

James Mark **Baldwin** (1861–1934), widely known American psychologist and philosopher, had published *The Story of the Mind* in 1898 – probably the work to which Wells refers.

19 / To H.G. Wells

10 Adelphi Terrace WC
4th September 1906

[HLS: Illinois. Holograph letter entirely in Charlotte Shaw's hand.]

The BL has a somewhat different version which makes it clear – despite Charlotte's postscript – that GBS had a part in writing the draft. In any case, the letter was relevant to the Shaw/Wells relationship; hence its inclusion here. Wells was in America for two months gathering material for The Future in America, *pursuing an arduous itinerary and interviewing public figures from President Theodore Roosevelt to Jane Addams. He spent the summer months in writing this book and dealing with the publication of* In the Days of the Comet *(a novel about social change and, more especially, sexual freedom), which appeared in September. He worked also at writing the report of his committee.*

*The Webbs visited the Wellses 15 July, and Beatrice wrote in her diary that they found him 'grown in self-confidence ... with a corresponding contempt for us poor drudgers,' so that 'there is little room for friendly and hopeful discussion' (*The Diary of Beatrice Webb, Volume Three 1905–1924 *[1984], p. 43). In* The History of the Fabian Society *(1916) Edward Pease was to comment that the 'inner history' of the Committee was 'never revealed.' In any case, Wells drafted a report for the members to approve. Janet Dunbar says in* Mrs. G.B.S. *(1963), 'Wells ... sent a copy to Charlotte to sign, though, he said, he would understand if she were not in perfect agreement with his ideas' (p. 219).*

If I am not 'in perfect agreement'! My dear Mr. Wells! You must know quite well I cant sign this report.

You have let me in in the most abominable manner, you treacherous man, over this business. You must remember that before the Committee was formed you assured me over & over again that the past work of the Society formed no part of our business: that we were to devise forms of activity for the future & sketch out new work. I explained to you then that if your Committee meant criticism & discussion of the past work & methods of the Executive *I* could not be on it; as I was part of the Executive & it reduced the matter to an absurdity that I should criticise myself. But in spite of this understanding – as I conceived it –

the Committee has been nothing from its very first meeting but a Committee of Public Safety to try the Executive; with the foregone conclusion that we were to be condemned.

Dont misunderstand me. I dont object to criticism of our methods & proceedings, nor do the others. We welcome it; & shall presently begin to enjoy it, when the time comes to defend ourselves! But you cannot reasonably expect me to plead my own indictment. Try to realize that I am the accomplice of the Executive; that I am married to the Executive (just as poor Mrs. Wells is married to the Committee!); and that I really believe in the Executive & approve of it, & am in a state of continual astonishment at all it has done with its means. If I had to choose between the Committee & the Executive to govern the Society in future, do you suppose I should hesitate which to choose (even if I weren't married!)?

I have been very anxious, all through our sittings, to keep friendly to your Committee & I feel quite friendly still. But I dont agree with you & I wont sign your Report. I *know* what happens at & about the Executive & you dont; & what you have put in the Report about it is not what I know but what you dont know. There are certain things in the Report I like, & should have been so glad to help to push. For instance, the Constitution of the Groups & about elementary tracts & small books. But the impossible triumvirates, the magnificent publishing business, the grand suite of offices, the bringing everything to the test of ordinary business success: in short, your Commercial Utopia: all this you would have to cut out to get my signature; & then what would be left?

I dont know what the other members of the Executive will do. I have not seen or heard of either of them for some months. Mr. Headlam is always original, & *may* produce a minority report: Mr. Taylor is so new a member (of the Exec.) that he is not yet really one of us. What I will do I cannot say until the Report has been discussed. What I *wont* do is quite certain: I wont sign this.

G.B.S. has a scientific play [*The Doctor's Dilemma*] nearly finished which he would like to read to you. If only there were any chance of its being finished by Sunday I should propose a Folkestone week-end; but it has only reached the 4th act – & there are to be five.

Yours ever
C.F. Shaw

P.S. I have discussed the Report with G.B.S. of course; but he has neither part, nor lot, in this letter: it is mine!

20 / To Charlotte F. Shaw

Sandgate
5th September 1906

[HLU: BL 50552 ff 13–14]

No! Dear lady, you have betrayed me. You want everything better & everything just the same & it can't be done. I'm sorry you can't see your way to sign. I think I will try and push things through on the lines I propose. I daresay I shall get beaten – even then I shall have been greatly stimulating.

Isn't Shaw on my side? Are you all so happy in this ugly world, that the sacred fourteen is worth all chance of change?

By **the sacred fourteen** Wells means the existing Executive Committee of the Fabian Society.

21 / To H.G. Wells

10 Adelphi Terrace WC
11th September 1906

[TLS: Illinois]

The Shaws spent part of the summer in France (where GBS sat to Rodin), Ireland, and Cornwall, Shaw writing The Doctor's Dilemma. *A week after Charlotte's exchange with Wells, Shaw wrote the letter that follows. The 'Boot tract' was Wells's paper 'This Misery of Boots,' which he had read to the Fabians 12 January. It was published in 1907 as a special pamphlet of the Society, not in its series of regular tracts. Pease had told Wells that its publication would depend on the deletion of some personal taunts directed at Shaw and Webb.*

This Misery of Boots *concludes with a chapter called 'Socialism Means Revolution,' which embodies a scoffing criticism of the Fabian approach to Socialism – the commitment to what it perceived as a historical process; the belief in the necessity of gradualism; the policy of 'permeation'; the sense that the achievement of socialism must involve changes in bureaucratic structures and operation at every level of public service; and so on. 'You cannot change the world, and at the same time not change the world,' Wells wrote. 'You will find Socialists about, or at any rate men calling themselves Socialists, who will pretend that this is not so, who will assure you that some odd little jobbing about municipal gas and water is Socialism, and back-stairs intervention between Conservative and Liberal the way to the millennium.' Again, 'Socialism is a common-sense, matter-of-fact proposal to change our conventional admission of what is or is not property, and to re-arrange the world according to these revised conceptions. A certain number of clever people, dissatisfied with the straightforwardness of this, have set themselves to put it in some brilliant obscure way; they will tell you that Socialism is based on the philosophy of Hegel, or that it turns on a theory of Rent or that it is somehow muddled up with a sort of white Bogey called the Overman, and all sorts of brilliant, nonsensical, unappetising things.'*

Horatio Gustavus Wells

First, my hearty curse on you for compelling me to write you a letter when I am horribly pressed with necessary business, Fabian and other.

You sit down and write to Pease telling him that the Boot tract is at the disposal of the Publishing Committee (or the Executive) to strike out any passages they think injudicious.

Some time ago Gilbert Chesterton enlivened a Daily News article by mentioning, quite gratuitously (except for the satisfaction of the boyish impulse to put out his tongue at the man on the other side of the street) 'Mr Wells' prigs of Samurai.' Remonstrance being made by some sane person who was shocked at this breach of good manners, Gilbert owned up, and said he really didnt mean any harm.

Now suppose we publish something of Chesterton's in this new series of tracts. Suppose he gives us a good socialist article to republish, which would be very good business for us. And suppose, when it is read at the publishing committee, it is found to contain an important assurance that Socialism does not mean making us all into an impossible lot of prigs called Samurai, and that on the Publishing Committee requesting him to omit that sally, he refuses to alter a line of the article on the grounds (a) that Wells would be the last man to endorse the ridiculous objection of the committee, and that (b) it is to him (Gilbert) quite vital to disavow the priggish conceptions of Socialism that have got into circulation, what would you expect us to do?

Come! indicate our line of conduct in this hypothetical case, and distinguish it, if you can, from your own. And remember, as the mantling blush oerspreads your extensive cheek, that you discussed these very passages with me personally at Spade House as ever was, and admitted – nay, chucklingly gloried in the obvious fact – that they were deliberate jibes, and would naturally come out in the permanent Fabian edition of the paper.

Remember also, that the municipalization of gas and water is Socialism in gas and water, and that the contrary belief (of which the Social-Democratic Federation is the recognized exponent) is gas and gaiters. Remember also, that there is such a thing as intellectual loyalty, and that though it is quite natural and proper for the stockbroker on the Leas to sneer instinctively at Nietzsche, it would be for the Fabian an act of unpardonable Philistinism and for you personally an act of the blackest treachery. From your Martians to your Samurai, what have you been preaching all your life but the Superman? and what have you to say of Brer Nietzsche that does not recoil on your own head?

Write to Pease by return of post – wire – take a motor car and tell him in person, with ashes on your hat.

yrs ever
G. Bernard Shaw

PS. I have read your report. It is Webbism gone mad. However, I will explain that to you later on. Meanwhile (since you never think of such things) remember that it is not etiquette to issue your report until the sub-committees have reported; so be careful to conciliate them on this score or there will be ructions.

Gas and gaiters was one of two slang expressions used occasionally by Shaw for 'nonsense' – the other being the more common 'gammon.' The origin of 'gas and gaiters' is uncertain, the favoured one being that it is sailors' slang for a loud-mouthed, gaiter-wearing gunnery instructor (Granville, *A Dictionary of Sailor's Slang,* 1962).

22 / To H.G. Wells 10 Adelphi Terrace, London WC
14th September 1906

[TLS: Illinois. Several handwritten lines occupy the l.h. margin of p. 2.]

On the day when Shaw wrote this letter the Times Literary Supplement *published an article that marked the beginning of a period of public criticism of Wells's views concerning sexual morality. The coincidence – whether or not Shaw had read the article before he wrote the letter – is interesting. Long before he went to America Wells was practising the sexual freedom that he championed in his novels and elsewhere (he himself implies in* H.G. Wells in Love *[written 1934–6; published 1984] that his initiatives in these matters began at the time when he was building Spade House – i.e., 1900). Eventually his actions and opinions scandalized the conventional-minded public and were the cause of a good deal of turmoil in the Fabian Society. That they caused his wife Jane great distress needs hardly to be said, regardless of her eventually coming to terms with them. Shaw, not disposed to be judgmental, seems to have made virtually no reference to them. The opening paragraphs of the following letter are more than a mocking criticism of Wells's* Comet *novel, however: they make clear, in GBS's teasing fashion, his sense of the stress that was on Jane, of whom Charlotte and he were both fond.*

My dear H.G.W.

May I without indelicacy ask whether Jane has been unusually trying of late? Can it be that during your absence in America that Roman matron has formed an attachment for some man of genius nearer home – I will name no names, but, say, one whose more mature judgment, more majestic stature, more amiable disposition, and more obvious devotion to her person, has placed you at a disadvantage in her eyes? At all events, when I take the opportunity presented by a letter of my wife's which I am asked to correct (and touch up), to invite myself to Spade House for a week-end, and when the recipient of that invitation (for such it was), instead of expressing the delight with which he looks forward to my arrival, morosely declines to take the hint and compels me to go up the river with Barker, I feel justified in demanding whether he considers himself a gentleman. Surely something is due to Hospitality in the abstract if not to me in the concrete. I am the last man to thrust myself in where I am not welcome; but I cannot help suspecting that some reason beyond the mere exhaustion of my conversation is at work here. What is all this in the Comet about a *ménage à quatre*? What does it mean? Why does the book break off so abruptly? Why not take some green gas and be frank? I have never concealed my affection for Jane. If the moroseness and discontent which have marked your conduct of late are the symptoms of a hidden passion for Charlotte, say so like a man. She takes a great interest in you – one which might easily ripen into a deeper feeling if ardently cultivated. It seems hardly possible that she can be tired of me: still, the first freshness is undoubtedly rubbed off our union. On the other hand Jane MUST be tired of you if you go on at her the way you have been lately going on at me. Well, a single example is worth all the fine writing and all the fictitious comets in the world. Jane is an extremely nice woman; and I doubt if you have ever appreciated her. I have always had an exceptionally open mind on these subjects. Do not let a mere legal technicality stand between us. If you would like to make it a group marriage, and can get round Charlotte, and Jane doesnt mind (if she does, I can at least be a father to her), you need apprehend no superstitious difficulties on my part.

As you say, we are a lot of rich and comfortable sentimentalists, fiddling while Rome is starving. And therein lies a peril to the poor Fabian. I have had 22 years of the Fabian. There must be an end of it someday. There are not wanting those who say that it has done its work. It hasnt; but *I* have done *my* turn. Webb has done his turn. The old gang has done its turn. Pease has burnt his boats and must stick to the ship because he cannot afford to drop his £150 a year; but you have no idea how strong the temptation is for the rest of us to unload on you. We have done enough for honor: why not let you walk over? If you really mean business; if you will steer that crazy little craft for five years to come, making the best of it no matter how ridiculously it may disappoint you, I will abdicate and the others will do the same. That is the real and hideous danger that confronts you.

You had much better come on the executive for a year of two before you commit yourself. You have no idea – nobody without actual experience can have any idea – of the instability of these little beginnings of social crystallization. They are like Prince Rupert's drops: they fly into fragments at the slightest nip. The energy that wastes itself in senseless quarrelling would reform the world three times over if it could be concentrated and brought to bear on Socialism. The whole thing is so ridiculous that if you once let your mind turn from your political object to criticism of the conduct and personality of the men around you, you are lost. Instantly you find them insufferable; they find you the same; and the problem of how to get rid of one another supersedes Socialism, to the great advantage of the capitalist. Lord Cardigan riding into the

Balaclava charge with his mind wholly preoccupied with the fact that Nolan had insulted him personally is a type of the sort of human material you have to work with. Here are you, a quite exceptionally reasonable and strong minded man, already turned completely from your message to the Fabian by an irresistible impulse to expose the futility of the lot of us. You want to play the part of the Comet; and you sit down to make yourself wretched by insisting on the jerkiness of Bland's literary style. Figure that to yourself from any point of view remote enough from Bland to prevent his blotting out the sun from you; and then imagine yourself with a committee of a dozen Wellses, bound to make the most of them, forced to recognize that so far from their being bad material, they are exceptionally good material, and able to do nothing unless you can drive them all twelve-in-hand, although their soft mouths and sore heads make it certain that the first impatient word that escapes you will send them all kicking and snorting in different directions. Then you will begin to see what you are up against just now.

I dont myself believe that you are going to do more with the Fabian than we have done; but you can use it, as we have done, as an instrument for increasing your own efficiency. You cannot go on spinning comets out of your head for ever. You have done Kipps; and you have done the Comet hero; and having done them you will dry up like Kipling unless by a continuous activity you push your experience further. You must get the committee habit: that is, you must learn the habits of the human political animal as a naturalist learns the habits of wasps, by watching them. And you must learn their possibilities by trying to accomplish definite political ends through them. You must acquire the personal force of the practised speaker (and not entrap a few poor devils in Croydon into engaging a public hall, and then leave ME to save them from ruin by taking your place on the platform). You must, in short, learn your business as a propagandist and peripatetic philosopher if you are ever to be anything more than a novelist bombinating in vacuo except for a touch of reality gained in your early life. We have all been through the Dickens blacking factory; and we are all socialists by reaction against that; but the world wants from men of genius what they have divined as well as what they have gone through. You must end either in being nothing, or in being something more than a man with a grievance, which is what your Comet chap is. I was accidentally and externally a clerk like him once; but really I was a prince. Your Kippses and people are true to nature, or rather to modern civilization, just as David Copperfield's dread of Littimer and his adventures with his landlady are true to civilization; but David Copperfield is not a man at all: Dickens has never for a moment given himself away in that book; and your Hoopdrivers & Kippses & Comet men, though excellent as demonstrations, are mere masks behind which you hide yourself. You are always bragging that you have been Kipps & that you know. This is a quintessential lie: if you had been Kipps you wouldnt know. If you said 'I am God: and know', it would be more to the point: Well, now that Kipps is demonstrated, you must learn a new trade – the Fabian trade. And the product will be, not a suite of offices & a million subscribers, but an approfounded and disillusioned and more variously effective Wells. – I am off to Ireland today & havnt time for more. Address: Castle Haven. Castle Townshend: Skibbereen. Co. Cork.

GBS

Harley Granville **Barker** (1877–1946) had met Shaw in June 1900. Barker was then several years into his career as actor, playwright, director and, later, Shakespearean critic. He had probably first met the Wellses in the Fabian Society. In Wells's *In the Days of the Comet* (serialized 1905–6; published in book form, October 1906), the tail of the comet, through which the earth passes, consists of a beautiful translucent substance – 'a veil of green drawn across the world' – the effect of which is to transform human nature and make possible a utopia of peace, goodwill, beauty, social equality, and freedom of sexual and familial love. **Prince Rupert's drops** were small glass bubbles with tails. If part of the tail was broken off, the bubble exploded.

James Thomas Brudenell, 7th Earl of **Cardigan** (1797–1868), was commander of the Light Brigade at the Battle of Balaklava in 1854. A notoriously quarrelsome man, he was incensed when Captain Lewis Nolan (1820–54) actually galloped in front of him at the beginning of the charge that Cardigan was leading, evidently in an effort to warn him that he had mistaken the order Nolan had brought to him. The catastrophic charge continued and, ironically, Nolan was almost immediately killed (by a Russian shell fragment), while Cardigan not only rode on, but was one of the few men of the brigade to survive – virtually unhurt. None the less, as the charge had already begun when Nolan tried to intervene, Cardigan's 'preoccupation' is more likely to have been primarily with the ill-judged order he had received than with the added stimulus provided by Nolan.

Littimer is the highly 'respectable' servant of Steerforth in *David Copperfield*, by Charles Dickens (1812–70). When Dickens was twelve years old his father was imprisoned for debt, and the son had to take work in a blacking (i.e., shoe polish and the like) warehouse to support himself. **Hoopdriver** is the central figure in Wells's early novel *The Wheels of Chance* (1896).

23 / To G. Bernard Shaw

Spade House, Sandgate
18th September 1906

[ALS: BL 50552 f 15]

According to Pease's History of the Fabian Society *(London, 1916), the report of Wells's special committee proposed, inter alia, the replacement of the executive of the Fabian Society by a council of twenty-five members, which was to appoint a triumvirate of three committees (for publishing, propaganda, and general purposes) of three members each. When the executive discussed the report on 12 October, Shaw was asked to draft a response that would include the executive's agreement to increase its size to twenty-one members; its objection to the idea of a 'triumvirate'; its objection to revising the Basis; and other points.*

My dear Shaw

You write the most gorgeous letters! I bow down. You are wonderful. The amazing thing is that just at one point the wonderfulness stops short. Why *dont* you see how entirely I am expressing *you* in all these things. Don't you see that to abolish that 14-in-hand, the executive has been the vague passion of your life? Fall in with my tri-umvirate. (They'll never elect me).

We are overwhelmed by the weekend we missed. For God's sake say it plain next time – & let it be soon. Then we will eliminate our last trivial differences.

Yours ever,
H.G.B. Shawells

Wells's coinage of the name **Shawells** in the signature implies playfully his perception – referred to in the letter itself – of the fundamental similarities between the objectives and habits of thought of the two men, a matter adverted to from time to time to the end of their correspondence. It is possible that Shaw, consciously or not, had Wells's word in mind when a year and a half later he wrote 'The Chesterbelloc: A Lampoon,' an article about G.K. Chesterton and Hilaire Belloc that is set in a framework of references to Wells. It appeared in *The New Age*, 15 February 1908, and was included in *Pen Portraits and Reviews* (1931).

24 / To H.G. Wells

Castle Haven
Castle Townshend
22nd September 1906

[ALS: Illinois]

The Shaws were in Ireland from 14 September to 6 October. Charlotte received a 'second edition' of the report in September and a further 'amended' one in October, to both of which she responded with acceptance of some parts, rejection of others, and suggestions. The following letter was written before she received them.

My Dear H.G.W.

The triumvirates will be wrecked by Democracy with a large D. A triumvirate would have no power at all, any more than the Czar has. It would be a fatal mistake for you to accept office as a triumvir; and I should refuse with a flourish, as the others would. The executive is in effect so autocratic that the society is always a little on the defensive; and when a new man gets on, he generally comes in to make a stand against the domination of the old gang. Muggeridge will tell you what happens. The new man finds that he has nothing to object to; that he has his say and is friendly entreated; and that he finds that if there is very little for him to do, it is because he is a fifth wheel to the coach, and not in the least because he is denied his place on the axle. Also he finds that the executive works well; that its smoking and joking lubricate its discussions; and that its business gets rather over- than under-debated.

Out of this comes the difficulty that it is not always easy to retain good recruits. For instance, we cannot keep capable women. Mrs Besant & Mrs Stanton Blatch were forerunners of a long string of really energetic women who have come on the executive and gone off again on discovering that they were fifth wheels – that the work was being done as well as it could be done by the old lot; that they were not being tyrannized or ignored; that there were no practical grievances; in short, that there was nothing for them to do that was not being done equally well without them. This was not quite true: once a year they made a difference; but that was not valuable enough for their time & trouble: they would not spend three years marking time for the sake of kicking a small stone out of the way three times or less.

It has been the same with all the men who have not found the executive atmosphere specially congenial to them. I planned for years to get the late William Clarke, for instance, on the executive; but he was a cantankerous man, and would not attend for the fun of the thing; so he really made no difference and dropped it. And here you have the real difficulty about new blood. We want a new set to unload on, and have wanted it for a long time past; but we automatically repel the capable, because the capable will not take up a burden which is being carried by somebody else in a manner which, on close examination, proves to be as efficient as is possible under the circumstances. If you came on the executive – which is a thing much to be desired by us – you would retire at the end of two years at the very outside unless you personally enjoyed it, or unless you could develop & lead a new policy (and we have tried all the new policies years ago). I think you would have a good chance of really catching on; but what is most to be feared in the event of your failing to acquire the executive habit – that is, of finding the executive, on the whole, rather amusing – is your becoming convinced that old Pease & old Shaw & old Webb & old Bland & the rest were getting all that was to be got out of the poor old Fabian, and saving your own time and energy for literature at large.

Fortunately, you are the sort of man who does not finish his education, and always wants a school. Well, the Fabian is a school for the exercise & development of certain personal powers – committee power, public speaking & debating &c – and that might hold you a little.

Now as to the democratic point. Democracy does not mean government of the Fabians by the Fabians & never can mean it; but it does mean government of the Fabians by consent of the Fabians. The Fabians put up with me because they know that they can chuck me when they please. And as I am tolerably confident that they wont please, I cling to the arrangement. My position as a triumvir would be far more precarious; and so would yours. If I supported the triumvirate scheme they would regard it (rightly) as an attempt on my part to make myself independent of them & boss them whether they liked it or not. I am already under suspicion of being a very lukewarm democrat because, as we all do, I deride the notions of crude democracy which the young revolutionist always boils with until he has ten minutes administrative experience. The more we fight against the dream of government *by* the people, the more we must stick to government by consent of the people; and that is, for the Fabian, represented by our present system of universal suffrage and direct election of the executive.

I still think that the whole strength & charm of your report lies in the group scheme, especially the Samurai groups. I believe if you developed that in the largest imaginative way, and even suggested rules of life for the central Fabian, the society would become enormously interested; you would become enormously popular; and you would carry your new basis & as much as would save your face of the rest –

Here is the post. I have not time even to read this over –

GBS

Henry Thomas **Muggeridge** (1864–1942) had been for some years a Fabian, and served on the executive in 1903–5. He was a Labour MP (1929–31) and the father of Malcolm Muggeridge (1903–91), author, editor, television personality. Mrs Annie **Besant** (1847–1933), social reformer and theosophist, had been one of the early Fabians and was a member of the executive in 1886–90. Harriet Stanton **Blatch** was a member of it in 1894–5, William **Clarke** (a journalist) in 1888–1.

25 / To H.G. Wells 10 Adelphi Terrace, London WC

17th December 1906

[TLS: Illinois]

The story of events in the Fabian Society in the autumn of 1906 and afterward has been told many times, most coherently and objectively by Norman and Jeanne MacKenzie in their biography of Wells, The Time Traveller *(1973), and in* The Fabians *(1977). The report of the special committee – the 'Wells Committee' – and the executive's reply to it were the subject of meetings of the Society on 7 and 14 December and five subsequent ones in 1907 (including the annual meeting, 2 March). Both the political manoeuvring and the feelings involved were affected not only by the perception that Wells wanted to alter the structure, aims, and leadership of the Society, but also by his publicly avowed support of sexual freedom – and the reputation for practising it that he was acquiring. At a meeting in October he had given a lecture on 'Socialism and the Middle Classes' that was in part 'an indictment of bourgeois marriage as the moral counterpart of private property' (MacKenzie) and advocated making the raising of children a state responsibility. Aside from other effects, the lecture ensured a large attendance, particularly of younger Fabians, at the 7 December meeting.*

At that meeting an amendment moved by Wells called in effect for the present executive to remove itself from office, making way for the changes in structure that Wells had envisaged. (In an undated note to Charlotte he had indicated that an early election was in his mind.) However, Wells's speech on the amendment (printed in the following week) was seriously flawed, and his behaviour to some members of the special committee – particularly its chairman, whom Wells had in effect brushed aside – markedly discourteous. The meeting was adjourned before Wells's amendment was put to a vote.

Hubert Bland, though himself a notorious philanderer, had been outraged by Wells's October lecture as well as the proffered amendment, and proposed that he speak at the ensuing meeting. In a note on 10 December, included with a postcard sent to many members of the Society urging them to attend the next meeting, Shaw advised Bland not *to speak: 'you had better leave the job to me. [Wells] came here on Saturday morning quite blithe and affectionate. He said, "Shaw: I apologize. NOW!" I tried to explain that this would not get him out of his corner. He said I was an Irishman – meaning, as far as I could make out, that I was vindictive.'*

*At the meeting on 14 December Wells – no match for Shaw in either oratorical or parliamentary skills – was obliged to withdraw his amendment. Beatrice Webb noted in her diary that if Wells 'had pushed his own fervid policy ... without making a personal attack on the Old Gang, he would have succeeded. The Old Gang are anxious to retire – are aware that ... they are played out, their work lying in other directions ... But his accusations were so preposterous, his innuendoes so unsavoury and his little fibs so transparent, that even his own followers refused to support him ... GBS, by a scathing analysis of his whole conduct, threw him finally to the ground and trampled on him ... An altogether horrid business' (*Diary, Volume Three, *p. 62).*

Shaw, although he had felt compelled to refute the amendment, was genuinely concerned that the Society should not lose a man of Wells's real stature and abilities.

My dear H.G.W.

Just a few lines in great haste provisionally. There will be no executive election until the regular one, probably; nor would it be desirable for you to have one. Just now you are at your zero electorally. But you can easily retrieve the situation if you will study your game carefully, or else do exactly what I tell you. We shall have a series of adjournments to discuss the reforms one after the other; and your Committee will no doubt move amendments to resolution 2, that the proposed 21 committee men be twentyfive councillors; that the sub-committees be triumvirates; that a fixed subscription be adopted; that the basis be altered by such and such clauses &c., keeping up a running fight with us. Now we shall no doubt score pretty well, and carry our resolutions against the amendments; but there is glory to be won in the engagements; and that glory will mean votes at the election. *Some* amendments will be carried against us, or at least accepted by us: I always make a point of accepting what I can. Your merry men will also have plenty of chances of making themselves known by speaking, which is the only way in which recruits ever get on the executive. These battles will carry us over until it is too close to the ordinary election time to make it possible to attempt a belated 1906 election.

Meanwhile, you MUST make up your mind to two things: first, that the moral superiority tack is an impossible one as against such strong and straight players as we are, and second, that you must carefully study the etiquette of public routine. You have outrageously disregarded the elementary rights of your people, and thereby driven Headlam to lead the attack on you instead of supporting you. Headlam had an absolute right to be summoned to all your conferences on the report, and to have a part in determining the procedure to be adopted at the meeting. Olivier had a sacred claim to move the committee resolution: the fact that he was thrust over into the five-minute ruck, and that I had to rise to claim unlimited time for him, was a horrible scandal. Your reckless mention of Coit and Mrs Reeves in your printed speech was simple madness from the point of view of the experienced parliamentarian. Now people will stand this and worse from a leader who will carry them to smashing victories, just as the Irish party submitted to unheard-of contempt from Parnell. But you havnt led your people to victory: you have delivered them helpless into our hands, so that your defeat was a mere mechanical operation. This wont do. You must win your committee back by giving up the leadership to Olivier, and contenting yourself with supporting his motions. And you must win back the Society too; for you made a mistake which is hardly exaggerable in refusing to alter that tract. You should have offered, with a noble air, to allow me to edit it exactly as I pleased: that would have won back most of your flying followers at a stroke. But you dont know these things yet; and they cant be learnt except by a very impersonal study of them.

Goodnight: I must stop.
G.B.S.

Rev. Stewart **Headlam**, Dr Stanton **Coit**, and Mrs Pember **Reeves** were among the members of the special committee.

26 / To H.G. Wells

10 Adelphi Terrace WC
16th January 1907

[ALS: Illinois]

Presumably there was little contact between Wells and Shaw in the month after the preceding letter was written. During the autumn the Shaws had occupied the house at Ayot St Lawrence that was to remain their principal base (although they kept for many years their London flat) until their deaths. On 30 December Charlotte received a note from Haden-Guest, a member of the special committee, saying that as Wells had now 'pro tem retired,' Guest was 'arrogating to myself secretarial powers' and proposing a meeting. She replied, 'The Special Committee ceased to exist when it had presented its report to the executive,' adding that she was writing to Mr and Mrs Wells to ask whether they shared her view. She did so, adding, 'We go up [to London] tomorrow morning, as G.B.S is rehearsing "Brassbound" for America, & shall be in Town the whole week. Is there any chance of our meeting? I do so very much hope there is – We both want to have a chat so much. Unfortunately we cannot *get down to Sandgate. Every possible good wish to you both.'*

The response to her note is unknown. Her reference to rehearsing is a sufficient reminder that both Wells and Shaw were extremely busy with their professional writing careers, for which the Fabian Society affairs, though too important to be neglected, were a distraction and to some extent a nuisance. In any case, Wells had written an angry letter for publication in Fabian News, *hotly critical of the treatment he had received at the 14 December meeting.*

Dear H.G.W.

Will you interrupt your labors for a moment to send a note to Pease (to arrive on Friday before the Exec.) withdrawing that long letter that you wanted put in Fabian News. Do this for the sound reason, which you can allege at any time if necessary, that I asked you to. Webb & I have tried to suppress the letter by main force; but the others want it in, which is another very good reason for you to want it out.

I am dead against this exhibition sparring – all the more as I do it so well that the sympathy goes to my opponent – and your cue for the moment is to come up smiling.

Anyhow, withdraw the letter: you didn't take any real trouble with it and you need not grudge it to the waste paper basket. Yours ever,

G.B.S.

27 / To H.G. Wells

10 Adelphi Terrace WC
15th February 1907

[APCS: Illinois]

[*Originally addressed to Spade House, readdressed ℅ The Hon. Bertrand Russell, Bagley Wood, Oxford.*]

Do not forget that next Friday, the 22nd, is the last day for nominations for the new Exec. I found tonight that nobody has been nominated except by the executive committee. If you are not nominated by next Friday, I shall nominate you myself unless you refuse to stand. You have no idea how people get caught out by neglecting these formalities: hence this reminder.

G.B.S.

P.S. Did Miss Maudie Darrell in the Cassilis Engagement strike you as being very like somebody?

Maudi (or Maude) **Darrell** (1882–1910) acted in *The Cassilis Engagement*, a new play by Edward Charles St John Hankin (1869–1909). It was performed twice by the Stage Society at the Imperial Theatre in early February. It is not known to whom Shaw's postscript referred 'as somebody.'

28 / To H.G. Wells and Sidney Webb

10 Adelphi Terrace, London WC
2nd May 1907

[TLS: Illinois. BL 50682, ff 27–30, is a typed draft of the following letter attached to which is Shaw's draft Basis (BL 50628). Neither is included here.]

Wells was elected to the executive of the Fabian Society in March 1907, and on 19 April the executive named Shaw, Webb, and Wells as a committee to propose a new statement of the Basis and aims of the Fabian Society. In preparing a preliminary draft, Shaw took into account two matters that had been of recent concern to the Fabians: 'that one of the objects of the Fabian Society is to establish the equal citizenship of men and women' (Minutes of the Executive, 5 December 1906); and the case put forward by Wells for having 'the parent regarded as the trustee and guardian of the child, and in no sense as its private proprietor' (Shaw's draft Basis).

At the meeting on 8 March 1907 it was proposed to take steps that would have led the Society to be more directly politically active. The proposal was strongly supported by Wells's followers, but was unsuccessful. One of its principal proponents was G.R.S. Taylor, a member of the executive, who reported the matter in an article called 'Fabian Folly,' which was published in the Labour Leader. *That action resulted in the proposal of a motion at the executive meeting of 10 May 'strongly disapproving' of Taylor's making public 'an account of a private meeting.' The motion was watered down so as to be simply a statement of principle, with no direct reference to Taylor's action, in an amendment offered by Sidney Webb; it was then passed. Shaw's letter suggests that Keir Hardie had prompted Taylor to take the action that he did. Taylor had written a letter of apology to the executive.*

Dear W(ells or ebb)

We may as well get this Basis job into hand and out of it promptly, by way of setting a good example to the new committees.

I therefore plank down a draft to start with. I am sending copies to both of you and retaining the original; so you need not circulate it. The paragraphs are numbered for convenience of comment or reference.

In drafting it I have assumed that we must limit the Basis to our specific objects and their political implications, so as to make the test for admission exclude nobody who is a socialist and a democrat, no matter what else he may be. I have, however, included Women's Rights and Wells's point about the children; and I have aimed at producing an effective filter to make our membership really select in the Fabian sense.

Will you either send it back to me with your comments, or else let us meet and discuss. We have to consider not only the draft itself, but the question whether we shall propose its substitution for the old Basis, or its institution as an additional test which candidates shall be required to read before being sworn in, or its provisional adoption as a gloss on the basis &c. &c. &c.

Also whether it would be worth while, when we have agreed on it, to send a proof of it with Fabian News to each member, asking whether, if brought forward, it would be voted for as it stands without amendment, or, if not, with what amendments.

We might even give the thing some sort of preliminary canter at the annual meeting on the 10th May, if we can agree on it in time. The Society would be more interested and encouraged by it than by anything else; and it would do something to wash out the nasty taste of the anti-Taylor resolution, which I wish we could get rid of altogether, as it is old history and nobody cares a rap about it now except Hobson, Bland and Chesterton, who suffered personally. Taylor has made it clear that K.H. was the real Machiavelli in the affair; and it is neither desirable to let this out, nor to have a bogus debate about Taylor with the truth up our sleeves.

Yours samuraitically,
G. Bernard Shaw

29 / To H.G. Wells

10 Adelphi Terrace WC
5th May 1907

[TLS: Illinois]

Wells's reply to the preceding letter has not been found. Its gist may be deduced from Shaw's response.

My dear H.G.

Good: I shall amend the document so as to make it clear that scientific as distinct from commercial research is the business of the State, and that the private man cannot equip his own laboratory or buy half a pound of radium.

As to the substitution of the idea of service for the idea of gain, what can you add to Ruskin (who is now for the first time cheap & accessible) on that point; and even if Ruskin had never written a word, what could you add to De Quincey & Carlyle, to Lord Shaftesbury & even Gladstone? Cancel them; and you still have 300 years of the Bible behind you. Why, the idea is in the very grain of our minds: Eton & Oxford, Harrow & Cambridge are saturated with it as thoroughly as Uriah Heep (before he found out that in practice it meant skinning him alive). Ask any member of the 80 Club or the Primrose League: not one of them will deny that your idea is the right one. 'The golden rule' they call it. What people want to know now is why it does not work – why honesty is *not* the best policy – why the idler flourishes & the toiler perishes etc.etc. Unless we have something to tell people that Sir Thomas More didn't know, and a basis that Ruskin would not have signed, we have no *raison d'être* apart from Headlam's Church of England. In the F.S. basis we must stick to the F.S's point. All the rest that you have to say you must say in your own books, as

I say what I have to say in mine. It is quite useless to try to expand the Fabian spout to take all your output.

As to the statement that we do not ask the nation to join the F.S., you imagine this is a jibe. It is not. The whole success of the Fabian – the whole failure of the S.D.F etc. – is explained by this substitution of the idea of service to the community for gain & Aggrandisement of the F.S. The old cry, 'Proletarians of all lands, unite – in our organization; and we will lead you to victory' is the folly that has damned every Socialist Society that ever existed. We have absolutely nothing but our ideas to offer; and to sell them in exchange for votes & subscriptions is 'the idea of gain' at its maddest. If you want a party, there are three or four to choose from; and we hope to see another – a Socialist one – formed. But we shall not give to party what was meant for &c &c &c &c &c &c.

I must hurry off to lecture at Oxford. Back tomorrow early.

What the devil are you doing in the Reform Club?

Yours ever
G.B.S.

Thomas **De Quincey** (1785–1859), Thomas **Carlyle** (1795–1881), Lord **Shaftesbury** (1801–85), and William Ewart **Gladstone** (1809–98) were all, like John Ruskin (see p. 8), critics of the social injustices of the nineteenth century, in differing ways and from differing points of view: the first two as writers, Shaftesbury as philanthropist, Gladstone as political reformer. Uriah Heep is 'the umblest person going' and unscrupulous student of the law in *David Copperfield.* The **80 Club** was a London club founded in 1880; the **Primrose League**, a Conservative Society formed in 1883 in honour of Disraeli. Sir Thomas **More** (1478–1535), statesman and author of *Utopia,* was executed by Henry VIII on the charge of high treason when he refused to condone Henry's divorce from Catherine of Aragon. The Social Democratic Federation (**S.D.F.**) was founded in 1883 as the Democratic Federation by Henry Mayers Hyndman (1842–1921), a financial promoter and journalist who drew many of his ideas from Marx. The S.D.F. was one of the more radical of the reformist groups of this period. Several early Fabians, including GBS, had been associated with it before establishing their own Society. Wells had been elected a member of the **Reform Club** – an Establishment political and literary club – in March 1905.

30 / To G. Bernard Shaw

Spade House
Sandgate
[*n.d.*]

[ALS: BL50552 f 9]

The Wellses lived at Spade House from December 1900 until the summer of

*1909. Lovat Dickson dates this letter 1909 (*H.G. Wells: His Turbulent Life and Times *[1969]), but does not state his grounds for doing so. Lacking firm evidence one might suppose an earlier date. Wells's engagement books show that he had been increasingly frequenting the Bland household through 1905 until – following six successive days in which it seems that it had been his central concern – there is no mention of it after 23 January 1906. If 'the Bland affair' means HGW's affair with Hubert Bland's daughter Rosamund, this letter may date from the summer or autumn of 1907. HGW wrote Violet Hunt on 9 March 1907, expressing his interest ('a pure flame') in Rosamund. Dorothy Richardson was then pregnant by him and miscarried that summer. By May 1908 he and Amber Reeves were lovers. One may guess that Wells's attempt to elope with Rosamund (if it happened at all and was not merely Fabian gossip) occurred between those dates. David C. Smith surmises that Shaw wrote Wells 'in an attempt to have Wells stop seeing Rosamund' (*H.G. WELLS Desperately Mortal, *p. 519). Michael Holroyd quotes from the following letter but mentions neither address, date, nor source (*Bernard Shaw, *vol. 2 [1989], p. 257). Shaw (whose letter has in any case vanished) may quite possibly have written to ask about a reply to his suggestion concerning the Basis, and gone on to mention the Bland business. But function is here smothered in surmise; the one certainty is that Wells had lost his temper.*

Dear Shaw

The more I think you over the more it comes home to me what an unmitigated middle-Victorian ass you are. You play about with ideas like a daring garrulous maiden aunt, but when it comes to an affair like the Bland affair you show the instincts of conscious gentility and the judgement of a hen. You write of Bland in a strain of sentimental exaltation. You explain his beautiful & romantic character to me – as though I didnt know the man to his bones. You might be dear Mrs. Bland herself in a paroxysm of romantic invention. And all this twaddle about the 'innocent little person'. If she is innocent it isn't her parents' fault anyhow.

The fact is yours is a flimsy intellectual acquisitive sort of mind adrift & chattering brightly in a world you dont understand. You dont know, as I do, in blood & substance, lust, failure, shame, hate, love, and creative passion. You dont understand & you cant understand the rights &

wrongs of the case into which you stick your maiden judgement – any more than you can understand the aims in the Fabian Society that your vanity has wrecked.

Now go on being amusing.
Yours ever
H.G. Wells

31 / To H.G. Wells

Hafod-y-Bryn. Llanbedr
Merioneth R.S.O.
14th August 1907

[ALS: Illinois]

Following a suggestion of Dr F. Lawson Dodd (1868–1962), a member of the executive, with money provided by Charlotte Shaw, the Fabian Society held in the summer of 1907 the first of a long series of annual summer schools. These were lecture holidays, intended mainly to encourage the interest and socialist views of the young people who, partly under the stimulus of Wells's thought and writings, were joining the Society. On this first occasion the Shaws took a nearby house, and Shaw participated energetically in the activities of the 'school.' On 7 August Charlotte wrote Jane Wells, inviting the Wellses to visit them for a few days. 'I know H.G. said nothing would induce him to come to the Summer School,' she began, '– but G.B.S. thinks he weakened just at the end of his last visit to Adelphi Terrace. Will you try to persuade him to?' Wells was not persuaded.

My dear H.G.W.

On the whole I think you had better see how much Jackson & Orage can get elsewhere before you put your hand in your pocket – at least to any depth. But I think the N.A. must be kept going. It is by chalks the best thing of the kind that has been done. No Socialist paper has ever before made even an attempt at serious day-by-day political criticism of parliament or of the movement. Of course we can pick holes; but they are the holes that can be patched only by our undertaking the editing ourselves; and since we are not prepared to do that we must remember that *le mieux est l'ennemi du bien.* I have purposely written a long screed that will fill three numbers of The Clarion to show the N.A. how such incidents as the Cromer grant should be tackled, and to rub off the silly class shyness that stands between us and the Labor Party. J. & O. will quite understand, as to Cromer, that this is what they ought to have said, instead of echoing the nonsense about his being 'the author' of Egypt's prosperity – such as it is. Also, I shall write to Jackson telling him that he must not put in puffs of Co-operative [*Quarries*] and booksellers whom he thinks 'decent chaps,' but must keep a hard fist over a serious paper. But, all deductions made, the paper must not be let drop. By the way, I had much rather have given them £100 than write the Clarion stuff; but money is no use except occasionally to throw back in the face of a man who wants to buy you cheap: it always ends in having to do a bit of work.

The movement is still childish. Upton Sinclair's book is in some respects heartbreaking. When I see all that hopeless tosh about capitalism becoming bankrupt by having more money than it can invest – stuff that I cut out of my edition of poor old Gronlund's Co-operative Commonwealth 24 years ago – when I come on such blatant inaccuracies as New Zealand being advanced because it was peopled by convicts!!! (convicts in respectable N.Z.!!!!) I really feel unutterable things. Kropotkin's European war that was to break up capitalism punctually next Tuesday week (same day Aveling was to pay you the five shillings or five pounds you had lent him), Hyndman's revolution of 1889: those dreams were at least romantic. But the Gronlund-Wilshire-Sinclair economics! – *what* are we to do with them? It is all such baby affectation of grown-up statesmanship, such *bloody BLOODY* nonsense. They mistake a silly reactionary anti-trust agitation for Socialism. How are we to teach them that only the complete and successful consummation of capitalism can give us the economic jumping-off place for Socialism. Write to Sinclair and ask him how he dare dedicate such trash to you.

The day before yesterday I had an interesting adventure. I went into a pretty rough sea; the tide suddenly turned; and when I tried to swim back I found the shore had walked away fifty feet, and was on its way to another fifty in spite of all I could do. You know what numbers 7, 8 & 9 are in every 10 waves in a rough sea. I had been diving through them until I was quite tired before I got swept out. But when you are trying to swim to shore, you don't bother about them; and they come up behind & snow you under and smother your head & sluice your stomach, and, when you try to take advantage of their sweep shoreward, drag you back with an almighty swirl just nicely for the next one. Loraine, bathing with me & following me out, shared my fate. For five hours (probably minutes) I swam without the slightest hope of escape, solely to put off the disagreeableness of drowning as long as possible, and noting how the tide was carrying me northwards along the shore and out. I gave up struggling to get back the moment I found that I was overpowered. My reflections [*sketch of the sea with GBS's head*] were of the most prosaic kind: I utterly failed to rise to the occasion dramatically. Chiefly I damned my folly for having postponed altering my now obsolete will, which I had brought down to Llanbedr for the purpose. My affairs were not in order. Charlotte would be a widow and would never make out about my translators, whose contracts are all higgledy-pigg – confound you (this to number seven) I must get my head up and get breath before number eight comes – *there* you are, you brute: now for number nine and a lull. When I think how carefully I ducked through them when we were in our depth! – and now I dont even look over my shoulder when I hear the rush and roar coming at my occiput. Where is Loraine? is he done for too? yes: there he is swirling like a tub in the suds, not gaining an inch, up against it, but not, like me, having had his fling. Can I help him? Good heavens, *I* help anybody! Number seven again, very eloquent on that point. Number eight rubs it in. Number nine half-hearted – a lull. No use telling him I am pretty nearly done: it might lead to his telling me that he is worse. Preserve a calm countenance, as of one who knew the coast and did this for pleasure every day. Can the people on the shore do anything? Clearly nothing. None of them know the sea as well as I do: if I cannot save myself nobody can save me: I cannot help Loraine nor can he help me. (What an idiot I was about that will!) They are all hulking about on the stones or talking in groups, without the slightest suspicion that we are not having a delightful swim. The dabblers in the surf are quite happy. Number seven again – eight – nine – Loraine swimming in foam – streaky foam – not in water at all – probably nearly done but keeping up appearances as industriously as myself. I am bound to try to save him; but as to doing anything! oh vanity of chivalry and unspeakable rebuke to safe-between-the-sheets estimates of one's courage and strength! – number seven – thank you: I am convinced; but aren't you a little before your time? hello! a stone: for a moment I can stand on it – only the tenth of

ontue. I went into a pretty rough sea; the tide suddenly
shore had walked away fifty feet, and was [illegible] on its
now what numbers 7, 8 & 9 are in every 10 waves in a rough
ved, before I got swept out. But when you are trying to swim
behind & throw you under and smother your head and
of that sweep shoreward, drag you back with an almighty
e & following me out, shared my fate. For five hours (probably
ly to put off the disagreeableness of drowning as long as
ds along the shore and out. I gave up struggling to get back
(THIS IS THE SEA: A = G.B.S.) were of the most prosaic kind: I
I damned my folly for having postponed altering my new

Detail of letter showing sketch of the sea with Shaw's head.

a second; but it rested me perceptibly – damn! my toe is doubled back by another stone or rock or something – this is that beastly spit of rocks & sand that is to the north – swirl again, swim again, why? I am in my depth (not the slightest exultation, but great physical relief) – where's Loraine? gone – gone down – no use: I cant go back and fish for him: if all the kingdoms of the earth depended on my going back into that wallow I could not swim another stroke: I have reached bottom at last: I am absolutely *beaten*, BEATEN. Talk of the treasure of the humble! Beaten.

I turned to look at the sea generally; and there was Loraine, who had been carried behind me and swept past me during the last 7–8–9 (I suppose), stumbling among the rocks, hardly up to his waist. The incident being over, I switched off with my usual inhuman suddenness, and went off to fetch my shoes, which I had left opposite the place where we went in. When I came back to the bathing boxes I passed Loraine's, remarking to him casually 'A bit of a shave, that.' 'Yes,' said Loraine. We kept up appearances to the last.

Conclusions. Whenever you get a serious call at the apparent approach of death, you may depend on it that your imagination is only at play, and that your organism hasnt the slightest intention of dying. The only really true fiction about death is the story of the American soldier dying at Gettysburg. 'Are you saved?' said the chaplain. 'Now IS this a time to ask coh-nundrums?' said the soldier, exasperated. If anybody had suggested a discussion on religion or immortality or the ethical aspect of my past to me, I should have given him my last kick for obtruding such heartlessly unreal and irrelevant stuff on me under such circumstances. Nothing of the kind occurred to me for a moment. The business inconvenience of my death preoccupied me completely. I was also concerned about drowning, not as death, but as a disagreeable inevitable, exactly like a dental operation. That was the sole personal aspect.

Also, though I was reduced to such a depth of utter selfishness as I have never experienced since I was a small child (that was how it felt when I missed Loraine & left it at that) this supreme result was the effect of fatigue, not of panic, of which I had no symptom at all. The question presented itself as 'Will you let Loraine drown?' but the answer was 'I would rather die than face the effort of keeping myself afloat and raising a ton of lead and pulling it in.' And yet I was not out of breath, not even discomposed. But my arms were deadly tired; and though the hopelessness of a rescue was also at the back of my mind, the main thing was the intense fatigue of my upper arms near the elbow and my thighs near the knees. But it passed off rapidly: I did not feel it after I saw that Loraine was safe. It was a purely local fatigue: my heart & lungs were no more distressed than they are now.

I learnt afterwards that Loraine had a much worse time than I. Although I am not much of a swimmer (the modern swimming-bath athlete would not admit that I can swim at all) I have been accustomed to the sea since I was a small boy; and I have exceptionally capacious lungs. In the sea I keep myself afloat mechanically, wallowing about in any attitude & only swimming when I want to swim. Loraine is not at home in the water to this extent. He tried resolutely all the time to fight his way back; and the big waves not only smothered him under their forward rush, but also dragged him under in the recoil – a thing that has never happened to me. Twice he was so tempted to give up and go down that it was only by a dogged assertion of will & concentration of his purpose to get back that he resisted it. His impression about me was that I was going strong, and that though it was an unheroic thing to allow the great brain of G.B.S. to become a salt water sop, he could hardly keep going himself, & had better not say anything. Fortunately he is a young and powerful man; and his muscle and will-to-live pulled him through. He got badly cut about on the stones, though. He said he felt 'grateful' when he escaped. Not a rag of such sentiment passed through my mind. I realized the safety just as I had realized the danger. This shows what a brute I am in some respects, as you have no doubt discovered for yourself.

I also conclude, in the light of the experiments of Irving Fisher and Chittenden in America, that Loraine was badly handicapped as a meat eater. But that is a controversial point. Still, the extraordinary difference in favor of the vegetarians in the Irving Fisher experiment of holding out the arms for a long time, taken with the fact that this is just the sort of fatigue I felt, is suggestive. Renounce, H.G.: abstain.

I have just read this carefully through, to eliminate all dramatic lies. I have found only one – the phrase 'for five hours (probably five minutes)'. This is a flourish of the 'for a moment that seemed eternal' order. As a matter of fact I dont believe our estimate of the time was affected beyond our power of automatically adjusting to allow for the effect of anxiety. When we went into the water, the sand was covered, and the water up to the stones above high water mark. When we came out there was a strip of sand as broad as, say, two thirds the length of Spade House, uncovered. I should put the adventurous part of the bathe at over five minutes and probably under ten.

Whilst I was dressing in the bathing box the waves in which I had been swimming were vivid before my imagination. When I went out and looked at the reality, my disgust – also Loraine's – was unspeakable. Simply nothing. A little rough, no doubt; but good Lord! make a fuss about a swim in that!! Rubbish! Mere imagination – funk – folly.

Here I am dragged off to bathe again. Charlotte & her sister were not present on that occasion, fortunately. It was too cold & windy & rough for them to come down.

Yrs ever
G.B.S.

The New Age, founded in 1894 as a journal of social and political comment, had come up for sale, and in April 1907 Pease reported to the Fabian executive that it had been sold to A.R. **Orage** (1873–1934) and Holbrook **Jackson** (1874–1948). The purchase was made possible by a gift of £500 from Shaw and a similar amount from a sympathetic London banker. Evidently Wells also had been approached, and had asked Shaw his opinion. ***The Clarion*** was a weekly newspaper founded in Manchester by Robert Blatchford (1851–1943) in 1891. Evelyn Baring, first Lord **Cromer** (1841–1917), British administrator in Egypt, had been largely responsible for reforming the Egyptian financial system. In 1884–5 Shaw had edited Laurence **Gronlund's *The Co-operative Commonwealth***, a book about German socialism published in Boston. Upton **Sinclair**'s book was probably *The Jungle* (1906), of which Charlotte had sent Wells a copy in March 1906. Prince Pyotr **Kropotkin** (1842–1921), Russian revolutionist and anarchist living in London, had published his book *Mutual Aid* in 1906. Edward Bibbins **Aveling** (1831–98) was a biologist, evolutionist, secularist, and one of Hyndman's Marxian followers. Shaw and he debated Marxist economic theory, which Shaw attacked, on various occasions. Marx's daughter Eleanor, a friend of Shaw's, lived with Aveling in a common-law relationship. When he deserted her she committed suicide, only a few months before his own death. According to Hesketh Pearson, Shaw said of Aveling that 'as a borrower of money and a swindler and a seducer of women his record was unapproachable' (*Bernard Shaw* [1942], p. 123). Shaw's mention of '**Wilshire**' presumably refers to *Wilshire's Magazine*, which in August 1906 published a lengthy comment on the economic argument of *Mrs Warren's Profession*. (See *CL*, vol. 2, p. 632).

Robert **Loraine** (1876–1935) was an actor and aviator, with whom Shaw made a balloon ascent in 1906. Irving **Fisher** (1867–1947) was an American mathematical economist whose interests included public health organizations and vegetarianism, as did those of the educator Russell H. **Chittenden** (1856–1943).

32 / To G. Bernard Shaw [Spade House, Sandgate]
23rd August 1907

[ALS: BL 50552 ff 17–18]

Dear Shaw

Wasted chances! You shouldn't have come out. There you were – lacking nothing but a little decent resolution to make a distinguished end. You should have swum to Loraine, embraced him & gone to the bottom – a noble life wasted in an insane attempt to rescue an actor-manager. It might have finished you up freely and well and it might have been of infinite benefit to the socialist cause. As for me I could have sailed in with one or two first class obituary articles and put you right with America and Germany. I should have invented a series of confidential conversations & practically gutted your 'serious side'.

Also I might have induced Gosse, Sidney Lee & others to organize a memorial – a Rodin I think, marble stiff and weedy with all the poor nude toes expanded.

But fundamentally you are a weak man. You & I know it. No advice of mine will save you from a fourth act and too much. You will probably die around 1938 – obscurely.

H.G.

Sir Edmund **Gosse** (1849–1928), well-known critic and biographer, was a translator and editor of Ibsen. Sir Sidney **Lee** (1859–1926) was editor of the *Dictionary of National Biography* from 1891 to 1901, and author of a biography of Shakespeare.

33 / To H.G. Wells 10 Adelphi Terrace WC
2nd March 1908

[APCS: Illinois]

No correspondence between Shaw and Wells from August 1907 to March 1908 has come to light. Both were busy with their professional writing, and Shaw with productions of several of his plays, in London and elsewhere. On 16 October 1907 Charlotte wrote Wells to acknowledge receipt of 'proofs' that GBS was now reading – possibly of New Worlds for Old, *which was to be published in the following spring – and promising to 'send it on to the Webbs by & by.' Wells was busily engaged in writing* The War in the Air. *His interest in the Fabian Society declined, and his attendance at the weekly meetings of the executive, which Shaw almost invariably attended, became sporadic. At a meeting on 11 October he resigned from standing committees to which he had been appointed, on the grounds (as recorded in the minutes) that the distance of their meetings from his home was too great and that the committees were too large; however, he continued as a member of the executive and of the Basis committee. The public attack on him for his views on sex, marriage, and the family expressed in* In the Days of the Comet *had been renewed; and gossip about his sexual adventures was growing both in and outside the Fabian Society: gossip in which the Shaws appear to have had no part.*

Social and personal relations between the Wellses and Shaws continued friendly. On 3 January 1908, Shaw sent a postcard to Jane Wells from Edstaston, in Shropshire, where he and Charlotte had spent Christmas:

'I have been all this time trying to screw up my courage to refuse. If you knew how I loathe dinners – how I create a public scandal by refusing to drink the King's health (an Irish habit) – how I always confirm the worst suspicions of the opposition – how I have sworn again & again that the Vedrenne-Barker dinner was to be my very last, you would not press me to do this inhuman and hated thing. Now, thank Heaven, I have collapsed & had to come down here to recuperate. We have bought a motor to recuperate, & I get frozen hard every day and thawed out every evening.

Don't – Don't – DON'T – ask me to dine at that horrible club. It will poison my life until it comes off, & embitter my memories for ever after. Ask Cecil Chesterton. He LIKES eating.

Spare me if you have a heart. Anything – ANYTHING but this.

G.B.S.'

On 28 January the two couples were among the participants in a copyright performance at the Savoy Theatre of Harley Granville Barker's Waste, *which the censor had refused to licence because an abortion operation was a crucial event in the narrative. When* The War in the Air *was published, Wells sent Shaw a copy. Shaw's reference to* my *balloon concerns an ascent that he made on 3 July 1906 (see* CL, *Vol. 2, pp. 633–4).*

Book just arrived. Will look through it presently.

Why didn't you consult an experienced aeronaut (me, for example) before you romanced about balloons? The great rip saw trick was done a few years ago by an aeronaut who came out of a cloud & found himself just crossing a break on his way out to sea. He took his chance & ripped. The lower part of the balloon folded up into the top & the balloon became a parachute. He & his party got down safely. It was not so desperate a stroke either, because balloons often come down pretty nearly empty. *My* balloon went up to 4000 ft, & came down to 400; & then went up to 9000 with a rush through expansion in the sun. When we cooled after that we dropped half empty.

G.B.S.

34 / To G. Bernard Shaw

Spade House
Sandgate
[early March 1908]

[ALS: BL 50552 f 17]

The enclosure that must have accompanied this letter is missing; but the subsequent letter from Shaw appears to be a reply. About ten months had elapsed since Shaw had written Wells and Webb about the proposed revising of the Fabian Society's 'Basis.' Wells seems not to have responded to Shaw's letter of 5 May, unless in conversation – for the two met from time to time during the summer at executive meetings. Shaw and Webb went ahead with some discussions, which in the absence of Wells were inconclusive, and were discontinued. Wells was (like the other two) busy with his career and other concerns. With the completion of New Worlds for Old, *which was published in March 1908, he returned to the Basis question: somewhat abruptly it must have seemed, as he had not recently been attending executive meetings.*

My dear Shaw

What do you think of a Basis Cttee meeting soon? Here is my idea of a revised Basis. Suppose we were to put that before the Society in the *Fabian News* & ask groups to discuss it, pass resolutions upon it & report their opinions to us (with the number of votes behind them) in order that we might make a first revise & bring the thing before the A.G.M. of 1909 as a definite motion.

Yours ever,
H.G. Wells

It will I feel sure be genuine help to the educational work of the propaganda to get rid of the old rather illiberal basis.

Or we might call in Sanders first as an expert adviser on the propaganda side of this question.

William Stephen **Sanders**, a Fabian lecturer, had become assistant to Pease, whom he eventually succeeded as secretary of the society.

35 / To H.G. Wells Ayot St Lawrence, Welwyn
10th March 1908

[APCS: Illinois]

The Liberal government of the day was engaged in legislating changes in the Poor Laws, including improving the lot of the children of the poor, in both education and health.

Rather a tidy little basis, but with a devil of a lot of Liberal Children's Bill to a very little Socialism and no Democracy – not even Women's Suffrage. You would not have a ghost of a chance of getting it through without hideous emendatory disfigurements, ending in no improvement on the present basis. Most really sound Anglican Tories would sign it as it stands. It will end in our sending in a report containing our several drafts, with an intimation that we are not likely to get much farther. I am just finishing the first draft of a play & cannot give my mind to this basis job properly. Webb is also heavily preoccupied. Stir me up again in a fortnight or so, if you are not yourself absorbed by a new job.

G.B.S.

The **play** to which Shaw refers is *Getting Married.* He had begun it in the previous August.

36 / To H.G. Wells Ayot St Lawrence, Welwyn
22nd March 1908

[ALS: Illinois]

Wells had written Webb as he had Shaw on 9 March. Webb replied that he was for the time being too busy to take up the matter, and that he disagreed with Wells's proposals. Wells responded in annoyance that 'if you'd only departmentalize a little & let me do what I want to do all could be well. That old Basis keeps the movement on the old hardshell lines & its the worst enemy the Webbs have in the Fabian Society. I happen to be something of a teacher & I want to get rid of that piece of apparatus very much. Why won't you & Shaw let me throw it out now? ... You two men are the most intolerable egotists, narrow, suspicious, obstructive, I have ever met' (BL 50552 f 20). Webb sent this letter on to Shaw with a footnote: 'I have answered this in a tone of gentle expostulation saying I am really very much occupied just now, & there must be joint action if anything is to get through. S.W.' Shaw's response was to write the following letter to Wells.

My dear H.G.W.

There are various things that you are forgetting.

Imprimis, you have chucked Women's Suffrage out of the Basis as well as all the other democratic implications of Socialism; and this would make it absolutely impossible from the start to get it through without amendments.

Further, you are forgetting your committee manners – if a man can be said to forget what he never knew. Just consider what you have done. When the committee was formed, Webb & I got to work at once; and within a fortnight we had spent a day together down here at Ayot over the job & sent you down a draft for discussion. This remarkable document you absolutely ignored, saying you were too busy to be bothered about it & would do a proper basis yourself later on when you had finished your book, we to await your convenience in the meantime. The meantime proved to be just a year, during which we had to read through your confounded book for you & neglect our own immortal works for your sake. Then you send us a new basis with the proposal, not that we shall consider it, but that we shall immediately send it out to the Fabian groups in order, as you naively tell us, that they may override the committee by an overwhelming rally to the side of your popular pen.

Now *I* dont mind this. But if I were an opponent desiring to thwart you, and at all hostile to you personally, I might seize the opportunity to take serious offence, and put you hopelessly in the wrong before the society. You will remember (or rather forget; for you never remember anything) that one of the reasons why I gobbled you up so easily at the great Special Committee corobbery was that you insanely accused us of deliberately and maliciously delaying the report when as a matter of fact we had done in six weeks what you had dawdled over for seven months. This time the proportion is more glaring still – Shaw & Webb, less than a fortnight, and the strictest consideration for you as our committee colleague: Wells, over eleven months, and the gross insult to his colleagues of absolutely ignoring their work & proposing to send on his draft to the groups & the society without meeting them or discussing it with them.

Now I tell you you mustnt do these things. You can treat me privately without the least ceremony; and though you annoy Webb extremely by your unruliness and by your occasionally *cold* incivilities, he has to put up with you. But in public work we must proceed on publishable lines. I cant get up at Fabian meetings & put the matter to them as a series of private larks between us. We must proceed in proper form. You may call us all the fools, liars, egotists & nincompoops you can lay your tongue or pen to; but you must be careful all the time not to take liberties of a technical kind. You may draw caricatures of us; but you must not copy our signatures at the foot of cheques. There is an art of public life which you have not mastered, expert as you are in the art of private life. The fine art of private life consists almost wholly in taking liberties: the art of public life consists fundamentally in respecting political rights. Intimate as I am with Webb, I should no more dream of treating him as you have treated him than of walking into the House of Lords & pulling the Lord Chancellor's nose. It was your duty – your DUTY, Herbert George – to send that draft of yours in with the intimation that you were now ready for a meeting to collate it with my draft & discuss it; and when we asked you to let it stand over until we were through with some pressing work, you should have cordially awaited our convenience as we did yours.

Also, though this does not touch our committee, when you address a public meeting, you must do so according to the forms of public meeting, and not publicly insult the chairman by not only assuming his duties & privileges, but actually thrusting him bodily out of his place. You may do that with impunity with worms who know no more about 'order' than you do. But have you any idea of what would happen to you if you tried it on with, say, Lord Courtney, or with the Speaker of the House of Commons? Learn, rash egotist, that if you were a thousand H.G. Wellses, there is one sacrosanct person who is greater than you all, and that is the chairman of a public meeting. To be ignorant of this, to fail in respect for the Chair, is the lowest depth of misdemeanor to which a public man can fall.

I have yet another technical lesson to give you. When you first spoke at a Fabian meeting, I told you to hold up your head & speak to the bracketed bust of Selwyn Image on the back wall. To shew that you were not going to be taught by me, you made the commonest blunder of the tyro: you insisted on having a table; leaning over it on your knuckles; and addressing the contents of your contracted chest to the tablecloth. I will now, having tried to cure you of that by fair means in vain, cure you of it by a blow beneath the belt. Where did you get that attitude? IN THE SHOP. At the New Reform Club, when your knuckles touched the cloth, you said unconsciously, by reflex action 'Anything else today, madam,' and later on 'What's the next article?' Fortunately, you were inaudible, thanks to the attitude. Now I swear that the next time you take that attitude in my presence I will ask you for a farthing paper of pins. I will make a decent public man of you yet, and an effective public speaker, if I have to break your heart in the process.

And this brings me to a matter of immediate importance. As I, thank Heaven, am an ORATOR, and not a mulish draper's assistant, the announcement that I am to speak at the Queen's Hall on Tuesday has sold the whole house out like a shot, without a single advertisement. Clear profit, at unnecessarily low prices, over £100. I think it possible that if you were to undertake another such oration, and stand on your heels instead of on your knuckles, you might do the same. Remember, there is a good deal to be made as a professional lecturer if you prefer to emancipate yourself from Fabian auspices & simply let the Lecture Agency take you on as a speculation. They implore me at brief intervals to let them make my fortune & their own. But if you prefer to do as I do, there is still the fact that you can become a platform athlete in propaganda if you choose to. When there is no table handy you are already a very tolerable speaker; and the rest is only a matter of practice and of a little daily exercise over the alphabet. What is more, when you become a rhetorician, you will have acquired a new literary power. Why is it that you cant write a play, and I can? You think it is because you dont choose. Yah!

That reminds me that I have just finished a dramatic masterpiece [*Getting Married*] – unities so perfectly preserved that I have got two & a half hours drama into a single act & a single scene. I should like to read it to you & Jane. Jane could not but be impressed by the contrast between my splendid skill in the most difficult of all the literary arts and your wretched texts for sensational illustrations in sixpenny magazines. Jane is a woman of spirit: she will not long be content with a Second Best. The real motive of your attempts to pick Fabian quarrels with me, and to put a stop to the intercourse which previously existed between our families, cannot be hidden from so shrewd a woman. Some comparisons make themselves, ignore them how we will. I say nothing of the facts that I am three feet taller than you; that the greatest living sculptor spent a month enthusiastically modelling my features; that my father's second cousin was a Baronet (no professional cricketers in *my* family, thank Heaven: Alfred Shaw was an impostor); that Jane, an exquisitely small woman, naturally admires big men; that, in short, Jane and I were made for one another. But I *do* say that I can write a play and you cant; that I can make the back row of 4000 people hear every word I say whilst you dare not look your customer straight in the eye – only look *up* at him (her) with a propitiatory smile; and whilst women are women such contrasts will not be lost on them.

It is up to you to cancel your natural disadvantages by a strenuous effort of genius & by years of perseverance. Otherwise I shall not answer for the second chair at the Spade House fireside retaining its occupant for long. I say no more. You are warned. The path is pointed out to you. Follow it or perish. And we will consider the Basis when Webb is a little less rushed.

GBS

[*The initials occupy half the final page.*]

Leonard Henry **Courtney** (1832–1918), later Lord Courtney, was an economist, journalist, and Liberal MP. He had been a strong candidate for the speakership of the House of Commons in 1892. He was a brother-in-law of Beatrice Webb. Selwyn **Image** (1849–1930) was an artist who became Slade Professor of Fine Art at Oxford. Alfred **Shaw** was a well-known cricketer; Wells's father had at one time bowled for Kent, though his professional career was ended by an injury, and he became a frustrated shopkeeper.

37 / To G. Bernard Shaw [*no address; n.d.*]

[ALS: BL 50552 ff 27–30]

Although the letter is undated and without an address, it is clearly a response to the previous one, probably written therefore on 23 or 24 March 1908, at Spade House.

My dear Shaw

Is this a firm offer? Do you propose to take Jane off my hands? Or are you just talking big & wild. Jane is a serious person & her affections are not to be trifled with. I know. You are an eloquent & engaging person & I am doing my best to conceal my personal merits. All I can say is – I write not as friend but as a humanitarian – look out! This sort of thing [*drawing of Jane arriving at Shaw's*] might inconvenience you.

For the rest your letter is just bosh! I think I wrote & told you that in the matter of the Basis (though not exclusively) you are an ass! I consider that is my contribution to that discussion. You & Webb have about as much capacity for running an educational propaganda as – Bland. If you were modest & respectful instead of being resentful, suspicious, greedy & constitutional & habitually [red haired?], you might supplement my obvious, beautiful, gigantic & attractive defects & the world have a splendid lesson in the superiority of 2 to 1 plus 1. Instead of which the sense of your fundamental inferiority to me, a thing for which I am in no way to blame & which I do my utmost to mitigate by speaking always with my chin down, wearing frock coats too long for me & pins in my lapel, *gnaws*. You are obsessed more & more by the craving to be disrespectful to me, to be impertinently familiar, to point to the frock coat & the pins (which everyone can see). You shindy about & try to distract people from me when nobody is looking at me, you strike attitudes & play for effects upon me when you know as a matter of fact that *I can see you.* You invent explanations of me & subtle unnecessary detractions. What good is all this liveliness? Here I am.

If you want the present hopeful expansion of Fabian influence & socialist training to go on under the most favourable conditions, you must alter the Basis. You can get that done, I can't. It isn't in my line of aptitude. I've given my indications. You can prevent it being done or you

Wells's 'picshua' of Jane arriving at Shaw's, carrying a handbag and saying 'Yours!' while GBS looks at her in consternation. Reproduced with permission.

can do it wrong. I regret to say that I don't care a damn, such is my faith in God. I have done what I can and I'm ready to come & lose my temper thoroughly when you & Webb are free to discuss the matter further.

We want to hear your play. I have always thought & spoken very highly of your plays. They lack characterization & modelling & the last act of the *Doctor's Dilemma* was disgraceful. But I know of no other playwright quite like you.

God bless you both.

H.G. [*very ornately inscribed*]

(Just compare this beautiful signature with your thin scratchy GBS. Note your middle class hold of the surname. You are G.B.*S.* I am H.G.)

38 / To G. Bernard Shaw Sandgate [*n.d.*]

[ALS: BL 50552 ff 21–2]

*Shaw's response to the preceding letter is unknown. The 'Basis committee' never presented a report and it is doubtful that they ever met. Both Shaw and Wells were present at meetings of the Fabian executive in May, but Wells was finding that body increasingly frustrating. In a letter dated 16 September announcing his resignation he remarked on the disregard in the existing Basis for the rights of children and the freedom of women, and referred to 'the petty growth that has been going on' as 'a mere mockery of the things we might have done.' He had additional reasons: not only that he was busy with some of his best fictional writing (*Tono-Bungay *and* Ann Veronica *were both to appear in 1909), but that his sexual entanglements had embarrassed some Fabians and made others furious. Dorothy Richardson's resignation was reported to the Fabian executive on the same day as his (28 September). He and Amber Reeves were having a 'brazenly indiscreet' relationship (MacKenzie), and there had been his affair with Rosamund Bland. One need neither extend the list nor lay all the blame on Wells. It seems probable that his resignation elicited a private response from Shaw that would have given rise to the following letter (in early October?).*

My dear Shaw

I think you do me an injustice – I don't mean in your general estimate of my character – but in the Bland troubles.

However, you take your line. It's possible you don't know the whole situation.

Well, I had some handsome ambitions last twelve month & theyve come to nothing – nothing measured by what I wanted – and your friendship & the Webbs among other assets gone for my gross of green spectacles. Because it's all nonsense to keep up sham amiabilities. I've said and written things that change relationships and the old attitudes are over for ever. On the whole I don't retract the things I've said and done – bad & good together it's me. I'm damnably sorry we're all made so.

And damn the Blands! All through it's been that infernal household of lies that has tainted this affair & put me off my game. You dont for one moment begin to understand. Youve judged me in that matter & there you are!

Yours ever,
H.G. Wells

In Goldsmith's *The Vicar of Wakefield,* the lad Moses Primrose goes to the fair to sell the family's colt in order to raise money for the purchase of a horse, and returns with '**a gross of green spectacles** with silver rims' that prove to be mere copper, in place of the needed money. W.G. Wills's adaptation of the love story in Goldsmith's novel, under the title *Olivia,* had a popular revival at the Lyceum Theatre in January 1897, with Ellen Terry in the title role.

39 / To H.G. Wells

10 Adelphi Terrace WC
17th January 1909

[ALS: Illinois]

Wells!

Attention! Business!

Anthony Hope Hawkins, Hewlett and myself – have been made a subcommittee of the Society of Authors to confer with certain publishers – Longmans, Methuen, Hutchinson & another – upon their appeal to us to save literature and ourselves from ruin by squashing the sevenpenny clothbound copyright novel. Longmans is a pathetically decent sort of chap, who, in an honest trade, would have done well in the XVII century. He and his little unofficial committee don't object to sixpenny reprints on flimsy frowsy paper, unbound, nor to shilling books, nor to anything but the clothbound library book at sevenpence. They tell the usual bookseller's anecdotes – customers ordering six shilling books & changing at sight of the sevenpennies whilst the parcel was being tied &c &c. They say the six shillings will be killed as a customary price by the 7d; that the author who once appears at 7d will never get six shillings again from the public; that no novels will ever be published at all (by new authors) &c &c &c.

We listened to this with due gravity, and then interviewed Buchan (alias Nelson). It was clear enough that Buchan is the Atlantic & Longmans Mrs Partington with her mop; but Buchan does not pretend that the bookbuying public is yet large enough for another author to get a living out of 7d novels; so we shall probably report that the 7d book has come to stay, and recommend authors to stick to 6/- for two years & then go into Buchan's machine.

I bought Kipps yesterday for 7d at Kings Cross, and saw The Food of the Gods announced. You are in the machine already. I want you to write me a letter of advice about it to be read to the sub-committee (Hawkins, Hewlett & myself as aforesaid), as you may be able to improve our report. I also want to know for my own guidance whether I ought to abolish the six shilling Cashel Byron &c, and let Buchan have it if he ever asks for it. He says that his public does not know one author from another, and that the good stories sell & the others dont, no matter who writes them.

Is two years an excessive time limit to recommend?

What do you get out of Kipps? The odd penny? Any advance? Has there been time to measure the value of the 7d edition, as an advertisement bearing – favorably or adversely – on your later books?

ever

G.B.S.

P.S. What do you make of Barker's condition?

Anthony Hope **Hawkins** (1863–1933) was a lawyer and novelist. John **Buchan** (1875–1940), Scottish novelist and historian, later to become (as Lord Tweedsmuir) Governor-General of Canada, was editor and literary adviser to Nelson, the publishers. His biographer, Janet Adam Smith, says he disliked the Irish and detested Shaw (*John Buchan*, London, 1965).

Mrs **Partington** is said to have had a house in Devon, very near the sea. During a violent storm in 1824 she was observed attempting to mop up the Atlantic waves that were washing into it. The episode was made famous by Sydney Smith (1771–1845) – clergyman, journalist, famous wit – who saw in it a metaphor of the House of Lords resisting the Reform Bill of 1832.

Wells's novel **The Food of The Gods** (serialized in 1903, published as a book in 1904) appeared in a cheap edition in 1909. **Cashel Byron** here means Shaw's novel *Cashel Byron's Profession*; its early publishing history is contained in the Preface that GBS wrote in 1901. Granville **Barker** had been seriously ill with typhoid fever in the early winter. After a long convalescence in Ireland, he and his wife, the actress Lillah McCarthy (1875–1960), had spent Christmas with the Wellses.

40 / [*To G. Bernard Shaw*] [*no address*]
24/08/09 [*dated by GBS*]

[ALS: Illinois]

*It is impossible to say precisely what action or actions of Shaw's gave rise to this letter. Clearly he had attempted, probably more than once, to persuade the Fabians – particularly the Webbs and the Reeveses in addition to Wells – to come to civilized terms over the situation that had developed. Amber Reeves having become pregnant in March or April, she and Wells moved to France for a brief period, then returned to England, where Wells rented for Amber a cottage at Woldingham in Surrey. In July she married G.R. Blanco-White (1883–1966), a young lawyer and Fabian who had proposed to her in the past and who was aware of her current situation. In a letter to Beatrice Webb, from Parknasilla, in Ireland, on 30 September, Shaw referred to advice he had given Wells (*CL*, Vol. 2, p. 869); and in her diary on 4 October Beatrice – who had been horrified and angry over the entire affair – wrote of a visit she had made to Amber, and of GBS's continued efforts to reconcile Amber's parents to the situation. Obviously Wells's letter refers to an earlier move of Shaw's.*

My dear Shaw,

Occasionally you dont simply rise to a difficult situation but soar above it and I withdraw anything you would like withdrawn from our correspondence of the last two years or so. There is no use in going into details about this affair. The world being full of asses and cowards it will be very detestable for Blanco-White & his wife if these stories got any decent backing, that is all. Matters are very much as you surmize. We should all be very happy and proud of ourselves if we hadnt the feeling of being horribly barked at by dogs. Amber has got a little cottage at Blythe (Butler's Dean Road) Woldingham. B.W. works in London & goes down in his leisure time. I like him & am unblushingly fond of her & I go down there quite often – the Reeveses dont know how often & the Heavens will fall if Reeves does. My children are staying there now while Jane moves to London. It would be very nice & amusing if you ran down to Blythe one day with Mrs Shaw. Amber is going to have a child early in the New Year & she cant go about and see people.

Yours ever,
(in a gust of violent friendliness)
H.G.

[*Note by GBS*: received 25/8/09 at Parknasilla.]

41 / To H.G. Wells [*postmarked London*]
3rd February 1910

[APCS: Illinois. Russell photograph of Wells on obverse.]

The expected child was born to Amber Blanco-White (as she now was) on 31 December 1909. Ann Veronica, *the novel based on Wells's affair with Amber, had appeared in October, and although it was highly successful, Wells found himself the object of attack in the press and of social embarrassment among many of his erstwhile friends. While the letter that gave rise to the following is unknown, it is reasonable to guess that Wells, having heard nothing from Shaw, inferred that GBS also had turned against him, and had written an enquiring note. Shaw had been busy with writing* Misalliance, *and was now rehearsing it for Charles Frohman's repertory season at the Duke of York's Theatre. He was also electioneering for Keir Hardie and the Labour Party in Wales.*

Inference totally unwarranted. Elections, rehearsals, preparations for the Repertory Theatre campaign have distracted me from these ephemeral gallantries as to which the other parties have kept me fairly well informed. When I learnt that my view of B.W.'s position had been adopted (with the necessary whitewash) and nothing was going to happen, I regarded the matter as disposed of. Is there anything that I am not likely to know?

G.B.S.

42 / To G. Bernard Shaw

17 Church Row
Hampstead
[*n.d.*]

[ALS: BL 50552 f 33]

In 1909 Wells sold Spade House and moved his family to 17 Church Row in Hampstead, which they kept as a London base until May 1913.

Shaw had become a vigorously active member of the Shakespeare National Memorial Theatre Committee. As a fund-raiser for the enterprise, he wrote The Dark Lady of the Sonnets *in the summer of 1910 and attended its first performance, a charity matinée, on the afternoon of 24 November at the Haymarket. It is unclear to what episode Wells refers.*

Dear Shaw

Oh what have you done? What *have* you been up to? The Hampstead Committee of the National Memorial Theatre was meeting yesterday & it was proposed that you should be asked to come up & address them. The Curate who lives opposite me & is a *great* friend of mine said: 'After what happened last week I don't think that we should care to ask Mr. Shaw' and a lady (unknown) said 'Certainly not.' The matter then dropped. No further light was thrown on the scandal & my earnest enquiries have failed to elicit any particulars. Was it a Police Court affair? We're tremendously agog. They asked *me* to come on the Platform. Really Shaw! The dignity of letters!

H.G.

43 / To H.G. Wells

10 Adelphi Terrace WC
18th November 1910

[APCS: Illinois]

Wells's Ann Veronica *(1909) was followed by* The History of Mr. Polly *(1910) and* The New Machiavelli. *In the latter Wells drew on his experience with the Fabian Society, satirizing that body and in particular, with bitterness, the Webbs. He experienced a good deal of difficulty in getting the book published; it appeared first in serial form in the* English Review, *May to November 1910.*

My dear Wells

I have just come across a passage in William Blake – in Vala, alias The Four Zoas –

'What is the price of Experience? Do men buy it for a song? / Or wisdom for a dance in the street? No: it is bought with the price / of all that a man hath – his house, his wife, his children.'

This would be a good motto for The New Machiavelli, which, by the way, is a frightfully unfinished masterpiece; for the truth appears to be that the parties will live happily ever after.

GBS

The quotation from Blake's ***Vala*** occurs in 'Night the Second,' where the words are spoken by the Voice of Enion. 'Vala' was Blake's original title for the poem that, when rewritten and enlarged, he called *The Four Zoas* (1804).

44 / To H.G. Wells

Reims
22nd June 1911

[APCS: Illinois]

The Shaws spent the summer of 1911, from 19 June to early October, travelling on the Continent. Shaw's message is on two picture postcards sent first to Wells's Hampstead address and forwarded to Pont de l'Arche. The cards show relief sculptures in Reims cathedral depicting the dead leaving their tombs on Judgment Day.

These things remind me of your tale of the Judgement in The Butterfly, and suggest a real need of the age which we could supply: a comic Bible. If we could secure the collaboration of a really able artist the thing would have an overwhelming success, and would revive genuine religion throughout Europe. It would kill all the ridiculous legends and bring out the reality of the serious part of the scriptural narratives. For instance, imagine a thoroughly natural and effective picture of the Ascension, with the bystanders exhibiting all the ludicrous & staggered astonishment of men and women who see somebody going up like a sky rocket for no mortal reason & by no discoverable means! All the mere arguments against the thing would be as nothing compared to a vivid illustration of its absurdity and its unworthiness. There was a French comic Bible beginning with a god in a dressing gown and slippers – a real old gentleman – and the author attained a sincere piety in the end by thus facing his conceptions.

G.B.S.

Wells's short story 'A Vision of **Judgement**,' was included in *The Country of the Blind and Other Stories*, published in 1911 soon after *The New Machiavelli*. It had previously appeared in the journal *The Butterfly*, in September 1899. The **French comic Bible** was *La Bible amusante pour les grands et les petits enfants*, by Gabriel Jogand-Pagès, with drawings by Frid'rick (Paris, 1882).

45 / To G. Bernard Shaw

Maison du Canal
Pont de l'Arche
postmark dated 28-6-11

[APCS: BL 50552 f 34. Photograph of Wells on reverse.]

While keeping the St James's Court flat for a London base, Wells arranged to rent from Lady Warwick the Old Rectory at Dunmow, Essex. Before moving there, the Wells family went to France for the summer. They were based at Pont de L'Arche, near Rouen, from where the postcard was sent. It is improbable that the Shaws went to Rouen, which was far off the southward route that they had planned.

Try & get round to us here. We are at the north end of the Bridge at Pont de l'Arche, & it will do you good to talk to me.

Post cards to hand from Rheims.

H.G.

46 / To H.G. Wells

10 Adelphi Terrace
London WC
16th February 1912

[TLS (holograph postscript): Illinois]

Wells had not given up his hope of achieving success with a play, and in 1912 he and Rudolf Besier (1878–1942) collaborated in a stage adaptation of Kipps. *Besier, of Dutch extraction, had been educated in Guernsey and at Heidelberg. He was a journalist, playwright, and translator and adapter of plays, mainly from the French. He is best remembered for* The Barrets of Wimpole Street

(1930). Kipps *opened at the Vaudeville Theatre in London on 6 March 1912, for a run of 51 performances.*

My dear H.G.W.,

They tell me that you want Christine Silver for Ann in Kipps; and I judge from a recent conversation with Besier at the Dramatists' Club that he is much taken with the young lady.

I do not want to stand in her way by holding her to Fanny, of which she must be deadly sick; but are you sure it is a wise cast? Unless you have shifted Ann to a much higher social stratum, Christine will be as wrong as she could possibly be. The woman you want is Hilda Trevelyan; and you could give the understudy to Evelyn Marthèze. In fact, if you cannot get Hilda, you might do worse than have a look at Evelyn.

You will find it extremely important in your work not to depend too much on acting. Try rather to get as many elements as you can of the real thing. A good many actresses who are quite attractive when they are playing parts which lie in their own class, are irritating and even disgusting when they are trying to mimic other classes. Others have a certain general humanity about them which enables them to get into the skin of all ranks and conditions with sympathetic verisimilitude. Unless you get this sort of actress for Ann, you may knock the whole production into a cocked hat – unless, of course, she is much less important in the play than she is in the book.

It is just possible that Besier, who is a Guernsey-Dutchman, may have that blind spot as to class which is characteristic of foreigners, and which makes tragedies of so many international marriages. Also, he may be enamored of Miss Silver, in which case you may class him for casting purposes as non compos.

Do not impart my opinion to him in greater detail than may be necessary in acquainting him with the fact that I should not dream of casting Miss Silver for Ann if it were my show, and that my notion is somebody like Hilda Trevelyan.

Yours ever,
G. Bernard Shaw

P.S. Christine is charming in delicate, dainty, refined-child-charm parts.

Christine **Silver** (1884–1960) left the role of Fanny O'Dowda (in *Fanny's First Play*), which ran at the Kingsway for just under a year, to take the role of Ann Pornick in *Kipps*. Many years later, near the end of her career, she acted in *Ann Veronica* (1949), adapted for the stage after Wells's death. Hilda **Trevelyan** (1880–1959) had played in *'Op o' Me Thumb* in 1904, but her real successes came in the plays of J.M. Barrie, especially as Wendy in *Peter Pan*, a role that she played repeatedly through many years. Evelyn **Marthèze** acted in various minor roles, but her theatrical career was mainly in administration.

47 / To G. Bernard Shaw

Little Easton Rectory
Dunmow
2nd September 1913 [*dated by Shaw*]

[ALS: BL 50552 f 37]

Wells moved his family to Little Easton early in 1912. The lease was short, and they renewed it on a long-term basis in the spring of 1914, then carried out extensive alterations and renamed the house – by September 1914 – Easton Glebe. Shaw wrote Androcles and the Lion *in January and February 1912, but it did not open until 1 September 1913, at the St James's Theatre, with Lillah McCarthy as Lavinia. The performance was preceded by a curtain-raiser,* A Harlequinade, *written by Dion Clayton Calthrop (1878–1937) and Granville Barker.*

My dear Shaw

Androcles is one of your greatest creations – the holy silly man – & the whole thing is delightful. Lillah's speeches are very typical of you, I could write a book on them & your qualities, the mixture of inspiration, deliberate wisdom and a kind of amiable quackery. Nobody has ever praised you at all, I think, for one of your most conspicuous qualities, more conspicuous than ever here, your invention. I am so pleased by this play I could almost find it in me to try an imitation.

But oh the horrors of that dreary Harlequinade. The staleness, the playfulness of a dug-up baby.

Yours ever
H.G. Wells

My frantic appeals got me an excellent seat which we tried to indicate by our smiles.

48 / To H.G. Wells Folkestone
6th September 1913

[APCS: Illinois]

On 8 August Charlotte had gone to France, where GBS was to join her in September for a motoring vacation. The first week of her absence was the occasion for his romance with the actress Mrs Patrick Campbell (1865–1940), to culminate in her rebuffing him. He recovered as best he could, partly through involvement in rehearsing Androcles, *which Barker was producing.*

I have to go to Mont Dore to fetch Charlotte, who has been there for a month past. I am shivering on the brink of the channel, and cannot foregather with you & C.B. until about the middle of October, when I must return.

I am very strongly in favor of an imitation of Androcles; but you won't take the theatre seriously. When I think of Kipps & Besier, I can only stretch my hands to the heavens and leave my feelings unuttered.

I have bought a novel (Bennett's Regent) and am reading it. I could turn that sort of thing out at sixpence a mile. I blush to recollect that I have written five novels. I refuse to treat you as my equal until you have written half a dozen good plays.

Palace Hotel Sarciron
Mont Dore
Puy de Dore is my next address

G.B.S.

C.B. may have been Charles Brookfield (1857–1913), the playwright who had recently been named Chief Examiner of Plays (i.e., censor); but this is uncertain. Brookfield died only a few weeks after this letter was written. Arnold Bennett's *The Regent: A Five Towns Story of Adventure in London* had been published earlier in the year.

49 / To H.G. Wells 10 Adelphi Terrace WC
6th March 1914

[TLS: Illinois]

Shaw was preparing for publication the volume containing Misalliance, The Dark Lady of the Sonnets, *and* Fanny's First Play, *with their respective prefaces. The preface to* Misalliance, *entitled 'Parents and Children,' had proved difficult to write – as he indicates. In the latter part of 1913 Wells wrote* The World Set Free – *'the most curiously prophetic of all his books' (MacKenzie,* The Time Traveller, *298) – which ran first as a serial* in The English Review, *December 1913 to May 1914.*

My dear H.G.

Whatever you are doing, just chuck it for an hour or so, and read the enclosed proof sheets of the Preface to my forthcoming volume of plays. I want you to tell me, out of your experience as a parent, whether there is any blunder or omission that betrays too flagrantly the childlessness of the author. I have tried it on a couple of fathers and a mother; but I want to try it on you as an extra scientific parent with a cultivated consciousness of your own experience. The thing expresses nothing more than a violent reaction against the present system; for I cannot form any definite conception of what children would be like on any other system: I have gone ahead simply because it seems to me that the tamed animals we now produce are as incapable of the sort of political and social work that we must get done or perish as the Chimpanzees in the Wonder Zoo.

I like your stuff in the English Review. I am convinced that the right line about war is to treat it neither as a calamity nor as a glory, but simply as an unbearable piece of damned nonsense.

This confounded preface has held up my book for some years.

yours ever
G. Bernard Shaw

50 / To G. Bernard Shaw

Little Easton Rectory
Dunmow
[*n.d.*]

[ALS: BL 50552 f 36]

BL dates this letter 1911, but it is clearly a reply to the preceding one from Shaw, and probably written on Monday, 7 March, 1914.

Dear Shaw

Your Preface needs thinking over and my brains are corrugated. In a few days (2 or 3) you shall have one of those Feats of Conscientiousness that make me so deservedly unpopular.

Yours ever,
H.G.

51 / To G. Bernard Shaw

Little Easton Rectory
Dunmow
[*n.d.*]

[ALS: BL 50552 f 35]

BL dates this letter 1911, but it follows on the preceding two. Shaw's rejoinder being dated 13 March, this one was probably written on the 12th.

Dear Shaw,

You know what I ought to say about that Preface. And being your light hopeful nature you cling to a fancy that I won't. Because I regard such work as Androcles & Catherine with unstinted admiration & say so you think I shall find some virtue *you* can't find in this stuff & let you print it. Shaw you did it when you were ill, you started without a plan, you trusted to your wit & luck to pull you through. They haven't done so. This isn't a preface, it is the lamentable product of an indigestion. It is a collection of disconnected half truths. It isn't connected enough to be wholly wrong or wholly right. It just *isn't*. You have never in your life thought hard for a week about this [business] of children. Your mind, early corrupted by public speaking & later almost entirely destroyed by the committee habit, cannot rouse itself unaided to grasp a question comprehensively. This Preface is like something that has had a series of amendments by Lawson Dodd, Aylmer Maude, Guest & so forth. My only counsel is that you should destroy it. Then come out and have a wholesome talk to me & then sit down & write, in your own beautiful & wonderful manner – the outcome. I cannot in a letter dispute & dispose of its innumerable errors. From the first paragraph onward.

Yours ever,
H.G. Wells

52 / To H.G. Wells

10 Adelphi Terrace WC
13th March 1914

[ALS: Illinois]

Come now, H.G.: none of that. Sit up and behave yourself.

Is there anything I have left out that you can remind me of? I want help, not cheek. I have owed that debt to the childhood of the world since I was a child myself; and this will probably be the last of my great prefaces – great because they say the things that are staring us all in the face and that nobody ever says. You have been a child, and a preciously spoiled one too; but your sensitiveness probably gave you a sufficiently bad time to enable you to say with authority either that the preface is good enough to blow the gaff on Education, or to point out where a crime against childhood has escaped me.

In great haste,
GBS

53 / To G. Bernard Shaw

Little Easton Rectory
Dunmow
[*n.d.*]

[ALS: BL 50552 f 39]

Clearly Shaw was anxious to have Wells's comments on the Misalliance *preface spelled out, and Wells was willing to oblige him, as the two following notes testify if the dates fit. The second of them bears the date 18.3.14, handwritten, but not in the hand of GBS or HGW. That day was a Wednesday; both men were in London (despite the letterhead); the proposed arrangement is sufficiently convincing. Whether Shaw's preface was subsequently altered is unknown; the volume containing it was published later in 1914.*

Dear Shaw

I shall be at 52 St James's Court on Thursday at tea time & shall be in London until Saturday morning. Today I am engaged for lunch & dinner but free in the afternoon 4 to 6.

Yours ever
H.G. Wells

54 / To G. Bernard Shaw

Little Easton Rectory
Dunmow
18.3.14

[ALS: BL 50552 f 38]

Dear Shaw

I will try to get to tea with you at 4.30 on Thursday

Yours ever
H.G.

55 / To G. Bernard Shaw

Easton Glebe
Dunmow
Monday, 19th June 1916

[ALS: BL 50552 f 40. Day and month written by Wells, year in another hand.]

Androcles and the Lion *had just been published in a volume that contained also* Overruled *and* Pygmalion, *together with a preface for each play and a non-dramatic 'sequel' – as Shaw called it in writing to Mrs Pat Campbell – to* Pygmalion. *The sequel was an effort to correct the romantic interpretation given the play on stage by that actress and Beerbohm Tree, which had infuriated Shaw's artistic sense but added greatly to his fame and fortune. In the sequel he not only referred to Wells's distinction as a writer, but playfully described how Clara Eynsford-Hill (of the play) met him 'in the flesh ... His pleasant neatness and compactness, his small hands and feet, his teeming ready brain, his unaffected accessibility, and a certain fine apprehensiveness which stamped him as susceptible from his topmost hair to his tipmost toe, proved irresistible.'*

My Dear Shaw

It was pleasant of you to send me Androcles & Company. I've told you already how greatly I admire both Androcles & the Lion, I admire it none the less now that I've read it. Your preface hasn't a simple thesis & isn't to be discussed in a letter but my inclination is to say that you've modernized Christ overmuch & disregarded the other worldliness element of his alleged teaching. After all why drag in Christianity & this extremely problematical person? The problem of religion continues to be as the Americans say right here & now.

I forgive you the personalities at the end of Pygmalion. They do much to correct the unpleasant shock of Will Rothenstein's recent portrait. Also we have to thank you for a very pretty map.

Yours ever
H.G. Wells

William **Rothenstein** (1872–1945), artist and writer, was principal of the Royal College of Art from 1920 to 1935, and was knighted in 1931. He had been a near neighbour of Wells in Hampstead and they had a long friendship. Rothenstein made several portraits of Wells. It is impossible to know what the **very pretty map** was.

56 / To G. Bernard Shaw

52 St James's Court
Buckingham Gate SW
[*n.d.; probably early December 1916*]

[ALS: BL 50552 f 41]

The Wellses gave up their Hampstead house in May 1913 and took a flat in St James's Court. In January 1914, Wells made a brief trip to Russia with Maurice Baring (1874–1945).

There appears to have been no correspondence between GBS and HGW for many months. It does not follow that there was no contact between them after their discussion of the Misalliance *preface; both were deeply involved in their professional and public affairs. According to a statement quoted by the MacKenzies, on the 1914 August Bank Holiday weekend when war broke out, the Shaws were visiting at Easton, and the news of the outbreak brought on a 'heated discussion' between Wells and Shaw (*The Time Traveller, *p. 297), Shaw saying it 'served us right' and Wells that 'we must have a levée en masse.' It is difficult to reconcile that account with the Shaws being at a hotel in Salcombe in Devon when the news came through, and Shaw's sending from there a cable to Siegfried Trebitsch dated 4 August (*CL, *Vol. 3, p. 243). What is certain is that the Shaws proceeded at once to Torquay, where GBS then spent two months at the Hydro Hotel writing* Common Sense About the War, *which appeared as a supplement to* The New Statesman *on 14 November. It is also certain that both Wells and Shaw had seen the war coming and had written articles to the press about the approaching danger; and that their respective initial reactions to the outbreak of fighting differed greatly.*

None the less, they had for the most part maintained friendly personal relations. Shaw lectured several times in 1915 to large audiences, and gave the first and last in a series of lectures arranged by the Fabian Society in the autumn of

1916. Wells's letter almost certainly was his response to Shaw's lecture of 1 December, on Religion.

My dear Shaw,

I used the ticket and liked your lecture very much & it was good to see the old faithful Fabian breed still gathering to the feast. I applauded your Republicanism & endorse your theology except that your phrase (Guest's I believe originally) of the 'Life Force' embodies an almost encyclopaedic philosophical and biological ignorance. But you are all wrong about Russia & rather out of [timing] about Germany. For the latter you need to read *When Blood Is the Argument* by Hueffer, a book with a lot of superficial vanity & silliness & much wisdom & knowledge. As for Russia, the Russians are more like the Irish & English than any other people in the world. Petrograd, where they discuss political assassination at the dinner tables, is amazingly like Dublin. Put Castleism for Czarism. You rage at Russia as an autocracy; you might just as well rage at Ireland as a Vice-royalty. Neither is true of the people & the country; it is their misfortune not their fault. I'm no fool, I've got eyes & ears & I assure you that the Russians belong to the North European system much more than the Prussians do. They are, to use your disgusting race cant, *whiter.* And don't you bother about Russia's mission in China. China will see to any mission work that is needed there.

Yours ever,
H.G.

When Blood Is the Argument, by Ford Madox **Hueffer** (who in 1919 changed his surname to Ford), had appeared early in 1915 and been reviewed by Wells in the *Daily Chronicle* for 25 March.

57 / To H.G. Wells

10 Adelphi Terrace WC
7th December 1916

[TLS: Yale]

Shaw refers to writing this in the country, doubtless at Ayot; obviously he had a supply of London letterhead with him.

My dear H.G.

I am all right about Russia. The longer I live the more I see that I am never wrong about anything, and that all the pains I have so humbly taken to verify my notions have only wasted my time.

Lemme explain. The Russians are beyond all comparison the most fascinating people in the world. And anybody who has heard their language sung will never listen to Italian with any more emotion than to school Latin. To talk about the production of a play to the Moscow people is not only a means of making three hours pass like twenty minutes, but to make it impossible to believe that it was the same play that was produced at His Majesty's Theatre, or even that it exists in the same world. Everything we write in England seems sawdust after Tchekov and the rest of them. And this is not the effect of any susceptibility of mine: they bowl over you and Granville Barker and everybody else in the same way. When Sasha Kropotkin tells me that Russia will give a soul to the world, I quite understand her. And I notice how very pretty she is, although an Englishwoman with her features would be ridiculously ugly. We also are the pets of the Russian smart people at present. On Friday a pretty girl stopped me as I was leaving the hall and said, 'I'm a Russian. You are so wrong about us. We adore the English.'

Stepniak used to say that the future of Russia lay between the western and the eastern streaks in her; between enterprise and fatalism; between Turgeniev and Tolstoy; and though he was very much on the side of Turgeniev, he felt the Tolstoyan side all the more because he saw that it was this side that fascinated the English. 'In Russia,' he said, 'if a man embezzles money he is cried over and forgiven when he comes out of prison; but in England he is never forgiven; and the English are quite right: it is weakness that makes the Russians forgive everything.'

All the charm of Russia was in the Russia that Peter the Great loathed and tortured and tried to stamp out. He would have made you a grand duke for saying that the Russians belonged to the north European system and resembled the English. Catherine II boasted that she was like an Englishman. Accordingly, they struck west, at Sweden, at Poland, at European Turkey and Hungary.

Now I am quite willing to be invaded by Karsavina and Nijinski, but not by Peter and Catherine. There is no room for Russia in the west and no work for her. In the east – well, look at the map! Manifestly her destiny lies there when she has any energy to spare from her internal development. This being so, what time has she to spare to make love to us? We may amuse her as the Solomon Islands might amuse her if she knew of their existence. We may be a convenience to her in her push for Constantinople, just as we were an inconvenience to her when we bolstered up the Turk to prevent her getting there. But until the world is much smaller than it is today – and today a square mile of Siberia is much larger than a square mile of Old or New England – Russia's relations with us, like Moscow's with you and me, will be only like Stevenson's flirtations with the South Sea Islanders. We have our work: they have theirs; and the surest way to quarrel is to attempt to live in the same house. They are, as you say, very like the Irish. Do you find that encouraging as to the success of a union of hearts?

The greatest obstacle to that integration of nations which is clearly the next step in political development is Anacharsis Klootzism, with its Tennysonian tag about the parliament of man, the federation of the world. If we try to bite off more than we can chew, we shall fall back for 20 years (equal to half a Victorian century) of petty nationalism. I think that the comparatively democratic west can be made fairly friendly and solid from Poland to the Pacific. I think Russia and Japan may break down the exclusiveness of China and make an eastern proposition of Asia. I think that Latin South America and the Latin South of Europe may make a third combination, and that each of the three may be too strong for any of them to dare fight over the partition of Africa. But if this is Utopian it is so because the units are too large, not because they are too small. If we try to make our end carry Russia and Japan because they are 'of the eight great Powers,' the thing will break by its own weight, or else, like the Concert of Europe, avoid the catastrophe only by holding its breath and doing nothing.

But I am old – over sixty – and nobody trusts me. The New Statesman took my money greedily enough, and then turned into a suburban Tory-Democratic rag and forced me to kick myself out, to the great relief of Webb and Bennett. The paper has its uses, but not for me: it is ungenerous and has just pluck enough to hit people of its own size and smaller, besides being always three weeks inside the margin of safety. Webb could keep it much closer up to the mark if he took any real interest in Welt Politik, or could now feel the slightest confidence in any solution that he has not worked out in his own way with Beatrice.

He has reason enough for this, as most of the solutions that are offered to him are wrong; but he does not see that war and political leadership do not admit of his method, as the materials for investigation and research are never available until fifty years later. In this war I began by putting in three months hard work into studying it; and I have found that when I try to fortify myself by facts and documents I could make nothing of it (Sarolea has read 600 books about the war and knows no more about it than you or I), and that when I went on my knowledge of human character and experience of the ways of men, and guessed and calculated accordingly, disregarding all but the quite unmistakable facts, I came out right enough for practical purposes. In fact the whole difficulty in political emergencies is that the safe methods – the Webb methods – cannot be applied: you have to divine the factors instead of ascertaining them, and integrate them instantaneously without stopping to write chapters about them. And, having done your best, you must back your conclusion with no guarantee whatever that it is not a frightful mistake. The only alternative is to be safe and dull the day after the affair. And so the New Statesman knows me no more.

One bother that I have often had with Webb I have sometimes with you. Both of you, when the world was your oyster, opened it by passing examinations. Anything that was good enough to score a mark in your papers was good enough to tuck into your head without further criticism. And you have never swept this rubbish out. You will find chunks of Nassau Senior and Mill and Fawcett sticking in Webb's mind like shot in a partridge. Hastily bolted and still undigested nonsense that passed as science in your South Kensington days still suddenly asserts itself and gives you a sort of Katzenjammer when anything reminds you of the blind and bloody fools of the Neo-Darwinian lunacy, when it was scientific to think of Darwin as a giant and Butler as a nobody. My biology is all right: I explained it before the amazed Saleeby at my first lecture. You will find it all in the third act of Man and Superman, in the creed of Mr Britling, and in the passage from my essay on Darwin in which I sweep away the silly controversy about the inheritance of acquired characteristics – as if, Good God! there were any habits but acquired habits to an evolutionist – and explain exactly how the inheritance occurs. I am simply the greatest biologist of this age if every man had his due; and dont you forget it. Whats the good of saying theres no

Life Force – or whatever you choose to call it? Did you write Britling or did you not? What made you write it?

It is a very fine book, by the way. I read snippets of it in The Nation and Collier's, and was completely misled as to its weight and mass. Serial rights are serial rights; and Jane must be fed and the boys kept at their schoolbooks when they ought to be reading us; but the result was a fearful injustice to Britling. I had two copies: one I bought and one you sent me; but as one was grabbed by everybody in London and the other by everybody in Ayot St Lawrence, I did not get hold of it fairly for months. It is among other things a priceless historical document.

A youth named Hesketh Pearson, whose God is Frank Harris, asks me is it not monstrous that an important book Frank Harris's Life of Oscar Wilde should be dismissed by the Manchester Guardian in ten lines whilst your lot of stuff about such trumpery as the war should have two columns. Probably he wrote to you to complain. Be kind to him and do not grudge Harris his worshipper: you saw him play in Androcles.

Harris, by the way, is now editing the American Pearson's, and is describing his feats as an editor in London, when he rescued from starvation and obscurity Kipling, Wells, Shaw &c &c. His book on Wilde only needs an authentic portrait of the author, instead of the Christlike figure of Frank the Saviour, to be quite the best there is on that subject. Harris tried to get Oscar on board his lugger at Erith, and Oscar preferring ignominy and imprisonment to a voyage with Captain Kidd, is the funniest thing in it.

This letter is too long: but you need not read it. I am alone here in the country and can scribble a frightful lot in shorthand without noticing. Happily it doesnt need an answer. You might however, come to lunch some day and tell us about your Italian escapade. Are you in town for the winter? Charlotte will fix up a day like a shot if you will come.

Ever

G.B.S.

P.S. [*handwritten*] On coming up to town, I find Charlotte in bed with 'trench influenza'. She wont be safe company for a week at least.

Shaw had been a principal mover in introducing the plays of **Chekhov** to the London stage in 1911. Sasha **Kropotkin** was the daughter of Prince Peter Kropotkin (see Letter 31). Sergius **Stepniak** (1852–95), whose real name was Sergius Michailovitch Kravchinski, was an exiled Russian nihilist and an author. In the four years before the war, the Diaghilev

Ballet (whose dancers included **Karsavina** and **Nijinski**) performed repeatedly at Covent Garden. Robert Louis **Stevenson** (1850–94), famous novelist and man of letters, travelled to the South Seas in search of health, settling in Samoa in 1888. He took an active interest in the affairs of the Pacific Islands.

Anacharsis Clootz or Cloots (1755–94) was an idealist revolutionary who led a group of self-styled 'ambassadors of the human race' in the French National Assembly in 1790. He was executed in the Reign of Terror. 'In the **Parliament of man**, the Federation of the world' is a line in 'Locksley Hall,' a poem by Alfred Lord Tennyson (1809–92), published in *Poems* (1842). An outcome of the Congress of Vienna (1814–15) that followed the Napoleonic wars was the formation by the principal European powers of an agreement for joint diplomatic action on matters of European concern. This so-called **Concert of Europe** proved to be too loosely based to be effectual.

Charles **Sarolea** (1870–1953), a Belgian, was a historian, editor, publisher, and Professor of French at the University of Edinburgh. During the war he worked tirelessly for the Belgian Relief Fund. Nassau **Senior** (1790–1864), John Stuart **Mill** (1806–73), and Henry **Fawcett** (1833–84) were eminent English economists. Caleb Williams **Saleeby** (1878–1940) was a physician, public-health campaigner, and eugenist. A **Katzenjammer** ('cat's misery') is the equivalent of a hangover, though not necessarily related to dissipation. Mr **Britling** is the protagonist of *Mr. Britling Sees It Through* (1916), Wells's highly successful novel about England in the early years of the First World War, written before he visited the battlefields. It appeared in serial form in England in *The Nation*, and in the United States in *Collier's*. Hesketh **Pearson** (1887–1964) was for some years an actor, then turned to writing. His books include a biography of Shaw. Frank **Harris** (1856–1931) was born in Ireland, became an American citizen, and lived many years in London as an author and editor. A member of Oscar Wilde's group of friends, he became notorious for his 'buccaneering' (as Shaw called it) style of life. In *Oscar Wilde, His Life and Confessions* (1916) he described graphically his futile efforts to persuade Wilde to escape from England at the time of his trial by boarding a yacht moored at **Erith** (on the Thames), which Harris had hired for the purpose. Wells visited the **Italian war front** in the summer of 1917.

58 / To G. Bernard Shaw

52 St James's Court
Buckingham Gate SW
[*n.d.*]

[ALS: BL 50552 f 42]

The letter is undated but is clearly a reply to the preceding one from Shaw. Since Wells was prompt with such responses, one can assume that he wrote this on 8 or 9 December 1916.

Dear Shaw.

Why do you say such silly things about science? Why do you mix science & Webbs together? The Webbs play at research in imitation of Herbert Spencer & he knew as little of science as you do. <u>He launched that</u>

absurd word Evolution in [*illegible*]. I'd be glad to come & quarrel with you about these things when Mrs. Shaw is better, after Xmas.

Yours ever
H.G.

Herbert **Spencer** (1820–1903), a philosopher highly regarded in his own time by social thinkers including some early Fabians, did not coin the word 'evolution'; but he developed his own definition of it and as the *New English Dictionary* (1897) says, 'greatly influenced not only the technical but also the popular use of the word.' His equating evolution with progress was emphatically rejected by Darwin and Huxley – and Wells.

59 / To H.G. Wells

10 Adelphi Terrace WC
9th December 1916

[TLS with holograph PS: Illinois]

Alfred Warwick Gattie (1856–1925) was an actor and playwright – author of The Transgressor, Sir Jackanapes, The Millionairess, *and other plays – but made his name as an inventor when he designed a scheme for a central railway 'Goods Clearing House' that would serve all London and eventually be adaptable to the needs of any densely populated centre, such that 'the heaviest goods train [could be] unloaded and reloaded in 6 or 8 minutes.'*

My dear H.G.

Go to see the Gattie machinery at Battersea – you know what I mean: the Railway Clearing House business. Never mind Gattie; never mind Henry Murray; never mind Roy Horniman: go. I held off for years for exactly your reasons. I thought that everything that there was in the clearing house notion was obvious on the face of it to any intelligent Socialist, and that, as Webb said, Gattie was only 'a crank with a crane'. The truth is he has invented one of the most extraordinary applications of electro-magnetic traction I ever saw or heard of, and that as it will certainly ruin the vast commercial interests bound up in the waste of the present system, every nerve will be strained to squash it. I am so violently and dangerously converted that, as I dont want to make a fool of myself, and know that you have a special flair for inventions of this sort, I implore you to go and see what you think of it. You must give them notice and treat them with respect; for they dont shew you a model:

they actually do the trick on full sized trucks on a full sized length of railway; and what they do is much more interesting, and much less credible, than going up in an aeroplane. You think you know what shunting is. Well, wait until Gattie puts you on a truck and shunts *you.* I say no more. Dont lose it for anything. I shall make Webb go. We have been too clever about Gattie: God fulfills himself in more ways (personally) than ours.

I am quite sober; and the place was devilish cold; so take an overcoat.

Ever
G.B.S.

P.S. I dont despise science. I have been trying all my life to rescue it from quacks & idiots. It's no use coming South Kensington over me: I know all about it, as far as anyone can, though I profess no technique. One proof that my biology is right is that you have been driven to it as inevitably as Thomas Hardy. In vain do you kick against the pricks.

Roy **Horniman** was the author of a book describing Gattie's scheme, called *How to Make the Railways Pay for the War* (1916). Henry **Murray** was one of the authorities on transportation quoted by Horniman. Shaw's **postscript** suggests that Wells may have replied to his letter of 7th December, but no reply has been found. Thomas **Hardy** (1840–1928), novelist and poet, might have been a little surprised by the strength of Shaw's claim. He had indeed, like Shaw, dismissed rationalist materialism as a tenable creed. Yet there is a great difference between his purposeless Schopenhauerian 'Immanent Will' and Shaw's 'Life Force' with its striving for greater degrees of consciousness. As late as 1926, in the preface that he wrote for *Late Lyrics and Earlier,* Hardy could write of being only 'forlornly' hopeful 'notwithstanding the supercilious regard of hope by Schopenhauer, von Hartmann, and other philosophers down to Einstein who have my respect.' (*Late Lyrics and Earlier* [1922], p. xvii).

60 / To H.G. Wells

10 Adelphi Terrace WC
11th January 1917

[TLS: Illinois]

The Commander-in-Chief of the British Forces in France was Field Marshal Sir Douglas Haig. Wells had visited both the Italian and the French fronts, and had written accounts of his visits for the Daily News. *Shaw's were to appear in the* Daily Chronicle *in March; subsequently he included them in* What I Really Wrote about the War *(1930).*

My dear H.G.

I have received an invitation from the Commander In Chief to go to the Front. Naturally the temptation to accept is very strong, as pure mischief is always fascinating. But I notice that your articles in the Daily News have been delayed, and – especially in one instance where you were giving your opinion of our general staff work as compared with that of the French – you have given such short measure as to suggest that somebody, like the man in Pickwick, had been dipping his beak into the jug.

What I want you to tell me is whether they demand any pledges from you as to what you shall say or not say, and also whether the fact of having been at the Front marks you out for special censorship even in respect of books. If that is the case, I wont go.

If you can give me any tips even as to boots and overcoats and baksheesh and the like, I should be glad to have them.

If I can save you the bother of writing by calling, or if it would be more convenient for you to look in on me, your secretary could arrange it over the telephone (Gerrard 331).

I am pulling the leg of the Fabian Society by proposing a republican manifesto to the Executive, but have no hope of creating anything thereby except an unquiet recalcitrance. They all have the fine old Victorian conviction that it doesnt matter; and these convictions are not to be upset by merely empirical considerations like facts.

By the way, I wish you would develop your thesis of the Resentful Employee more carefully. You snatched at it as a stick to discipline the Labour people; but I think it was thrown away on them because I believe that the R.E., on the whole, enlisted to escape from his drudgery. The C.O. represents a special brand of cantankerousness which is both resentful and anarchic, but is very much the contrary of the shirking slacking good-for-nothing temperament, and generally extricates itself from galling slavery as you and I did. The mere R.E. would be sulkily incapable of co-operation with Trevelyan and Ponsonby, whom he would disparage as toffs, and be too shy and unsocial to approach. You would not find any of that shyness about Norman or Clifford Allen. What I should like to speculate on is the effect of army service on the R.E.: in fact, the most interesting part of the whole question is the effect of soldiering on the civilian.

I allow, of course, for the fact that dread of bullying and field punishments and the like must have produced a good deal of shirking among R.E. weaklings; but their efforts to escape would take the form of pleas for exemption: they would not face the pains and indignities of the Conscientious Objector except in paroxysms of the quite unreasoning sort of cowardice which makes a man who is going to drown himself in the river run away when a sentinel threatens to shoot him.

Ever,
G.B.S.

When Mr Pickwick (in Dickens's *Pickwick Papers*, 1826–7), gave a fellow-prisoner a half-sovereign with which to buy 'burnt sherry,' Mr Smangle recommended that he be watched 'just to see that he didn't drop his beak into the jug by accident.'

Shaw, a believer in the socialist concept of compulsory national service, nonetheless had been a defender of *bona fide* conscientious objectors (**C.O.**'s) from the outset of the war. The Rt. Hon. (later Sir) Charles **Trevelyan** (1870–1958) and Sir Arthur (later Lord) **Ponsonby** (1871–1946) were both prominent political figures, the latter a socialist and pacifist, the former a Liberal MP who resigned from the government at the outbreak of the First World War. He later joined the Labour party and became president of the Board of Education. Clarence H. **Norman** (1886–1974) was a journalist, shorthand writer, Fabian socialist, and pacifist and conscientious objector. He was twice imprisoned, at least once at hard labour, for refusing military service. Clifford **Allen** (1889–1939), a Fabian socialist prominent in the Independent Labour party (he was its chairman from 1922 to 1926), eventually created Lord Allen of Hurtwood, was sentenced to two years at hard labour for the same offence. Shaw discussed the cases of both men, whose treatment he regarded as barbaric, in letters to *The Manchester Guardian* (See *What I Really Wrote* ..., chap. 9).

61 / To G. Bernard Shaw

Easton Glebe
Dunmow
[*c.* 14 January 1917]

[ALS: BL 50552 f 54]

The letter is undated but is clearly a reply to Shaw's of 11 January; and as Shaw departed for France on 28 January and obviously had preparations to make, Wells's response must have been prompt – as was his habit. Shaw visited the front in both France and Belgium. For a résumé of his tour, see CL, *Vol. 3, p. 448. The account that Wells had written for the press appeared subsequently in book form as* War and the Future *(1917).*

Dear Shaw

The swine do impose the right to censor (severely) your articles on the front but not the rest of your literary career. My work on the front is held up now by G.H.Q. on the score of that criticism of the staff work.* But if you go & see them they get timid & make concessions.

Thick boots & *waders.* The mud is terrible. Macintosh & a fur-lined coat.

Be careful how you tip the French chauffeur. He is frequently a rich embarqué. Northcliffe tipped in the manner of the West End. Otherwise generous normal tipping.

Stick to the republican issue; its vital.

Yours ever,
H.G.

* But in the later part of the book which deals with the war generally & not the 'front', I get it all in – uncensored.

Viscount **Northcliffe** (1865–1922), born Alfred Harmsworth, was a journalist who became proprietor of *The Times* (London) and *The Daily Mail.*

62 / To H.G. Wells

10 Adelphi Terrace WC2
17th May 1917

[TLS: Illinois]

Wells's philosophical tract God the Invisible King *had just been published.*

My dear Wells,

Your tract arrived duly, and has been devoured by everybody in the house.

Since 1880, when I finished my second novel, and found that I could get no further with rationalism, I have been more or less on this job; and all its moves have become so familiar to me that now that I am growing old and stale, I no longer have any confidence in my notions of what this generation needs to have said to it. But instead of making a violent and unnatural effort to freshen myself up to your date (remember that though I am only ten years older I began in Ireland, virtually in the XVII century) I had better keep as Victorian as I can in my criticism of it.

First, then, this pre-Constantine movement, like the pre-Raphaelite movement, may be necessary as an attempt to recover lost qualities in our religion; but it is not a step in advance. It may easily lead to such a revival of theological wrangling (you are yourself up to the neck already in a Duality as opposed to the Trinity) that it may end in some new Constantine putting his back to the door like Lord Melbourne in the Cabinet, and saying 'I dont care a damn what lie we tell; but you shall not leave this room until you have all agreed to tell the same lie.'

Then there is the historical side to be considered. There is nothing in your tract to exclude the possibility of your following in the footsteps of Münzer, John of Leyden and Cnipperdolling, and Paul Kruger. They started theocracies on your lines; and though Kruger was saved up to a point by the Bible and his mother wit, the Kingdom of God in Münster ended so hideously that when I looked up at the Münster Church tower and saw the iron cages in which they hung up what was left of John to starve to death after they had torn him with red hot pincers as far as they could without killing him, I could almost smell his burning flesh still. And this was not altogether, as the Socialists used to say, because the princes and the bourgeoisie were abominably cruel, but because John, on conceiving himself as the agent of God, the Invisible King, went on in such a way as to make Frederick the Great, a professed atheist, far more to be trusted as a ruler. The truth is, the doctrine, in its crude state, is a fearfully dangerous one.

Then there is modern science to be taken into account. You have ventured to ignore evolution. By doing so you not only leave the contradiction of a benevolent agency producing snakes and tetanus bacilli and all sorts of evil unsolved, but ignore the really vital controversy of our time: the controversy of the Mechanists and Natural Selectionists with the Creative Evolutionists. This leaves you rather in the air, which is not a bad place to be on some accounts; but the earth has finally to be reckoned with.

Your suggestion that the realization of a theocracy is a matter of a few years rapid crystallization of a solution saturated with your conception of God is obviously very sanguine. God is known only as an impulse. When you get an impulse you have first to decide whether it is atavistic or not. And if you are convinced that it is not, then you have to reason hard to discover the way to carry it out into practice. Otherwise you may go drinking and cutting off widows' heads with two handed swords like John of Leyden, or instituting meatless days to cure a scarcity of bread, like our 'practical business men.'

Sometimes your terminology bothers me for a moment until I adjust myself to it. Your demonstration that God is a person is in effect a demonstration that he is not a person; and when you say he is finite, you seem to mean that he is limited in power though eternal in duration: that is, infinite.

As you have ventured to give advice as to personal conduct in the case of the clergyman and barrister, I think you should say something about the Socialist demonstration, which seems to me quite valid, that we must reform society before we can reform ourselves, and that personal righteousness is impossible in an unrighteous environment. In practice a parson finds that if he proclaims his apostasy and walks out of the church, the effect will be to dip every village in England up to the neck in the blood of the Lamb, and that he had better stick to his pulpit to keep the Nicean out. And the barrister always satisfies his conscience by holding that the best way to arrive at the truth is to place before a disinterested body of men two statements of the case from opposite points of view, one advocate making the best of the assumption that the horse is black and the other that he is white. This is quite reasonable; and if I were a barrister I should do my best to save a murderer client from hanging, just as, if I were a doctor, I should do my best to cure him if he came to me for medical advice.

These are all the holes I can pick in the book. They are perhaps more interesting as shewing the grooves in which my mind runs than useful for your next edition; but such as they are, here they are. There is an excellent author whose works you ought to read through occasionally. His name is H.G. Wells. Morris used to say of Ruskin that he said splendid things and forgot all about them ten minutes after. Are you sure you have not the same want of tenacity? There is a stage trick which I keep before me when I write. It is that of the clown who pretends to pick up potatoes or what not, but never picks up one potato without dropping another. You must not become famous as a writer of palimpsests.

Ever
G.B.S.

Shaw's second novel was *The Irrational Knot*, written in 1880, serialized in *Our Corner* (1885–7), and published in book form in 1905. The Roman Emperor **Constantine** the

Great (d. 337) formally declared Christianity a lawful religion in the Roman Empire and did much to promote its cause. In 325 he summoned the First Council of Nicaea, an ecumenical meeting of bishops, to deal with the Aryan heresy, which denied the doctrine of the Trinity. The Council adopted the formal Nicaean (or Nicene) creed, the earliest of such statements of the Christian faith. Wells, eventually unable to accept the adaptation of Christianity to the jingoistic patriotism of professed Christians that had become prevalent, had written his tract in an effort to inspire his countrymen to 'live and die for greater ends' and 'to personify and animate a greater, remoter objective' (*Experiment in Autobiography*, p. 575).

Lord **Melbourne** (1779–1848) was twice prime minister of Great Britain. Shaw's reference (with language that polite historians may have glossed over) is to the occasion in 1841 when Melbourne, having unwillingly agreed amid much cabinet wrangling to the repeal of the taxation known as the Corn Laws, called to his ministers as they left the meeting, 'Stop a bit. What did we decide? Is it to lower the price of bread or isn't it? It doesn't matter which, but we must all say the same thing.' (See, e.g., David Cecil, *Melbourne* [1965], pp. 501–2.) Thomas **Münzer** (c. 1489–1525) was a religious and social radical, associated with Luther and subsequently the Anabaptists, whose essential doctrine he nevertheless rejected. When the Peasants' War ended he was beheaded. Jan Bockelson (c. 1509–36), known as **John of Leyden**, and Bernhardt **Knipperdollinck** (c. 1480–1536) were two of the three principal leaders of the Anabaptists, who made Münster their centre, taking full control of it and fortifying it. When it was recaptured, they were executed with hideous cruelty. Shaw would have read *Rise and Fall of the Anabaptists* (1903) by his 'friend and fellow heretic' – as he called him – Ernest Belfort Bax (1854–1926). Paul **Kruger** (1825–1904), president of the Transvaal, led the resistance by the Boers against the British that culminated in the South African War (1899–1902). Wells's **advice as to personal conduct** is in the tract under discussion.

63 / To Mrs H.G. Wells

10 Adelphi Terrace WC2
29th March 1919

[TLS: Illinois]

Although it is addressed to Mrs Wells, this letter concerns HGW also. As he tells in his autobiography, the Wells's sons were sent at the outbreak of the First World War to Oundle School, near Peterborough in Northamptonshire. The headmaster there was F.W. Sanderson, whom Wells greatly admired, and when Sanderson died suddenly in 1924 he wrote The Story of a Great Schoolmaster *as a tribute to him. In 1919 the Oundle pupils gave a performance of* Arms and the Man *in which Gip Wells, the elder of the two sons, played Bluntschli. The Shaws and the Arnold Bennetts were with the Wellses in the audience. The school magazine,* The Laxtonian, *reporting on the 'electric' evening, said, 'All concerned were indeed sensible of the signal honour conferred on them by the presence of Mr. Bernard Shaw, whose acceptance of his 'call' was, as he observed, the first to which he had acceded since the original production of the play – 25 years ago.'*

Jane: what a lark! The place seems remote from all lines of communication except the main road through Hitchin, Bedford & Higham Ferrers; so I will venture in our little station car, a most untrustworthy vehicle.

I am quite in the dark as to the hour of performance; but unless warned to the contrary I propose to start from Ayot after lunch and arrive at Oundle (if the car ever does arrive) between 5 & 6. Oundle is printed in the postal guide in the capitals appropriate to a populous city; so I suppose I can find quarters for the car and the chauffeur (really the gardener) for the night. If not, he can go to Peterborough.

The result of my visit will probably be the withdrawal by indignant parents of all the boys who have not already been withdrawn on H.G.'s account; so Pip will have the whole school to himself next term.

By the way, where do they get the girls? Is it a mixed school? I was fearfully disappointed to gather from Pip's letter that they were real girls: boys give extraordinary vividness to female parts. I foresee that Pip will marry Miss Edge, write revues, and patronize the poor old governor and Daddy Shaw and all that lot. Why do we encourage these young upstarts?

I shall be at Ayot tomorrow (Sunday), in London on Monday, & back again at Ayot on Tuesday. Letters coming by the first post on Monday should be directed to Adelphi, as I have to arise with the early village cock and leave before the postman dares and take the winds of March with beauty. But as I have written as well as wired to the head, everything is in train without further letter writing.

Do you dig in at Oundle or retreat to [*double deletion*] – dash it! I have misspelt it twice – well, Petrograd: there!

G.B.S.

Pip was a nickname for the younger of the two boys – possibly used only by Shaw. Whether they referred to him as 'Daddy Shaw' is not clear. Miss Winifred **Edge**, who appeared as Louka in the school production, had spent her childhood in Russia and been hired by the school to teach Russian when Wells urged Sanderson to add that language to the curriculum. Though Shaw suggested a London stage career for her, she remained at Oundle, marrying a member of the staff later in 1919.

64 / To H.G. Wells

10 Adelphi Terrace WC2
12th June 1919

[TLS (c): Illinois]

Sir Thomas Barclay (1839–1921) was a wealthy business man, traveller, and promoter of international goodwill.

My dear H.G.

Sir Thomas Barclay, the Friend of Man and of Ententes, has introduced to me Mr Liang-Chi-Chow, former Minister of Finance and Justice to the Chinese Republic, and, I learn, regarded in China as a Man of Letters in the most Celestial sense. As he is staying at Claridge's, I fully accept this assurance of his importance.

To me Liang-Chi-Chao sends V.K. Ting, Director of the Geological Service of Pekin (probably a young necromancer); and Mr Ting informs me that the Celestial purview of English literature includes, in alphabetical order, only five illustrious names, Ah-Bennet, Ji-Kai-Chesterton, Jan Galsworthy, myself, and Aytch-Ji-Wells. I am held to be the patriarch of the group; and the rules of Chinese politeness oblige me to introduce Mr Liang-Chi-Chao (only one letter between him and chaos) before he can present himself or entertain us all at Claridge's.

Accordingly I do now solemnly present this gentleman to you, and ask you as a man and a brother to bear me up, and receive with distinguished consideration the approaches of Mr Ting, a Celestial Knut of modest and affable manners, much better dressed than any of us. The next move is with him.

I am sending this letter in quadruplicate to the whole galaxy. Dont bother to answer me. I presume you will have to answer Mr Ting when he approaches you.

Forgive me; but what can I do?

Ever
G. Bernard Shaw

65 / To H.G. Wells

10 Adelphi Terrace
London WC2
1st July 1921

[TDU: BL 50552 ff 43–4]

The date of this letter has been crossed out, presumably by Shaw. A holograph note by him, preceding the text, reads, 'This letter was not sent. Next day I substituted for it the Napoleon scene in Back to Methuselah, Part IV.' Several minor alterations were made in the draft. (See Shaw's letter to Wells dated 4 December 1922.) Wells's 'sketch and summing up of Napoleon' are in The Outline of History, *which was published in 1920.*

My dear Wells,

I have just been reading your sketch and summing up of Napoleon. You are clearly on the needful reaction against the legend; but there is one omission which not only robs you of the crowning proof of his lack of originality, but also takes away all sense from his replunging of Europe into war at Marengo and Hohenlinden. There is something comic in it too, as if you had written a life of Dante without knowing that he was a poet, or of Newton without knowing that he was a mathematician.

This omission is nothing less than the fact that Napoleon was an extraordinary soldier, was indeed extraordinary in no other way. Take that away from him, and Stein is obviously greatly his superior. Talleyrand could have wiped the floor with him if he could have outbid him as a purveyor of glory. It was the only leg he had to stand on. Try and conceive your own predicament if the only fluid with which you could write was freshly shed human blood, and your works were all the more eagerly read because of it – and that men would even stab one another to fill your bottle with yells of triumph and adore you for giving them the chance. Would you stop writing? *Could* you stop writing? Remember, the stoppage would not only cashier you to the rank of a nobody, but involve the suicide of your genius.

That is precisely how Napoleon was situated. If he hadn't been a soldier he would have been a nobody. He tried writing and everything else that he could try in his youth, and failed them all. He was useless even as a subaltern: only for the revolution he would have been kicked out of the army as a disgrace to it. But from the moment when he got a military command he never looked back until he was defeated, and then he was nothing. All the other things he did could have been better done by other men. Peace was fatal to him: it was the smashing of Paganini's violin, the locking up of Paderewski's piano. He spoke as an artist when he described a field strewn with corpses as a beautiful sight. What else could the poor devil have done, being born with this specific talent in an overwhelming degree, and being otherwise open to your reproaches as a duffer, a cad, a snob, and anything else you please except – and you have a little undervalued the exception – that he had prodigious industry and no sense of comfort.

And he was beaten by Wellington because Wellington, who was no pedant, when he found himself face to face with an academic tactic of artillery preparation and a concentrated blow delivered by columns, could improvise a new tactic of thin red lines and so forth. But Napoleon could play the academic gambit better than anyone else because he had not only an amazing memory in general, but an instinct for topography and for what one may call the vectors of manoeuvering: he seemed to know, if he started a force across Europe on the first of June exactly where and when it would turn up on the fifteenth of August; and it always did. In the days when there were no railways this must have been an enormous advantage. I don't mean that other men could not have calculated these movements; but they could not catch up with a man who knew it without calculating it.

The moral seems to be that Napoleon was as great as Peace the burglar was great, except that people persist in admiring warriors though they have sense enough to suppress petty burglars.

I have no other criticism: the outline is enthralling; but the sketch of Napoleon evidently does not account for him, as there were plenty of other chaps about who had all his bad qualities (what about Barras, for example?): therefore you must show the ace that he held to explain his success.

Ever,

[*unsigned*]

PS By the way, some of his recorded sayings have wit enough in them of a sort to suggest that he could at least grin occasionally; and he was idiotically in love with Josephine, and put up with her longer than some men would have done. Also I think that the fact that he did not drop his family, but took the lot on his back just as he took his boy brother when he was desperately poor in Paris, must be counted to him as evidence that he had the virtues of his narrowness and provincialism. How many Wellses and Shaws would you and I have taken on in his place? He was actually grateful to Joseph.

Baron Karl von **Stein** (1757–1831) was a reforming Prussian statesman who in 1807–8, when Prussia was under the domination of France, was largely responsible for a series of reforms that changed it from a feudal state to a modern one. Napoleon dismissed him from office in 1808 and forced him into exile. Charles Maurice de **Talleyrand** (1754–1838), French statesman of the Napoleonic period and later, won his most famous diplomatic success as France's representative at the Congress of Vienna. Niccolō **Paganini** (1782–1840), was the most famous of violin virtuosi and a composer. Ignace Jan **Paderewski** (1860–1941), Polish pianist and composer, was active also in the political life of Poland. Charles **Peace** was a member of an elusive gang of thieves who in the early years of the seventeenth century were active in the vicinity of Dunmow in Essex, where Wells had his country home at the time when Shaw wrote this letter. The Vicomte de **Barras** (1755–1829), a revolutionary leader in France, played an important part in Napoleon's rise to power.

66 / To H.G. Wells

10 Adelphi Terrace, London WC2
7th July 1921

[TLS with holograph PS: Illinois]

The following letter deals mainly with vivisection, a subject on which Wells and Shaw held totally contrary views. While the 'stupidest letter' to which Shaw refers has vanished, it must have comprised Wells's comments on Back to Methuselah, *which was published on 23 June.*

My dear H.G.

This won't do. There is something to be said for not throwing out dirty water until you get any fresh; but there is nothing to be said for pouring the fresh into the dirty water. You have a lot of second hand and very dirty pseudo-science at the bottom of your bucket. You should have emptied that out when you made your discovery of God. I shall not mind your emptying it over me if that will be any satisfaction to you; but it has to be thrown out decisively and for ever, or you will never get a step further. When I reached the age of 24, and finished my second novel, I found that I could not get a step further on mechanistic lines. I felt my way for awhile, trying how the square root of minus x would work, just as you tried how God would work. It worked very well; and I very soon found an integral position. I backed Butler because Butler had arrived at my position; but his horrible education and infamous controversial manners (see my review of Festing Jones's Memoir in *The Manchester Guardian*) prevented him from doing it justice, very much as the same malicious tradition and training sometimes prevent Inge (who has a first class mind) from doing himself justice when he is dealing with temporalities. Bergson is unspoiled in this way; but when I wrote Man and Superman I had never heard of Bergson; and I backed him, too, because he had arrived at my position through another path. Just so with Scott Haldane. I pounced on him because he was putting in the laboratory work that must be done before the St. Thomases can be persuaded to believe in Creative Evolution. But Scott Haldane has not yet grasped, any more than you have, the implications of the fundamental change from Natural Selection to Creative Evolution. This will not lame his mind because he is going on with his work on the right tack. But it may play the devil with yours because you are not observing any science with an open mind: you write to me about Butler like Robert Tyrrell and about Bergson like Ray Lankester. You are where Archdall Reid was twenty years ago; but A.D. [*typist's error for A.R.*] has extricated himself, whereas you offer to me – to ME, Bernard Shaw – the sort of stuff that the British Medical Journal thinks good enough for the Anti-Vaccination League. You have produced the unnatural phenomenon of the most gifted man who has read my book writing me the stupidest letter about it – the sort of letter that Gladstone or Lord George Hamilton might have written about the Outline of History. Take it away, H.G. Hector: thou sleepst: awake. None of your third quality goods for me, thank you. Why did you, who have put your finger with ridiculous ease on dozens of political absurdities that have duped generations of Englishmen, never put your finger on the absurdity of that experiment of Weismann's with the mice's tails, or spotted that great hit of his: that death is an evolved expedient and not an eternal condition of life? Why did you not see from the very beginning of the most idiotic of all controversies, that the moment you gave up the Garden of Eden you were committed to the conclusion that *all* habits are acquired habits? Why, above all, were you, with such an unerring eye for a fool in every department, taken in by chumps like Victor Horsley, who found his level at last as a simple honest teetotaller? I bewildered poor Horsley, when he was the leading champion of vivisection, by saying, 'The question at issue is not whether Miss Frances Power Cobbe is a liar, as you, with your childish belief in the possibility of infallible accuracy on scientific subjects, assert, nor yet whether the experiments of Farrier have enabled you to cure epilepsy by trephining, but simply whether you are a scoundrel or not.' He fled the field. But to do him justice he did not forget his common observation of human nature to the extent of telling me that a horror of cruelty is feminine. Is the ideal Victorian female so deeply rooted in your imagination as that? 'Oh woman in our hours of ease, uncertain, coy, and hard to please etc. etc.' Get out. Why, when you wrote Love and [Mr.] Lewisham you knew that experiments were put-up jobs. Have you never followed that up to the knowledge that thought alone discovers, and that though thought can be faked, and is faked daily to prove whatever the thinker passionately desires to prove, the experiment is not even fake: its artificiality is open and confessed, and that no sound man ever believes a thing until his intellect is satisfied as well as his senses?

I am not now thinking of vivisection only: that question is child's play. If it is expedient that one dog should die for the people it is expedient that Gyp should die for the people: you could have found out a lot by boiling him when he was a baby. Why didn't you? Was it only the law that withheld you? Or was it a feminine weakness that funked cruelty? Really, H.G.! Yah, H.G.! Yah, yah, yah, YAH! Wake up, and realize that history would have no outlines at all if men of your quality always went on that way.When you get a real grip of science (like mine, eh?) you will see that its importance is so enormous that the difference between a human baby and a canine one, which seems so great to a nursery maid, utterly vanishes in comparison, as the difference between a six foot man and a five vanishes from a height of a thousand feet: consequently the man who once argues himself into torturing a guinea pig will presently find himself torturing a baby. I saw the danger signals soon enough to refuse to go down that railway to folly and madness. If we cannot fight our way out of disease we shall not escape it by trusting to fools to hack a way out for us. So I remain a vulgar suburban Anti-Vivisectionist just like your Christ, whom Belloc or somebody thought a vulgar suburban Communist.

I haven't time to write any more: besides, you are tired of my debating tricks. But you have to write such a lot that you will get into a habit of writing, not without thinking, but without thinking *enough*, unless I bash you about the head occasionally to keep you up to the mark.

I hope to look in on Friday; but I am not linguist enough to be of any use.

Ever,
G.B.S.

[*Hol.*] PS In the matter of the World State you are up against my celebrated demonstration that Psychological Homogeneity is indispensable to political combination. The conditions, as far as I could work them out, were (a) a common language (one in which marriage, justice, honor etc. meant the same thing, whether you used the French, German or English dialects) and (b) intermarriage without any sense of miscegenation. You might get a Teutonic Protestant League, a Latin Catholic League, a Yellow League, a Black League, and a Brown League to come to an agreement about so obvious and universally noxious [a] thing as war and even about unsectarian super-Christianity; but if you attempted such a complete amalgamation as is implied in the World State you would get Babel. You may get something practically homogeneous from the Urals to the Rockies, but not from the Rockies to Japan by the Atlantic route. I have come to think that League-of-Nations Societies will always be futilized by Anacharsis Klootz unless they sit on his head. An invincible majority is as much as we can hope for yet.

How unkind of you to compliment me on my technique! When I was in my prime nobody ever noticed that I had a technique: you dont notice the technique of the torturer when you are on the rack or of your sweetheart when you are in love. Now everybody begins to notice my technique. That means that I am beginning to dodder. Alas! I know it only too well.

Shaw's review of *Samuel* **Butler**, *Author of Erewhon (1835–1902): A Memoir*, by Henry Festing-Jones, was published in *The Manchester Guardian*, 1 November 1919. It was included in Shaw's *Pen Portraits and Reviews* (1931). William Ralph **Inge** (1860–1954), clergyman and author, was Dean of St Paul's Cathedral (1911–34). John Scott **Haldane** (1860–1936), was a biologist admired by Shaw. Robert Yelverton **Tyrrell** (1844–1914) was a classical scholar and translator at Trinity College, Dublin. Sir Edwin Ray **Lankester** (1847–1929) was a distinguished zoologist, educator, and author. Lord George **Hamilton** (1845–1927), politician, was chairman of the Royal Commission on the Poor Laws and Unemployment (1905–9), of which Beatrice Webb was a rebellious member. August **Weismann** (1834–1914) was a German biologist whose experiments (notably with mice) established his theory that acquired characteristics are non-heritable.

The Dublin-born writer Frances Power **Cobbe** (1822–1904) led in establishing the Society for the Protection of Animals Liable to Vivisection, better known as the Victoria Street Society, in the early 1870s. The society led in the prosecution of David **Ferrier** (1843–1928), an eminent physiologist, under the Cruelty of Animals Act of 1876, because of his experiments on the brains of monkeys. (The spelling 'Farrier' is obviously a typist's error, though not the substitution of **Hector** for Brutus in the brief Shakespearian quotation.) The prosecution failed on what were in effect technical grounds. The occasion on which Shaw **bewildered poor Horsley** is unknown. In ***Love and Mr. Lewisham*** (1899), Wells describes an episode in which two science students attend a séance and expose the contrivance involved in it. Three short chapters later they talk with a third student, a convinced spiritualist who organized the séance. He argues that he invited them to it simply to provide a demonstration of techniques used at such affairs; and that in the course of 'demonstrations' in science laboratories, similar contrivances are regularly employed.

67 / To H.G. Wells

10 Adelphi Terrace WC2
3rd October 1921

[TLS: Yale]

The letter has several minor alterations in Shaw's hand, suggesting that it may have been a draft. If so, the original has not been found. A portion of one sentence was quoted by Gordon N. Ray in H.G. Wells and Rebecca West *(1974).*

Wells met Rebecca West (Cicily Isabel Fairfield, 1892–1983), who had already adopted her Ibsenite pen-name, in 1912. Nineteen years old, she was just at the beginning of her career as a writer. She and Wells became lovers, and their son Anthony West was born in August 1914. When the following letter was written, their relationship had become very stressful for them both. None the less, both were deeply concerned about the sort of education that their son should have. Obviously Shaw's letter is his reply to a question raised – whether in conversation or writing – by Wells, and quite possibly by Rebecca also, for she regarded Shaw as one of her four literary 'uncles.' In any case, Anthony West grew up to become a writer.

My dear H.G.

There is no way in which a child can receive a musical education in this unhappy country, or in the world for the matter of that, except by (a) becoming a choirboy, in which case, though he receives a ridiculously one-sided musical culture, he does learn to read music (and if you don't learn this as a child you never learn it at all), and lays the foundation of a professional habit by having to behave himself and do certain jobs before the public at certain hours, whether he is disposed to or not, and (b) choosing parents who are so musical that they keep open house for string quartette players and conductors who are getting up choral works for public performances. I owe my early knowledge of music to the fact that we shared our house with such a conductor, and my mother was his amateur prima donna.

Now I don't see how it is possible for Rebecca to start a musical salon and keep it up. Besides, there would be no element of discipline in it. When our home broke up, and my mother crossed to London to see whether she could not start my sister as a professional singer and keep herself by becoming a professional teacher herself (my father being unable to keep us going) I was left able to sing or whistle all the stock oratorios and cantatas and several typical German and Italian operas, from end to end as thoughtlessly as a canary; but I could not read a note or play a bar on any instrument. Finding the deprivation of the accustomed music in the house intolerable, I had to buy a book with a diagram of the keyboard in it, and laboriously learn my notes and teach myself to play in a horrible manner. To this day I can't play decently; and I can't sing at sight at all. I repeat, you must learn it young, like riding, or you never really master it at all. I was left in a condition of complete illiteracy and technical inefficiency which prevented me from exploiting my large acquaintance with music except as a critic. One man offered to teach me the oboe; but my father was not only dismayed by the cost of the instrument, but shocked at the idea of my becoming anything so ungentlemanly as a professional bandsman; and this, if you please, though no attempt of any kind was made to qualify me for earning a living, and I was started in life with an introduction from my uncle which procured me eighteen shillings a month as junior clerk (office boy) in an extremely genteel office in Dublin.

You see the point. If Anthony is to be a musician, he must be taught musical notation, the keyboard, and to sing from notation at sight at the earliest possible moment. Otherwise he will be in the position you would have been in if you had never been taught to read and write.

When he has been equipped to this extent, the rest is a matter of hearing plenty of music and of having access to a piano and a well stocked musical library. You need not bother about harmony and counterpoint: Bach and Elgar never had a lesson: they had a choirboy training and were steeped in music from their childhood; and they did the rest for themselves. Wagner, after composing a lot, went in voluntarily for six months academic grind with old Dorn, and did not regret it. Elgar told me that a little book called Mozart's Succinct Thoroughbass, consisting of a few notes made by Mozart for his pupil Sussmayer, contains everything that it will save a composer trouble to be taught.

Elgar, by the way, was a fiddler, and not only worked as an orchestral player but at one time thought of becoming a virtuoso like Kreisler and Heifetz. Mozart was a violinist. Elgar, like Goossens, can play a bit on almost any instrument; and I should draw the moral that Anthony should be taught the fiddle as soon as he can hold one, and have a flageolet (which is only a seriously made penny whistle) among his toys at once.

In the old days, unless the father was a musician like Leopold Mozart, the boy was apprenticed to an organist or a nobleman's bandmaster (like Haydn), and fagged for him and picked up his trade as best he could. Verdi, for instance, was apprenticed to the organist of the nearest Italian church. There was no nonsense about the musician being a gentleman or having a liberal education. His self respect, which was often morbidly immense, was based on his being an artist: no mere British duke was ever so insolent, pretentious, and autocratic as Sir Michael Costa, who was only an opera conductor. But he was a musician and nothing else; and this was the strength of his position. The modern situation is different. Stanford and Parry stood as gentlemen and hallmarked University graduates, just as Burne Jones came into painting on an Oxford literary fashion; and the result was that Stanford and Parry never ceased to be amateur champions and it took B.J. many years to become as good a draughtsman as Hogarth or Van Eyck, though he did it at last. Wagner himself, hampered by his racketty boyhood as a university student, not knowing whether he was going to be a poet or not, and fancying music exactly like an amateur instead of facing it as his job, is more amateurish in Tannhauser than Mozart was as a child composer. Now it may be said that Wagner and Burne Jones went much further than the thoroughly professionalized tradesmen ever did; but I do not think their divided, confused aims and liberal education helped them to this advance: I think they simply delayed them. Wagner complained that the new generation of gentlemen musicians were no use to him; that they turned up their noses at their orchestras without being able to conduct them; that though the old sergeant major conductors hated his music and didn't understand it, yet when you gave them the score they could make their men play what was in it firmly and well, and that this was what he wanted, and not essays on music-aesthetics in culture journals.

Forgive me for bothering you with all this; but you see what I am driving at. If Anthony is to be a musician – and he will be too anarchically brought up to have much chance as a banker – dedicate him straight away. Don't be afraid of sacrificing his general education: music is a far more effective instrument of culture than any university course. It leads to languages, and, being itself a common language of high civilization, it carries with it a genuine international culture. No musician could possibly feel or talk about Germany as Henry Arthur Jones and Chesterton do; and, as you know, the University people were just as bad as Jones and Chesterton. As a training in accuracy, delicacy, sustained vigilant attention, and power of enduring simple drudgery, scoring a big orchestral work holds its own with any activity in the world, and beats most of them hollow.

So let Anthony begin today. Let Rebecca call in the builders and upholsterers, and have the room she writes in made proof against the extremity of distracting noises: indeed the house itself should be detached for the sake of the unfortunate neighbors. Let a piano be provided and a flageolet, and a tiny fiddle, and let Anthony be taught notation, sight singing, and the piano keyboard at once. Take him to the opera (I think my first pantomime must have been at something like his age), and if he likes it, get him a vocal score and let him fight its battles over again for himself on the piano. Don't plague him with piano lessons after he has been shown how to finger scales. Don't let him be set to play sonatas without telling him what a sonata is: otherwise he will be disgusted because they are not dramatic and exciting. Let him find his own way as soon as he has been taught to walk. By the time he wants to be an actor or a novelist or a playwright, let him be so much more effective as a musician that he will be no more able to escape from music than a sailor from the sea.

There: that is all I could say if the boy were my own. But the fact remains that I am not a professional musician; and nobody knows quite so well – capacity for capacity – as the one who has been through the mill. Do you know any musician who has brains enough to be worth consulting? Do you know Elgar among the older men, or, among the younger, Goossens, Holst, or Cyril Scott? They will not be able to express themselves as well on paper as we can; but it occurs to me that you – or Rebecca – might show one of them this letter and ask is there anything in it or is it all damned nonsense. Holst or Goossens might even take an apprentice in a modified sort of way if you could give them a lift with a premium. But this last is only a passing notion to which I have given no consideration.

You need not acknowledge this appalling infliction, as I shall see you on the Chaliapine occasion.

Ever,
G.B.S.

Shaw's reference to **old Dorn** is not entirely accurate or fair. Heinrich Dorn (1804–92) was already an established composer, conductor, and teacher at Leipzig when Richard Wagner (1813–83) – only nine years Dorn's junior – went there to study in June 1830 for six months. Wagner had not then done 'a lot of composing,' though he himself seems to have forgotten how little. On Christmas Eve of that year Dorn conducted the first performance of an overture that Wagner had written. Wagner provides an amusing account of the period and of that event in his autobiography. He and Dorn had a falling-out later in their careers and became bitter antagonists.

Sir Edward **Elgar** (1857–1934), English composer, was a friend of Shaw, to whom he dedicated his *Severn Suite*. He was not only a 'fiddler,' but an accomplished organist. Franz Xaver **Süssmayr** (1766–1803), Austrian conductor and composer, was the pupil to whom Mozart is said to have dictated from his deathbed the final section of his *Requiem*. Fritz **Kreisler** (1875–1962), Austrian by birth, and Jascha **Heifetz** (1901–1987), Russian by birth, were both American by adoption. They were perhaps the most famous violinists of the twentieth century. Eugene **Goossens** (1893–1962) was, at the time of Shaw's letter, conducting at Covent Garden, having for several years been first violinist in the Queen's Hall Orchestra and associated with Sir Thomas Beecham. Sir Michael **Costa** (1808–84) was a composer and conductor whose tastes differed from Shaw's, but whose ability to make an orchestra play well, even if it was through sheer terror, Shaw admired. Sir Charles Villiers **Stanford**(1852–1924) and Sir Charles Hubert H. **Parry** (1848–1918) were well-known composers and teachers. Sir Edward **Burne-Jones** (1833–98) was a painter and decorator, one of the Pre-Raphaelites. Gustav **Holst** (1874–1934) was in his most productive period, having written *The Planets* in 1914–15, and now turning to choral and operatic work. Cyril **Scott** (1879–1970) was an English pianist and composer who in the 1920s was enjoying an international reputation. Fyodor **Chaliapin** (1873–1938) was the most famous operatic basso of his time. According to his autobiography *Pages from My Life* (1927), he gave his first concert outside Russia after the First World War at the Albert Hall – on the date of Shaw's letter. The 'occasion' to which Shaw refers may have been that concert or a luncheon that Shaw gave in Chaliapin's honour, described by the singer in his later autobiography, *Man and Mask*, 1932.

68

[*no address*]
20th July 1922

[HLS: Boston]

In September 1922, the London Strand Magazine *published a report by the journalist Bruce Barton of an interview he had had with Wells, following up the worldwide success of the* Outline of History *(1920). Wells had been asked to name the six greatest men in history, and in response had listed – giving his reasons – Jesus, Buddha, Aristotle, Asoka ('ruler of an empire which stretched from Afghanistan to Madras; and he is the only military monarch on record who abandoned warfare after victory'), Roger Bacon, and Abraham Lincoln. In October the* Strand *published comments by five well-known writers, including Shaw; and in November, further comments together with Wells's 'summing up.' The manuscript versions of Shaw's and Wells's comments follow. They are not personal letters, but are included here as showing how the minds of the two might be engaged in the discussion of an essentially non-controversial topic – about which neither cared much.*

Mr. Wells has taken advantage of an idiotic question to do some more of his invaluable culture propaganda; but the question remains idiotic. Asking for the names of the six greatest men is like asking for the names of the six greatest tools in the carpenter's bag. Jesus, who knew something of carpentering, thought himself a good preacher and relatively an indifferent carpenter. If he had been apprenticed to a stone mason instead, and stuck to his trade, he would probably have been left out of sight by Michael Angelo; and Michael Angelo would certainly have been completely eclipsed by Mr. Chaplin as a movy-star. None of Mr. Wells's six would have had a dog's chance at an election against Titus Oates or Horatio Bottomley – two quite incommensurable characters, by the way; but I couple them because popularity is a sort of common denominator; and before you can compare men of different specific genius at all, you must find a common denominator for them.

Mr. Wells uses a common denominator which obliges him to discard Napoleon and Mahomet as inferior to men who never had to govern for a single day. If Mahomet had been crucified before he ever had to spend a farthing of public money or control a day's police work and Jesus had seen the Roman and Jewish power melt before him, and been made King of the Jews in earnest instead of in mockery, Mahomet would have been the pure unstained martyr and Jesus the soiled ruler and conqueror. Had Richelieu been a mathematician and Descartes a Prime Minister, Descartes would have been dragged down from the empyrean and Richelieu caught up into it. It is easy for an astronomer to be clean, but impossible for a sweep or a polar explorer. We all know that it is silly for the pot to call the kettle black: what we do not know is that it is equally silly for the alabaster urn to reproach the pot for its blackness. Shelley's denunciations of Eldon and Castlereagh win our sympathy; but if Shelley had had to do the work of a Lord Chief Justice or a Prime Minister, he would not now seem a luminous angel to us, however well he might have done it. Lincoln had the luck to be shot at the moment that the really difficult part of his job was beginning. Had Wilson, Lloyd George, and Clemenceau been shot between the Armistice and Versailles, they would now have some reputation left.

Great men are statues of our ideals. Our hopes and enthusiasms crystallize upon some name: that is all: Aristotle was no more (and no less) Mr. Wells's Aristotle than Julius Caesar was Mommsen's Caesar. I am a Great Man myself; and I Know.

G. Bernard Shaw 20/7/22

Titus **Oates** (1649–1705) was an unscrupulous English demagogue, anti-Catholic conspirator, and criminal. Horatio **Bottomley** (1860–1933) was a journalist and jingoistic entrepreneur who in the early years of the twentieth century fell into disgrace; he died in poverty. (Oates and Bottomley are again mentioned together in Shaw's letter of 3 January 1941.) Armand Jean du Plessis, duc de **Richelieu** (1585–1642), French churchman and statesman, was made a cardinal in 1622. A master of intrigue, he was virtual ruler of France through the last twenty years of his life. René **Descartes** (1596–1650), almost exactly contemporary with Richelieu, was a philosopher and scientist, one of the greatest of all mathematicians. Percy Bysshe **Shelley** (1792–1822), the poet, was persecuted in various ways for his outspoken radical views of religion, marriage, politics, and social injustice of all kinds. His denunciation of Lord **Eldon** (1751–1838) and Lord **Castlereagh** (1769–

1822), both prominent Tory politicians, arose partly from the judicial decision that he was not a fit father to have custody of the children of his first marriage; but it reflected his bitter hatred of oppression of whatever sort. With the phrase '**a luminous angel**' Shaw is recalling the words of Matthew Arnold: 'Shelley, beautiful and ineffectual angel, beating in the void his luminous wings in vain' (1886). Thomas Woodrow **Wilson** (1856–1924) of the United States, David **Lloyd George** (1863–1945) of Great Britain, and Georges **Clemenceau** (1841–1929) of France were three of the 'big four' leading statesmen at the Paris Peace Conference that resulted in the Treaty of Versailles in 1919. Theodor **Mommsen** (1817–1903) was a German historian, best known for his three-volume *History of Rome* (1854–6) – a work on which Shaw drew when he was writing *Caesar and Cleopatra.*

69 [*no address; n.d.*]

[AD: Boston]

Wells's draft response to Shaw's previous letter, which was published along with some by other hands.

I agree with Mr. Shaw's first sentence &, by the bye, with his last. The question *was* idiotic. But not as Mr. Walkley says 'merely futile.' The idiocy is no condemnation of the journalistic questioner; he knew his business, as Mr. Walkley witnesses. 'Futile,' says Mr. Walkley & puts his bright little man-of-the-world mind through its attitudes, *proxime accessit, cherchez la femme* & all the rest of it, for a nice long contribution. The futility is not to the interviewer.

And the game is so amusing that your invitation to say a few words more catches me replying. Mr. Zangwill is so tempting. What nonsense that man writes! There is hardly any evidence at all that this Moses of his ever existed. Harmsworth's Encyclopaedia is no proof. And Buddha's 'monkish gospel of renunciation'! After that Shakespeare as one of the six cardinal men is no astonishment.

Some of your other contributors display evidences of the Shakespeare cant – for cant it is. It may be worth while to say a word or two about that. Mr. Zangwill writes: 'The greatest writer the world has ever known does not even appear in the *Outline of History* whence his very name is banished. One might imagine it is because Mr. Wells like Kipling admires action more than thought.' But the name was never banished; it was never there. Why should it be? It would be amusing if we could get Mr. Zangwill explaining why the name of Shakespeare should come into an outline of history. What did Shakespeare do, what did he add to the world's totality? Some delightful plays, some exquisite passages, some deliciously observed characters. He was a great playwright, a great humourist, the sweetest laughter in the world. *All* truly English people must love him dearly, he is so intensely ours, so near our inmost hearts. But none of those plays were of main importance to the story of mankind – or even to the story of England. He had none of the power & patriotic pride of Milton. If he had never lived things would be very much as they are, there would have been so much less beauty in England & British literary people, native & immigrant, would have had to have some other name to cant about, but that must have been all.

Shakespeare's 'thought' amounted to very little. He added no idea, he altered no idea, in the growing understanding of mankind. I could believe that English people loved him more if they respected him a little less. The legendary Moses-Shakespeare monster is a bore. People should read & see his plays.

Alfred Bingham **Walkley** (1855–1926) was drama critic for the *Times.* Israel **Zangwill** (1864–1926) was a playwright and journalist. The ***Harmsworth Encyclopædia***, published in 1905–6, had been long out of print; it was succeeded in 1920–3 by *Harmsworth's Universal Encyclopedia*, presumably the work to which Wells here refers.

70 / To H.G. Wells

Ayot St Lawrence, Welwyn, Herts.
4th December 1922

[ALS: Illinois]

Wells's A Short History of the World *was published in 1922.*

My dear H.G.W.

I have read the Short History all through devoutly, and highly approve of it as a much needed piece of educational work. Barring the Outline, which I read also, it is the first attempt at presenting history in any sort of proportion to Little Arthur, and superseding his Old Testament & Macaulay outlook.

There is a Yellow Peril in it. It will be devoured in India and China; and when the east becomes self-conscious, the west will have to look out. Well, let it. What I want to know is how the Fool Peril is to be averted.

I find a certain pleasing irony in your being the great history teacher of the rising generation, because the odd thing about all your novels was they seemed to be written by a man totally ignorant of history. The world in them began in 1876, when I came to London. A reference in them to Queen Anne would have been as surprising as a reference to Hathor in Dickens. You never made allusions; and classical literature is made up nine tenths of allusions. Your command of contemporary stuff never gave out. If anyone had been intelligent enough to ask me what older body of thought – what history and philosophy – was at the back of *Tono Bungay*, I should have replied that I hadnt the remotest idea. And now the biographical dictionaries seem likely to say WELLS. H.G. – 18-- – 19--. After some early essays in fiction, the Father of British History, supposed by some to have worked in a book factory kept by Archbishop Laud Acton, devoted himself exclusively to his true métier &c &c &c &c.

By the way, when I read the Outline, I wrote you a letter about Napoleon. But instead of sending it I dramatized it and stuck it into Methuselah.

Love to Jane.
ever
G.B.S.

***Little Arthur's** History of England*, by Maria Graham (later Lady Calcott) was first published in 1835, went through several editions, was brought up to date in 1874, and reissued in 1875. Thomas Babington **Macaulay** (1800–59), writer, poet, historian, and parliamentarian, is best known for his five-volume *History of England from the Accession of James the Second* (1849–61). **Hathor** was the Egyptian goddess of fertility. William **Laud** (1573–1645), an ultra-conservative churchman who became Archbishop of Canterbury (1633–45), was condemned to death by Cromwell's government for his persecution of the Puritans. John Emerich Edward Dalberg **Acton** (1834–1902), a liberal Roman Catholic historian who became Professor of Modern History at Cambridge, was elevated to the peerage as Lord Acton in 1869.

71 / To H.G. Wells

10 Adelphi Terrace
London WC2
11th April 1924

[TLS: Illinois]

The letter has an added sentence indicated by an asterisk. It and the postscript are in Shaw's hand. Evidently Wells had been approached with a request for money, linked to a proposal that the man making the request might become Wells's Polish translator. He had turned for advice to Shaw, knowing that he was acquainted with the man in question. Wells's novel The Dream *had very recently been published.*

My dear H.G.

Sobieniowski is just what you see: an unfortunate foreigner with no taste for anything but literature and no other means of livelihood except borrowing money without the slightest prospect of being able to pay. I think he keeps accounts with Micawbresque scrupulousness: for he told me the other day that he was indebted to me to the tune of £94, and that I could secure repayment infallibly by guaranteeing his bank overdraft for £300, you guaranteeing the other half of £600 to buy a house which would only consummate his ruin. That is the kind of chap he is; but his nature is a noble one.

His parents, ruined Polack squireens, are practically in the workhouse. He got his university degree and supported himself by teaching until he came over here. He has a wife and son. They live with him in a single room and drive him distracted. Let him translate us by all means if he can get any publisher to accept him; but if you lend him five pounds he will return next week and ask for thirteen, giving you precise dates for repayment (he does not understand notes of hand) and also an explanation of his proposed plans for applying the money which will deprive you of all excuse for entertaining the faintest hope that he will not then be in worse difficulties than ever. In short, a miniature poetic Polish Micawber, who will one day make good, as he is sober and industrious and would be honest if he knew how and could afford it.

Thank you for *The Dream.* I'd better send you the one Charlotte bought: it is always handy to have copies about to give to people.* I was taken aback by the ending, as I had quite made up my mind that Smith was to murder Sumner and return to Sunray by way of the gallows and describe to her what a trial for murder was like and how very easy it was for quite decent sort of people to find themselves in the dock.

I wonder how much impression you are making on the middle

classes. When I was your age I never could feel that I was making any impression on anybody, which was perhaps all for the best as it set me free to hit recklessly. But I am not so sure now. I am staggered sometimes to find how much a casual phrase will do when it strikes on the box of some young nobody in a corner. I wonder how soon people will come to blows about these things that they find so amusing in our books.

* I have since consulted her; and she flatly refuses: she says she bought it and it is hers.

Ever
G.B.S.

PS I think you might have underlined the irony of Smith's virtuous indignation with his wife when he was trading on his sister's liaison with his employer.

Floryan **Sobienowski** (1881–1964), who translated Shaw's plays into Polish, was an unprincipled scrounger who made himself a nuisance to a number of writers. (Three years before Shaw wrote this letter, Sobienowski had blackmailed the writer Katherine Mansfield [1888–1923] because of letters that she had written him a decade earlier.) Shaw's assessment of his nature as 'noble' suggests that he had himself been somewhat taken in. Although he warned his friends against Sobienowski, Shaw viewed him with Dickensian humour, seeing a resemblance to David Copperfield's friend Mr Micawber, who also was constantly impecunious – and constantly convinced that something was about to 'turn up.'

72 / To Mrs H.G. Wells

10 Adelphi Terrace WC2
12th July 1924
[*Addressed:* Easton Glebe, Dunmow, Essex
Forwarded to: 120 Whitehall Court, London SW1]

[APCS: Illinois]

*This and the next letter are addressed to Jane Wells, but their two messages are intended for Wells himself. The latter had through two years been strenuously busy, to the point of exhaustion: travelling and working for the cause of the League of Nations until he lost faith in it, standing unsuccessfully for two parliamentary elections in England, and continuing his writing career. Also, his affair with Rebecca West had ended in the later months of 1923; and he had entered that extraordinary 'web of relationships' outlined by Anthony West in his study of his father (*H.G. Wells, *1984) and the subject of the third volume of Wells's autobiography (*H.G. Wells in Love, *1984).*

Floryan, seeing the possibility of bringing off the double event, applied his lemon squeezer simultaneously to me. I confronted him with the letter you enclosed; and he at once handsomely announced that as he had extracted enough from me to go on with, he would not press you any further except to ask you for copies of the books he means to translate. I then made some general observations on his character with my usual lack of delicacy. He said he had resolved to change his nature, and that there would be no more trouble. What could I do but laugh? Dont answer his future applications for money: just tear them up. G.B.S.

73 / To Mrs H.G. Wells

Gleneagles Hotel
Scotland
7th September 1924

[ALS: Illinois]

At the head of this letter is a note, presumably in Jane Wells's hand, saying, 'Told him the facts.' Shaw would have known that Wells was in Europe, where he had gone to Geneva to observe the League of Nations Assembly. He would not yet have learned that Wells had also plunged into another passionate and long-lasting love affair, with Odette Keun, university-educated in Holland, for three years a Dominican nun, then a journalist and novelist in Paris, now living in the South of France.

My dear Jane

I enclose a scrap (tear it up) of Sob's latest, to show how much impression my remonstrance made on him.

However, that is not why I write.

My American lawyers Stern & Reubens write pressing me to receive one Lavell who wants me to write for the McLure Newspaper Syndicate. They urge that Wells is supplying a set of articles (weekly for a year) at $400 per article, and Bennett for $500, but without any stipulation or guarantee as to the number: practically $500 for any article he sends them.

Now they are always after me for this very thing: a series of articles for a year; and by repeatedly refusing or quoting impossible prices I have found out how far they will go. The limit so far is £150 per thousand words, or, if I prefer it, a guarantee of $30,000 a year against 50% of the total monies received by the Syndicate for the serial rights.

As H.G. is, to say the least, as big a draw as I am, there is no doubt that $400 for an article of 1500–2500 is far below his market value, and that if he had demanded $1000 per article they would have given it. I always tell them to go away – that it is not worth the while of anyone who can get plays produced to do journalism at all – that I lose by every word I write for a newspaper instead of for the stage. This is true for H.G. also unless he can make a book of the articles that will sell as widely as a novel. So if you are his business man, you might try it on next time.

I just thought I would tell you.

We are here until the 17th in a new ferro-concrete hotel straight out of *The Sleeper Awakened.* Everything is done by electricity or compressed air. Even your boots are collected in electric trucks. Ford's factories are crude in comparison, and probably much less noisy. The clocks do not tick: they remain dead for 10 seconds, and then jump forward with a hiccup that makes you jump also. Even my placid nerves gave way the other morning when I was trying to work. I wrenched open the door of the clock's interior, and disconnected the wires. I then worked on in peace, happily unconscious of the fact that I had stopped every clock in the hotel (several hundreds I should imagine).

But Charlotte likes the luxury of our royal suite; and we are staying until the 17th.

I have not dared to ask the price.

ever
G.B.S.

Wells's novel *When the Sleeper Wakes: A Story of Years to Come* was published in 1899.

74 / To H.G. Wells Lochinver, Sutherland (on the wing)
11th September 1925

[ALS: Illinois]

A note of Charlotte's dated 17 October 1924 refers to 'our very nice dinner on Wednesday' – presumably 15 October. Through most of the ensuing year Wells was in France, and there seems to have been no contact between him and Shaw.

Shaw had, however, received a copy of Wells's novel Christina Alberta's Father, *written in 1924 and published in 1925.*

My dear H.G.

Charlotte insisted on my mixing up *C.A's Father* with *Waverley*, as she refuses to drag that volume about with us any more; and I had to finish it at meals to appease her, taking you between meals.

The inevitable comparison, however, is not with Scott, but with Cervantes. The subject is the subject of *Don Quixote.* Why didn't Cervantes, who was, I suppose, as clever as you or I, treat it your way, and solve his problem instead of collapsing when he could think of no more adventures, and making the Don a pious recreant on his deathbed?

I wonder will any critic have the gumption to see that the answer is the whole difference between the age of Shakespear and the age of US!

You make me feel fearfully old fashioned, as if I kept the Dark Ages in countenance whilst you put them out of it; but – like Scott – I am really not so bad for an old un; and I rejoice unspeakably in your pioneering.

We have been to Orkney and Shetland up to our eyes in scenery; but we must get back for October. I am tired of this Irish part of Scotland where you have to climb to the top of the wilderness of rocks to escape from the sense of being in a stone prison with a cloud ceiling: after a day or two I want Scottish Scotland and English England. I am also much of Morris's mind 'The Scotch have every possible vice; and I like them: the Irish have every possible virtue; and I *don't* like them.'

My hand, as you see, has writer's cramp. I now carry a Remington Portable with me; and it is a great comfort; but I take up the pen occasionally to see whether I can still write, with this rather negative result.

Our love to Jane. I presume the infants are now more than semi-detached. By the way, shouldn't Gyp call himself Fountains or something, so as to start fair? Think of Siegfried Wagner and young Mozart and Charles Dickens Junior! People *will* expect these unfortunate innocents to carry on the old man's business.

ever
G.B.S.

Waverley (1814) was the first of the series of 'Waverley novels' by Sir Walter Scott (1771–1832).

75 / To H.G. Wells

from Regina Palace Hotel
Stresa, Lago Maggiore
Italy
[*n.d.*]

[TLU: BL 50552 ff 48–9]

This undated unsigned letter, typed on Shaw's Whitehall Court stationery, is a transcript of BL 50552 ff 46–7, which is a letter drafted in Shaw's shorthand. Presumably Shaw sent the draft to his secretary Blanche Patch, who transcribed it and sent it on to Wells. The typed letter does not carry Shaw's signature or initials, but has Wells's instruction 'File' in the margin. The Shaws were in Italy from 4 August to 4 October 1926. Wells's novel of discussion The World of William Clissold *had recently been published. It is reasonable to assume that GBS wrote the draft letter in late August or early September.*

My dear H.G.

They sent on *Clissold* to me here; and I gulped it greedily. Charlotte is now improving her mind with it very appreciatively.

This preface business is swallowing up all our fiction. With me there is still a pretence that the preface is only a preface and that the play's the thing; but in *Clissold* the pretence is thrown over recklessly: the book is history and sociology with rudimentary survivals of fiction, and a gorgeous relapse into landscape painting, in which, nevertheless, the figure which asserts itself as significant is the farmer uprooting his olive trees to produce scent. There are pages in which you have forgotten that there is such a thing as a novel in the world, and are back again in the *Outline of History*. You appear as a sort of inverted Mr. Dick, trying to write a romance of Charles I, and unable to keep soul evolution out of it. The fact is, fiction as such is no longer more interesting than romance, but so far from it on the contrary quite the reverse. Your only chance – if you really want to make *Clissold* a novel, is to do what Fielding did in *Tom Jones*, when he, too, could not stick to King Charles's head: that is, divide the work into 'books'; and make the first chapter of every book an essay on the world as he saw it. Except that you will have to set apart, not one chapter, but all the chapters save one, for your Anschaung.

The only section that does not arouse my enthusiasm is the one that raises the issue between the Englishman and the Irishman. You are altogether too godlike, and incidentally too Anglo-Saxon, when you deny that the isms ever existed. It is true that when you go up high enough in a balloon or plane, the hills vanish, and nothing is visible but a dirty brown muddle with a few threads streaking it. But the hills are there all the same; and an engineer accepting your view would curse you by his gods when he got to work on it. When you say that there never was any such thing as Feudalism or Capitalism you are insisting in the Anglo-Saxon manner in making a muddle where there is no muddle, because muddle is the natural element of the A-S. Now lucidity is the natural element of Irishmen, whose failing it is to allege system where there is no system. But you cannot say that here there is no system. People are now reading George Trevelyan's *History of England* (a great advance on Macaulay); and they will not stand such a ten-thousand-feet up statement as that Feudalism may be dismissed from the historical landscape because there never was any such thing. It and Capitalism are the two most thoroughly argued out, most defined, most largely acted and legislated upon, and most powerfully established systems that have ever been proposed and accepted for the regulation of human society. What you are entitled to say is that neither of them have been understood by the rank and file of those who administrated them or submitted to them, and that this, which is true of all social strategies, gives a certain artificiality to them, and a very serious practical instability. No sooner is a system established in principle than all sorts of people who know nothing about its principles, in all sorts of emergencies, begin to knock all sorts of holes in it. But you would not say that there was no Cartesian mathematical system, or no Copernico-Newtonian system, or no undulatory theory of light, because the Forth Bridge fell and Einstein showed that the hypotheses of gravitation and the ether are superfluous, and, anyhow, not one person in a thousand ever knew of their existence.

Mr. Dick is the protégé and attendant of David Copperfield's Aunt Betsy Trotwood. He is attempting to write a 'Memorial'of King Charles I, but is persistently interrupted by the obsessive question of how the people at the execution of Charles could have 'made that mistake of putting some of the trouble out of *his* head, after it was taken off, into *mine*.' It was the Tay Bridge, not the **Forth Bridge**, that collapsed, 28 December 1879, in a storm.

76 / To H.G. Wells Ayot St Lawrence, Welwyn, Herts.
12th November 1926

[ALS: Illinois]

On 12 November 1926 it was announced that the Nobel Prize for Literature for 1925 had been awarded to Shaw. Wells, living then in France, must have cabled Shaw at once – though Shaw's reply leaves the nature of Wells's message (which has not come to light) ambiguous. Shaw's action was to accept the honour and direct that the money accompanying it be used for the furthering of Anglo-Swedish literary relations through the establishing of a special foundation.

My dear H.G.

Of course you cannot ask me to throw three or four hundred a year back in their faces; but you will not be surprised, and certainly not disappointed, when I tell you that this is precisely what I am going to do. It shall be done in my very grandest style; but it shall be done very emphatically.

When you are 90 they will no doubt crown you for some senile novelette, ignoring the Outline.

However, what can they do, poor devils, called upon to be God-Omniscients, but play for safety by registering the accomplished fact?

The cheek of it!

ever
G.B.S.

77 / To H.G. Wells Passfield Corner
Liphook
Hants.

[ALS: Illinois]

The following letter was written by Charlotte Shaw on the Webbs's stationery, with the note:

As from
Ayot St Lawrence
Welwyn Herts.
30 May 1927

In March 1927 Jane Wells joined her husband in Paris for the occasion of a lec-

ture that he gave at the Sorbonne. She returned to England, where Wells joined her in late April for the wedding of their son Gip. He went back to France, but in less than three weeks he was again in England, for doctors had discovered that Jane had inoperable cancer and would live only a few months. Evidently Wells wrote the Shaws about her, suggesting that they go to see her.

Dear H.G.

This very terrible news was broken to us in outline by Lady Russell a few days ago, & I have been thinking of you both ever since. It is one of the most tragic things that has come into my life, for, as you say, she is *valiant* & has been the gayest & pluckiest person I have ever known, I think.

And for you – but it is beyond words – we will see you this week.

We are here with the Webbs, but go to Ayot today & will be in London on Thursday morning next. I propose we should go to see Jane on Thursday afternoon at five o'clock. But if any other time during the hours you mention is more convenient, only let us know. We will go any time on Thursday afternoon or evening. But, if you say nothing, it shall be five.

My love & thoughts with you both.

Yours
Charlotte F. Shaw

I understand the hint 'gossip about things in general'.

Lady **Russell** was Elizabeth von Arnim (née Beauchamp, 1866–1941), a writer with whom Wells had had a passionate love affair. She married the second Earl Russell in 1916.

78 / To H.G. Wells Ayot St Lawrence, Welwyn
30th May 1927

[ALS: Illinois]

Shaw wrote the following letter on the same day as Charlotte wrote the previous one, after their return to Ayot St Lawrence.

My dear H.G.

I could hardly refrain from writing to you when I heard about it: I couldn't stand getting it as gossip; but I concluded that you had better choose your own moment.

Of course I am as helpless as everybody else. I am greatly relieved at the verdict of inoperable. Operation is as useless as it is horrible. Incurable means only that the doctors and surgeons can't cure it, which we knew beforehand. Whether Jane (or God) cannot cure it is not so certain. Cancer means that the life force has taken the wrong turning and finds it easier than the right turning, as it is downhill. It is making a lower class of tissue; and the problem is to get it back to the right road and the higher tissue. Instead of facing this problem the doctors have been wasting time and money in trying to give cancer to mice, and find a microbe. They found one, and succeeded in establishing that it was entirely innocent, and that the mischief lay in the conditions in which it was found, but couldn't define them.

When we are blankly ignorant, there is nothing for it but reckless empiricism. Raphael Roche insists that he has cured cancers by empirical homeopathy, his theory being that the moment you have a theory you are wrong. He once gave me some sugar for an exceedingly nasty lump in my scrotum; and whether by pure coincidence or not, the lump dissolved into lymph in three weeks and troubled me no more. In Jane's case I should be incurably sceptical about Roche; but I should spree £20 on him, and take his pinches of apparently harmless sugar. I should try starvation on water and orange juice, not very hopefully, but on the calculation that at worst it is as good a way to die as the other. I should let Lady Astor Christian Science me into pretending that there was nothing the matter with me. I should not bother much about Doctor Bell and the Battersea Hospital methods, because I know that vegetarianism does not protect. The one thing I should not do is follow medical advice, as that is known now to be at best useless and at worst mischievous.

We shall look in on Thursday: Charlotte has written to settle when. I cannot express my feelings: the thing is quite beyond that. There it is, blast it!

G.B.S.

Raphael **Roche** (1857–1945) was a well-known homeopath. Viscountess Nancy **Astor** (1879–1964), MP and outspoken promoter of social reforms, was a close friend of Shaw for many years. She belonged to the Christian Science movement. Dr Robert **Bell** (1845–1926), physician and author, was superintendent of cancer research at the Battersea Hospital.

79 / To H.G. Wells

10 Adelphi Terrace WC2
8th July 1927

[ALS: Illinois]

At the bottom of the first page of this letter Wells wrote 'about 4.' The Shaws were preparing to move from the flat in Adelphi Terrace that they had occupied for almost twenty-eight years – Charlotte for longer, in fact. The move itself was to take place in August, while they were in Italy.

Dear H.G.

We have been thinking about you & Jane constantly but it has been impossible to propose a visit before this because of the urgency of our move to Whitehall Court. We have been kept at work here getting rid of the accumulations of rubbish of 30 years.

Now we are fairly well through with it – do you think you would both like us to go to Easton on Monday next – 11th?

If so, shall it be luncheon – or hadn't we better go to tea? These light days there is *plenty* of time to get back after tea, & I think myself you will probably have quite enough of us if we turn up about 4.

We go to the country – Ayot St Lawrence, Welwyn, tomorrow: & our telephone number there is Codicote 18.

Yours with much love

C.F. Shaw

80 / To H.G. Wells

Regina Palace Hotel, Stresa
4th August 1927

[ALS: Illinois]

Wells remained with Jane, affectionate and attentive, throughout the months of her illness: he gives a moving account of this period in his introduction to The Book of Catherine Wells *(1928). His novel* Meanwhile *was published in this period, a time of intense economic and social problems that had culminated in the General Strike of 1926. It deals with a family who are rich owners of coal mines in the Vale of Edensoke, in Yorkshire, Geoffrey being a nephew of Lord Edensoke.*

My dear H.G.

I have just devoured Meanwhile. The fiction of a disgusted spectator of the strike telling his wife what he thinks of its protagonists in intimate letters not intended for publication serves its turn extremely well. As long as Baldwin and MacDonald do not know exactly where they are they will not be able to tell their respective right and left wings to go to hell; and we shall have nothing but guerilla warfare. Baldwin's position is not ascertainable: he is in the air between Capitalism not yet become impossible and Socialism not yet become comprehensible. MacDonald's position *is* ascertainable; but we have to ascertain it for him; the men of action and the parliament men have no time to think. That is why I have left 12½ plays unwritten to produce this book on Socialism with which the printer is now in travail.

You should now pick up some dropped strands from Mr. Lewisham, and deal with the appalling corruption of learning, of science, and of thought in every department except that which is fortified by an impregnable *chevaux de frise* of transcendental mathematics, by Edensoke-cum-Geoffreyism in the professions. You must grasp the horror of your own scientific education, by which the material side of physiology and anatomy was imposed on you as biology. Here I am face to face with Troubetskoy, who never reads, and is left desolate by the death of his wife. 'What did you make of the Paris surgeons?' I asked. He replied in one word 'Assassins.' These poor devils did what they had been taught and trained to do; and that is what it came to. And so I shall have to pose to him for a statue (he has done three of me already) because in no other way can I take his mind off the assassination; and I have already had to sacrifice a week of my holiday to answer your paraphrase of Lister's reply to Victoria in the Sunday Express. Why do you do it, H.G.? How can I ask you about Jane after it?

For heaven's sake, if you must believe that doctors are gods, call in Roman Catholic doctors. They too hold that as animals are for the use of Man, Man has no moral duty to animals. But they also hold that a woman is fundamentally different from a mouse, and that to treat a woman as a mouse or even think of her as a mouse is a mortal sin. The others make no such distinction. To them Jane is mechanically and chemically a morphologic variation on a mouse. Having investigated many thousands of mice they assure you that they know all about her. *I* say that having investigated so many thousands of mice they know nothing even about mice, or about anything; and to do them justice they dont pretend to when they talk to me.

I have met an old lady here: an Italian countess, who has turned her place into a menagerie, her speciality being vampire bats. I suspect this humanitarian of being your mother. Her features are not particularly like yours; but her eyes and her expression are so extraordinarily like yours in your sunniest moments that she gives you away. The dismal and uneasy apologist of vivisection is not the real man.

But all that you have said and all that I have said has been said over and over again and left things just where they have been since Galen, the father of lies. What we have to do is the positive work of suggesting experiments in genuine biology. Nothing else will overcome the inertia of the established routine. Bose has done something to bridge the change; but it is not enough to show what a homeopathic dose of snake poison does to a plant, or even reduce our common shop vivisection to utterly contemptible clumsiness and savagery by the contrast with his methods. We are not plants; and we must get to direct experiment on the human subject, leaving nothing to analogy and as little as possible to inference, before we can make our biological fictions and speculations (including your books and mine) scientific. Digging into the entrails of dogs and guinea pigs, and seeing what will happen when you extirpate this or ligature that is only ancient Roman augury pithed: I should have no patience with it even if it caused no suffering and did not turn decent medical students into the demoralized blackguards they are.

I don't know whether you have any clinical instinct: anyhow, it is not cultivated; and you cannot take Jane wholly into your own hands. But you can watch and wait with an undarkened mind. The official diagnosis comes to nothing, not only because none of the cases are identical, but because there is a 'pseudo' which saves face when the medical verdict has been wrong. If Jane is curing herself – if she has given up making the wrong sort of tissue and is replacing it with the right sort – then you have nothing to do but encourage her, and write nothing that will plunge her into despair. But if not, you must first ascertain whether she is being prevented by some purely physical lesion of the sort that the osteopaths are trained to feel and correct. It is no use putting the question to a registered doctor: he has not the technique: it takes a couple of years to acquire it. If the osteo. finds nothing, or his correction will not stay put, then Bose's snake trick seems to indicate that a homeopathic stimulus might give the life force (*vis medicatrix natura*) a lift. I, in your place, would then try Roche, as a pure empiric; for there is no science of drugs; and he is clever enough to know it. If that failed I should be tempted to get an opinion from his son, because his son is young, has attained the M.C. [*Master of Surgery*] degree which is the summit of professional qualification, and has been nursed by his father in anti-Harleystreetism. His youth will prevent him from trying to impose on you (you being who you are); and as he knows the latest he will not be out-of-date like the fully arrived panjandrums.

Here are three stones which you ought not to leave unturned if all is not well. Of course there are all sorts of professed healers about with more or less plausible systems and theories; but there is not time to try them all as last resources; and you could not reasonably reproach yourself for neglecting them. But there is evidence enough to try (1) osteopathy on a definite tissue, (2) homeopathy as a drug stimulus, and (3) the opinion of an up-to-date beginner with a tiptop qualification. To leave these obvious resources untouched simply because the Assassins can do nothing would leave you a prey to remorseful doubts if Jane were to perish at their hands. Besides, there are plenty of qualified men, inside and outside the Battersea Hospital set, who agree with me.

Charlotte says I can do no good by worrying you, as you will only be made more miserable. But I do not regard you as a miserable person; and I have had too many of my friends assassinated to feel easy about Jane whilst the Thugs are in command of her situation. If I worry you you can easily take it out of me without hurting my feelings in the least: I am just as pigheaded as you are.

But it would be very jolly to hear that Jane is all right. Send us a bulletin, however brief. Blank verse, *that.*

G.B.S.

Stanley **Baldwin** (1867-1947) had a distinguished career in parliament as a leading Conservative, and was prime minister at the time when Shaw wrote this letter. James Ramsay **MacDonald** (1866-1937) had been a member of the Social Democratic Federation, then of the Fabian Society. He became a Labour MP in 1906 and – although his pacifist views discredited him during the First World War – he went on to become the first Labour prime minister. In 1924 his government was defeated, though he remained leader of the Labour party. Shaw's **book on socialism** was *The Intelligent Woman's Guide to World Capitalism and Socialism*, which appeared in 1928. By **Mr Lewisham** Shaw refers to Wells's *Love and Mr. Lewisham* (1900). Prince Paul **Troubetskoy** (1866–1938) was a Russian sculptor who in the summer of 1927 was sculpting the life-size statue of Shaw that now stands at the entrance to the National Gallery of Ireland.

In June 1875 Queen Victoria, through her private secretary, wrote Lord **Lister** expressing her shock at the 'unnecessary and horrible cruelties' of vivisection and appealing to him to make a public statement of opposition to them. Lister answered that he could not comply with her request, acknowledging that he himself had often performed experiments of the sort referred to, without the use of chloroform and 'at a very great sacrifice of my own feelings.' He argued that 'the infliction of pain upon the brute creation is ... allowed by all to be justifiable when some important human interest is supposed to be served' and that 'indeed the term cruelty seems to me altogether misapplied in the discussion of this question.' (The letters are quoted in full in Sir Rickman Godlee's biography *Lord Lister*, 1917.) Wells had written 'Popular Feeling and the Advancement of Science. Anti-Vivisection,' an article that appeared in the *Sunday Express* 24 July and was later published in his volume of essays *The Way the World Is Going* (1928). The final paragraph of the article begins, 'The biological experimenter experiments because he wants to know. He is neither dismayed by pain nor does he desire that pain should enter into his experiments. He avoids it when possible. I doubt if his work is determined by practical ends.' A reply by Shaw, 'These Scoundrels,' appeared two weeks later. **Galen** (c. 130–c. 201), a Greek anatomist and physiologist and a prolific writer, was widely regarded until the sixteenth century as the primary authority on medical matters. Sir Jagadis Chandra **Bose** (1858–1937), an Indian physicist and plant physiologist, founded the Bose Research Institute in Calcutta. Alexander Ernest **Roche** (1896–1963), urologist and writer, was the son of Raphael Roche (see Shaw's letter of 30 May).

81 / To H.G. Wells

Hotel Regina, Stresa
Lago Maggiore
1st September 1927

[ALS: Illinois]

Dear H.G.

I have been anxiously waiting for a line from you to G.B.S. in answer to his letter – & it hasn't come.

I didn't want G.B.S. to send that letter, & did all I could to stop him from writing it. I thought it might vex you, just when I dont want you worried!

Please H.G. dont be angry with him. You know he is like that – he must sometimes let himself go in this aggravating way – & he means it all so more than well! He is very fond of you & Jane. I do think you are our most special friends, & G.B.S. is really worrying about you both dreadfully just now & would do anything in his power to help you. Then – by some evil fate he is impelled to do what I fear has hurt you.

Do – *do* – write a line – to *me*, even – & say you aren't angry.

We both of us revelled in 'Meanwhile'. I think it is among the best things you have done.

Our love – best – to you both; and how is Jane now?

Ever,
Charlotte

82 / To Dorothy Cheston Bennett

Regina Palace Hotel, Stresa
Lago Maggiore, Italy
4th September 1927

[ALS: Colgate]

The following letter was written two days after Charlotte's anxious note to Wells. The actress Dorothy Cheston, wife of Arnold Bennett, had written Shaw about her plan to produce Jitta's Atonement, *Shaw's translation of* Frau Gittas Sühne *(1919), by the Austrian playwright (and translator of Shaw's plays into German) Siegfried Trebitsch (1869–1956). The first half of his reply (omitted here) dealt with her questions. The Bennetts were close friends of the Wellses and visited Jane several times during her illness – the last occasion being only a fortnight before her death, which occurred on the evening of 6 October.*

My dear Mrs. Bennett

. . . . .

Can you tell me anything about Mrs. Wells? I can get nothing from H.G., and am seriously afraid that Jane will be sacrificed to his confounded scientific education, which makes him the slave of the doctors, who are no use in such cases. I believe I could cure her by making love to her if I were presentably younger. As it is, I believe Arnold could do it if you could spare him occasionally. Otherwise she will die of boredom and of the atmosphere of nurses and doctors who have made up their minds that her trouble is incurable because they cannot cure it or even get their knives into it. It is so curable that when the patient cures it for herself they say it was a pseudo, and not the real thing.

Anyhow, let me have your latest; for we have none at all. I wrote to H.G. suggesting a number of things that he might try, and damning him heartily for writing that abominable vivisection article at such a moment; but he has not responded to the stimulus, and may be sulking or despairing for all I know. My touch is not sympathetic enough for these occasions: they infuriate me; so let me know anything you can.

ever
G.B.S.

Although it has disappeared, it is evident from what follows that Wells sent a reassuring reply to Charlotte's note. She wrote him from Stresa on 16 September, 'Your charming letter brought peace to me and a great deal of thankfulness that you should be so understanding & so kind & so patient. We think of you & talk of you constantly.' She went on to speak of their returning soon to London and getting settled at Whitehall Court.

Less than a month after she wrote, she and GBS attended Jane's funeral at the Golders Green Crematorium. Wells sat beside them in the chapel, sobbing. When the coffin moved off, 'Bernard Shaw, who was standing next to me, said: "Take the boys and go behind. It's beautiful." ... That was a wise counsel and I am very grateful for it' (Wells's introduction to The Book of Catherine Wells, *1928).*

Charlotte, who found the occasion very distressing, went home and wrote a detailed account of it in a letter to T.E. Lawrence. Arnold Bennett noted it in his diary and, after remarking that only one man was in mourning, commented: 'Number of really A1 people present, very small; which shows how Wells kept out the "great" world and how the great world is not practically interested in Wells' (The Journals of Arnold Bennett, *ed. Newman Flower [1933], volume 3, p. 237).*

Virginia Woolf, who was there with the ballerina Lydia Lopokova (wife of John Maynard Keynes), wrote in her diary of 'how we saw the pale dove grey coffin of Mrs Wells slide through the gates at Golders Green. It had tassels like bell *pulls on it. Wells sat in a bottle blue overcoat by Shaw, sobbing ... Mr Page a shaggy shabby old scholar, read some typewritten sheets, by Wells, about "our friend Caroline [*sic*]." "Poor things, poor silly things" she'd say, in their days of ill repute ... Then the coffin slid away ... She had become part of the roses she loved & of the sun on the snow. Poor Jane! It was desperate to see what a dowdy shabby imperfect lot we looked ... Afterward we stood about congratulating; Lydia sobbed; Shaw said "You mustnt cry. Jane is well – Jane is splendid" & we went off – I to Fortnum & Mason's to buy shoes'* (The Diary of Virginia Woolf, Volume Three 1925–1930 *[1980], p. 163). Charlotte writes of GBS 'clowning' and even getting Wells to smile.*

83 / To H.G. Wells Ayot St Lawrence, Welwyn, Herts.
7th May 1928

[ALS: Illinois]

Soon after Jane's funeral Wells returned to France and to Odette Keun – whose company he now began to find tiresome and ultimately intolerable. He set to work at once on The Book of Catherine Wells, *comprising a prefatory account of that side of Jane that she had kept largely unknown, and a number of short poems and other pieces that she had written. He sent a copy to Charlotte Shaw when it was published early in 1928.*

Dear H.G.

I got the book you sent me with its beautiful little inscription to myself which touched me very much.

It is a wonderful little book – in some ways unique. I should like to talk to you about it. G.B.S. who read it with affectionate interest says your Preface is perfect.

Thank you for understanding how much I should care to be sent it – & thank you for itself.

We shall soon be in London. Are you thereabouts? Can we meet?

Yours ever,
C.F. Shaw

84 / To H.G. Wells

Restharrow, Sandwich, Kent
29th May 1928

[ALS: Illinois]

Shaw wrote this letter entirely in pencil – not his usual weapon. In addition to preparing for publication The Book of Catherine Wells *in the closing months of 1927, Wells completed a novel (*Mr. Blettsworthy on Rampole Island*) and* The Open Conspiracy, *in which he reworked, more formally and purposefully, many of the ideas that he had dealt with in* The World of William Clissold.

My dear H.G.

I have read *The Open Conspiracy* carefully; but the levity induced by the holiday here provokes me to begin by a series of purely mischievous gibes which you must bear as best you can't.

The middle chapters of the book are splendid; but their style is so extraordinarily like that of Beatrice Webb that were I not informed to the contrary I should suspect a collaboration with Beatrice as the senior partner. The method – the selection of a phrase 'The Open Conspiracy' (like 'the Common Rule' or 'Collective Bargaining') and the not-too-familiar manner – 'he who writes those lines' with its sequel in the third person (Mrs. Humphry Ward presents her compliments) – are intensely Victorian; and the terrific bump when you suddenly throw off the literary mask and tell the tale of the pig on Provinder Island gives away the whole show.

The open conspiracy must drop that style – the leading article style – frankly and for ever. Its association with pretentious muddle and snobbery is so powerful that the moment you drop into it you become a suspected person. Besides, it is almost impossible to be intellectually honest and lucid in it. It betrays you into its own worst tricks when you give in to it. For instance, can you read the following sentence without a yell of derisive mirth?

'The O.C. will build up an encyclopedic conception of the modern economic complex as a labyrinthine pseudo-system, progressively eliminating waste and working its way along multitudinous channels towards unity, towards clarity of purpose and method, towards abundant productivity and efficient social service'

Selah!

Alfred Mond would scorn to pontificate like that: he would 'call upon' Lord Inchcape for it. As to H.G.W., he simply mustn't. Out it comes when you reprint.

The opening chapters violate the Shavian rule, which is, never to write *about* your book, but to come straight to business and write it.

Now as to this Bible business. You announce a Bible; but what you describe is a Koran. The Bible of the O.C. will include your Koran and my Koran. It will include Shelley and Wagner, Marx and Ibsen, to say nothing of pre-XIX century prophets. Science will provide, at best, an apocrypha, because science has concentrated itself on physiology, anatomy, mechanics and chemistry, not only neglecting biology, but actually denying it bigotedly and trying to force its lifeless conceptions upon it. The tide has changed, but too recently to reach its flood and give us a biological Koran.

So look out for the word Bible in your next edition.

You repeatedly represent Capitalism as being the muddled vagueness that it is in the mouths and pamphlets of unlettered Labor orators. But you must guard yourself against being supposed to share their ignorance. Capitalism is perhaps the only system of social organization for economic purposes (or any other purpose) that has been worked out with exact definiteness to the last decimal. That is why it imposes so easily on lucid men like Balfour, Inge, and Asquith. There is no muddle about it. Capitalists are muddled about it just as Socialists are muddled about Socialism or farmers about the Copernican astronomy. But anyone who has read up and thought out the subject knows quite clearly and definitely that the issue between Capitalism and Socialism is one of distribution. My article in the Ency. Brit. is as sharp cut as any of the studies on physics. And the O.C. will never make headway (except so far as the stream of events may carry it along) against Capitalism until it knows exactly what Capitalism means. You must therefore postulate that as something to be learnt.

This will lead you to delete such a staggerer as – 'The ends of Big Business must carry Big Business into the O.C., just as surely as every other creative and broadly organizing movement is carried' (p 133).

The reader pauses and reflects on the Ruins of Empires, or Flinders Petrie's bag of scrapped civilizations, all ruined by Big Business. The sentence is in violent opposition to the *Outline of History*.

On p. 123 you renague [*sic*] by speaking of 'a childish fable of surplus value wickedly appropriated.' What do you mean by this? You will be taken to mean that Marx's 'Capital' is a childish fable, and Macaulay's cheers for the National Debt adult commonsense. You will be taken to mean that the 'economic harmonies' of Bastiat will be reached by the spontaneous evolution, not, as he thought, of Free Trade, but of Clissoldism. It is clear that the O.C. must 'eat and assimilate' Marx. But if that effort is to end in its getting sick and throwing him up again, the plea of indigestibility will not serve. If the O.C. cannot digest Marx it cannot digest anything later than 1850, and will die of stale bread on a weak stomach. To dismiss Marx contemptuously as a mystic is like dismissing Ptolemy as a flat earth man. Marx, an 1848 insurrectionist Liberal in politics, could not prescribe a practical policy for Lenin in 1917, and never had experience enough in government or in industry to do more than can be done on paper by a solitary reader, writer, and thinker; but he stood Macaulay and his world on their heads for all that; and all the King's horses and all the King's men cannot undo his work. When you mention him, take care of the perspective.

This is all the grumbling I have to do. Anyhow the morning is gone, and I must shut up. As my own proof corrections cost me £175, and my book was spread over 4 years, I do not expect the O.C. to be as impeccable as it or *The Outline.* But you might reconsider ch. XIII which has faults which are at bottom splenetic. Like Henry Arthur Jones you are liable to attacks of 'the spleen', a complaint which used to be more clearly recognized than it is today, when we no longer mention it. When I indulge it I cut it out on the proof; and I understand it so well that when you vent it on me it does no harm. But do not let it corrupt or break up the open conspiracy. It is the cause of that quarrelsomeness which makes it so hard to hold Englishmen together. Long before you ever heard of the Fabian Society I had my hands full keeping it from the splits that wrecked the Democratic Federation, the Socialist League, and all the rest of them. You were the only man who beat my powers as a Solvent, and yet you were the man whose adherence was most important. And the difficulty was pure spleen.

So revise always with an eye to the elimination of bile.

But bless you, I am and always have been, completely friendly and immensely appreciative.

ever
G.B.S.

Alfred **Mond** (1868–1930) was an industrialist, parliamentarian, and defender of capitalism. In 1927 he published *Industry and Politics*, advocating combination rather than competition in industry, and the development of partnership between employers and workers. Lord **Inchcape** (1852–1932) was a prominent financier who served on a variety of political commissions. For the thirteenth edition of the **Encyclopaedia Britannica** (1926) Shaw had written an article called 'Socialism: Principles and Outlook.' Sir William Matthew **Flinders Petrie** (1853–1942) was an eminent archaeologist and Egyptologist. Lord **Macaulay** (1800–59) in his *History of England* traced the origins and growth of the National Debt and scoffed at those who were alarmed by it: 'our National Debt, vast as it appears to us, will appear to our great-grandchildren a trifling encumbrance.' Claude Frédéric **Bastiat** (1808–50) was a laissez-faire economist and anti-socialist politician. Shaw's **book** was *The Intelligent Woman's Guide.*]

85 / To G. Bernard Shaw

614 St Ermin's
Westminster SW1
9th June 1928

[ALS: BL 50552 f 50]

My dear G.B.S.

My warmest thanks for your friendly letter which I found here on my return from France. I'm setting up a flat in Paris so as to lead a quadrilateral life, – here, Paris, Grasse & Easton (where God & my careless offspring are making me a grandfather). Your criticisms are very wise & valuable & also you are, as ever, quite wrong headed. But you are always sound-hearted & I am always, through all our disputes & slanging-matches

Yours most affectionately,
H.G.

I haven't read the Thousand & One Nights of Socialism yet, but I shall. It will please & annoy me extremely.

My salutations to Charlotte, without whom your errors might become at times excessive.

Grasse, in Provence, was where Wells lived with Odette Keun, in the house called Lou Pidou that he had built for them in the early part of 1927.

86 / To Mrs G.P. (Marjorie) Wells 4 Whitehall Court, London SW1
23rd October 1928

[ALS: Illinois]

Wells's son George Philip (Gip) married Marjorie Craig in April 1927. She had been H.G.'s secretary in the time of Jane's illness, and after Jane's death she took over much of the conducting of his professional affairs. Evidently she had written on Wells's behalf to ask for advice about French publishers. Aubier was the Paris publisher who published The Intelligent Woman's Guide *in 1929. The letter has a note in Wells's hand, 'apologies to Marjorie.'*

Dear Mrs. Wells

Aubier is an experiment. I tried Calmann Levy; but he got cold feet and backed out. Like all the old solid publishers he is still in the days of Louis Philippe; and the young nephew who realizes us can do nothing with his old uncles. My French translators collected all the renseignements they could get about Aubier, and interviewed him. The report was favorable. He seems a decent chap; and he has resources and ambitions, respectable and honorable. So I have contracted with him for the publication of my complete works at the rate of two a year, with, of course, power to withdraw if he turns out badly. He is a beginner, I take it, comparatively: at least his name was new to me. But so were all the alternatives.

I think your father-in-law may venture. He wont get any better security outside the Louis Phillipe period. And Wells + Shaw will give Aubier a prestige which will be good for both of us.

faithfully
G. Bernard Shaw

PS What's Gyp's full dress name? I don't know how to address the envelope.

87 / To G. Bernard Shaw

614 St. Ermin's
Westminster, SW1
24th October 1928

[ALS: BL 50552 f 51]

My Dear G.B.S.

Thanks for your report on Aubier. I met him in Paris & liked him &, as you say, we support each other if we go in together.

Marjorie is Mrs. G.P. Wells. G- for George after you & P. for Philip.

My salutations to Mrs. G.B.S.

H.G.

Wells was aware of Shaw's dislike of the name '**George**'.

88 / To H.G. Wells

Ayot St Lawrence, Welwyn, Herts.
21st July 1929

[TLS: Illinois]

In Experiment in Autobiography *Wells gives an account of his decision, following the success of* Outline of History, *to carry forward his project of educating 'Mr. Everyman' through two more large volumes:* The Science of Life *and* The Work, Wealth, and Happiness of Mankind. *In writing the former of these he enlisted the help of his son G.P., now a young biology teacher, and Julian Huxley, newly appointed to a chair at King's College, London. 'We worked very harmoniously throughout,' says Wells somewhat disingenuously, 'and, after a part publication, produced the book in 1930.' The book made its initial appearance in a series of inexpensive fascicles 'to be completed in about 30 Fortnightly Parts.' Reading them as they appeared, Shaw wrote marginal comments and sent them to Wells.*

My dear H.G.

This Science thing won't do as it stands: it has 1861 all over it; and what people expect from you is 1961, or later. Gyp is saving the situation by his tales of the latest things in monstrosities and in pure naturalistics; but you and your much stupider fellow fossil Julian are like *Pope* and *Pagan*, the imbecile giants in *The Pilgrim's Progress.* I havnt read such damned stuff since I was 16. Will nothing get the garden of Eden out of your blood? You spend a gallon of ink in passionate declarations that life could not possibly begin, and never can; and then you have to admit that it did begin, but – childish plea! – only once, and oh! it will never never do it again.

I have no time to educate you all over again; but I enclose a few pages which I have scrawled with insults. I have no great hope of any result; for your quicksilver brain apprehends everything and retains nothing, and Huxley's head is solid boxwood. But when I see you offering as a companion to the *Outline of History*, which was enormously needed and successful, this budget of obsolete Biblesmashing drivel I must just stick a gaff in your neck and haul you out of it.

When Haldane junior talked about Men of Science at the Fabian Society I asked him what he meant by men of science. For instance he seemed convinced that he himself was a man of science; but was I, or you. He said at once that I was not, as I had never performed any laboratory experiments, but after a long and painful hesitation he said that he thought you had worked in a laboratory at the School of Mines or somewhere; and therefore he wouldnt like to say.

That is the conception of Science which they impressed on your young sensorium when you were too young to see through it; and you have never reconsidered it. You must, before you damn yourself by issuing all that tosh in a single volume.

Come off it, H.G. Suppose another up-to-date-and-further chap comes along who doesn't like you, and lays you out publicly!

Won't have it I tell you.

Better come to lunch some day and bring the boy and the other idiot with you.

ever

G.B.S.

PS Give Huxley the Sanderson books to read. He will drop down dead.

Haldane junior was J.B.S. Haldane (1892–1964), physiologist, son of John Scott Haldane (1860–1936), a biologist admired by Shaw. John Burden **Sanderson** (1828–1905) was a physiologist who in 1895 became Regius Professor of Medicine at Oxford. He was at the centre of the current vivisection controversy. By **the Sanderson books** Shaw probably means the two-volume *Handbook for the Physiological Laboratory (1873)* of which Sanderson was the editor although not the sole author. The *Handbook* was a major topic of discussion by a royal commission looking into questions of cruelty to animals, in 1875.

A Marginal Correspondence

[Wells's pages and Shaw's 'insults' do not constitute a 'correspondence' in the strict sense, but they illuminate the exchanges that were to ensue, exemplify clearly the differences between the two men's views of life and science, and are in themselves amusing to read. What follows here represents an effort to reduce them to a series of alternating statement and comment: statements from the text of the book, and Shaw's marginalia. Some of the words ascribed to Wells may have been those of Gip or Huxley: a matter impossible to sort out.]

Wells: [*announcing the title*]: *THE BODY IS A MACHINE*

Shaw: Good God! Invented, doubtless, by a Divine Ford. Chorus of Biochemists – *IT AINT*

Now if you called it a *FACTORY*, you could at least have pleaded that there are some very pretty bits of machinery in it.

Wells: We shall begin this work as we shall end it, with man. There our interest in life begins and there it culminates.

Shaw: We have, you see, got as far as Pope, but not as Wordsworth (what is that young ribald Gyp sniggering at?)

Wells: Let us first take a Man ... and consider certain familiar but sometimes disregarded aspects of his daily life. We will say nothing here of his loves and hates, his dreams, and his political opinions. That must come later.

Shaw: – because the body is one thing and the soul another, God having stuck a soul into the body like a ramrod into a machine, with similar results.

Wells: So far as our knowledge goes, life arises always and only from preceding life. In the past it was believed that there could be a 'spontaneous generation' of living things.

Shaw: Spontaneous generation is a contradiction in terms. Adam was not generated: he was created. Cain was not created: he was generated. Readers (students) should be warned to make this distinction and keep it carefully in mind; otherwise they will confuse the terms and imagine that the silly experiments of Pasteur, Tyndall, and Charlton Bastian proved that there never could have been a First Man, whom you will have presently to introduce.

Wells: [*in a footnote to an illustration showing cell division*]: ... These experiments suggest that even the architecture of the living cell may some day be explained in terms of simple physical forces.

Shaw: – or vice versa.

Wells: [*ending his account of spontaneous generation*]: Gradually this error was dispelled ... It was only in the middle of the nineteenth century that the concluding dispute took place over Bastian's assertion that abundant bacterial life appeared in sterilised infusions of hay and other material. Pasteur and others demonstrated the insufficiency of his sterilisation –

Shaw: Why in an English work is Tyndall called '*and others*'? And why, seeing that it is common knowledge that the miracle of creation occurs only when a supreme necessity provokes a mighty orgasm, is the ludicrous spectacle of a couple of debaters solemnly trying whether the miracle would be performed for their amusement in a test tube mentioned in a serious treatise on biology as if such extremities of idiocy had anything to do with Science or could settle anything except the folly of which men are capable when they live too much in laboratories?

Wells: It is accepted now by all biologists of repute that life arises from life and in no other way – omne vivum ex vivo.

Shaw: Delete this disgracefully obsolete rubbish.

Wells: Life as we know it flows in a strictly defined stream from its remote and unknown origins, it dissolves and assimilates food, but it receives no living tributaries.

Shaw: A bandersnatch would be ashamed to pen so thoughtless a sentence.

Wells: It is at least possible that the distinctive properties of living things depend simply upon the complexity of their molecular organisation – in which case, spontaneous generation ... is at least credible.

Shaw: *NO*. Think, boy, think.

Wells: ... never in all human experience and observation has there come the slightest intimation of any life beyond our atmosphere.

Shaw: So the Martians say, probably. 'What I don't know isnt knowledge.' Extraordinarily inconsiderate stuff, all this.

[*On page 18 Wells returns to the question of the body as a machine and provides an account of a typical day in the life of Mr. Everyman – his rising and dressing, eating, working, &c.*]

Wells: So out he goes to lunch and then back again to his desk, or wherever it is that he works ... At lunch again he may seek the distraction of a book or paper, or talk with companions. There, perhaps, is something not quite like a machine –

Shaw: [*having underlined the foregoing sentence*]: Indeed! Is what precedes quite characteristic of a machine? It sounds rather like H.G.W. describing Mr. Polly [*hero of Wells's novel* The History of Mr. Polly].

[*The lower half of this page is occupied by a series of drawings of a rat at various stages of cleaning itself, the series being entitled 'Mr. Everyman at his toilet.'* *See illustration on p. 146.*]

[*Much later in* The Science of Life *comes an account of evolutionary theory and natural selection. Shaw's final marginalia surround pages 278–9.*]

Wells: We have insisted that Natural Selection is not a theory. But, on the other hand, this appeal to the fact of Natural Selection and the fact of hereditable variations as giving between them a full and sufficient explanation of the fact of Evolution, is a theory; it is the Darwinian Theory. To the majority of even highly educated people at that period, educated for the most part upon lines of a narrow religious orthodoxy, it brought home for the first time the neglected and repudiated fact of Evolution, and made it seem credible. Explanatory theory and fact to be explained appeared together in their minds, and so to this day, in common talk, Evolutionism, Darwinism, and Natural Selection are hopelessly mixed and muddled ...

Moreover, Darwin and his associates drew attention to the particular aspect of the question of Evolution that had hitherto been in the background ... He insisted that man was an animal and that if the facts of Evolution were true they applied to man. If other living things had not been specially created but evolved, so, too, man must have evolved. To do this was to challenge and

146

kept busy before he can attend to anything else. It is a very persistent clamour. It is even more persistent than his alarm-clock. He might stop his alarm-clock and go to bed again without immediate or talk with companions. There, perhaps, is something not quite like a machine. But whatever else he does, he eats. Before he goes to bed he will have to answer that imperious demand from within again.

Indeed! Is that quite characteristic of a machine? It sounds rather like H.G.W. describing Mr Polly.

Fig. 18. Julian Huxley theorising.

Shaw transforms the illustration into a comic cartoon simply by changing the title to 'Julian Huxley theorising' and attaching two words to one of the drawings.

bring the whole world of contemporary theology into the discussion. What had been a field of interesting speculation for naturalists became an arena of intense interest to the ordinary man.

Darwin's publication was followed by furious controversies ... But the controversies did much to darken counsel in these matters ... All sorts of secondary considerations have played their part in these disputes. There is, for example, a real dislike of the fact of Natural Selection on the part of such a fine and sympathetic nature as Mr. G.B. Shaw's. It seems to him unchivalrous and vile for science to recognize that the weakest do go to the wall ... He wishes things were not so, and he does it with great charm, confidence, and conviction. It pleases Mr. Shaw to tell the world at regular intervals that Natural Selection has been 'exploded', and it does not hamper the operation of Natural Selection in the very least that he should do this ... Wherever there are favourable or unfavourable hereditable variations Natural Selection must be at work.

Shaw: What a lie!

Wells: ... Darwinism has been criticized and tested in every conceivable way. It cannot be said that it has been destroyed, but it has undergone restatement in certain respects.

Shaw: What is Darwinism? Darwin was not a Darwinist. Weismann *was*. These loose epithets have no place in science.

Which of the three is responsible for this sentimental bunk? It certainly isn't Gyp. It is not one of Julian's reflexes; and he, poor chap, has nothing left but reflexes which start only when you say 'acquired habits' or 'somatic cells'. Thus by elimination I arrive at the infamous H.G., the traitor. He knows very well that I was the first great biologist to make an end for ever of the silly controversy about acquired habits by reminding the squabblers that to the evolutionist all habits are acquired habits, and that those who do not see this are still in the Garden of Eden. To solve the riddle of the apparent division of habits into inherited and uninherited I applied the scientific method of experiment and observation. I acquired a habit (balancing on a bicycle) and observed the process. I inferred the acquirement of habit by infinitesimal increments, their establishment as fully inherited habits, and their end as prenatal recapitulations. I used Weismann's foolish experiments with mice to show that an undesired habit imposed from without mechanistically could never produce a habit, and that imagination, desire, and will could produce it by creating the necessary mechanism. I pointed out that acquirement by practice was a delusion, the process being one of relapse after relapse until the miracle of creation occurred, and the creature who at noon simply could not, at one second after noon *could*, and could again even if 20 years of disuse had elapsed. As to Natural Selection, I lose no opportunity of reminding the ignorant world that it has been utterly exploded as an explanation of vital phenomena, and that a Neo-Darwinian is simply a fool out of his depth; but it is I who have explained in immortal pages how the facts of Natural Selection, and the completeness with which it accounted for many changes formerly attributed to divine providence, gave it an enormous vogue as a stick to beat the bible with. A very considerable number of the people for whom these fifteenpenny numbers [*i.e. the fortnightly sections of* The Science of Life] are being written know quite well that Back to Methuselah is a biologic classic. When they read here that its author is a sentimental sailor out of a melodrama who believes that a universe that would lift its hand to a worm save in the way of kindness is unworthy the name of Nature they will lose all respect for H.G.'s science and Huxley's XIX century superstitions, and read on, if at all, for the sake of Gyp's latest in the way of naturalists' stories.

All this dreadful dead wood must be cut out when you republish in book form, and replaced by modern Creative Evolutionary theory starting from the microzymes of Béchamp and including the latest theory of symbiosis by Reinheimer, Dr. Young (a female), Bach, Abrams' electronics, and all the rest of the neo-Vitalist stuff. A good deal of it may be rubbish; but at all events it is undetected and unexploded rubbish, and more amusing than the Victorian dust heap you are raking up. And it is at least full of hope and encouragement, whereas your stuff leads to nothing but cynical pessimism, despair and Schrecklichkeit. In a word, it is pre–Samuel Butler, which dates it to damnation.

G.B.S.

The poet Alexander **Pope** (1688–1744) affirmed in his *Essay on Man* (1732–4), 'The proper study of mankind is man.' William **Wordsworth** (1770–1850) was not less concerned with humanity, but his 'study' was rather of those moments when 'Our souls have sight of that immortal sea / Which brought us hither' ('Ode, Intimations of Immorality,' 1807). Louis **Pasteur** (1822–95) and John **Tyndall** (1820–93) were scientists who through experiments in their respective fields of chemistry and physics concluded that the theory of spontaneous generation was untenable. Shaw is mistaken in including with them Henry Charlton **Bastian** (1837–1915), a neurologist and bacteriologist who championed spontaneous generation and opposed Pasteur, as Wells goes on to indicate. Pierre Jacques Antoine **Béchamp** (1816–1908) studied the action of microzymes in relation to disease, Hermann **Reinheimer** (b. 1872) the relation between diet and cancer, Edward **Bach** (1886–1936) the use of herbs in treating disease, and Albert **Abrams** (1863–1924) the use of early electronic devices in diagnosis and treatment. The identity of **Dr. Young (a female)** has not been established.

89 / To G. Bernard Shaw

Easton Glebe
Dunmow
23rd July 1929

[ALS: BL 50552 f 52]

My dear G.B.S.

You're the same G.B.S. as ever & I quite believe your statement that you've read nothing about biology since you were sixteen. I'll try & save you from Gip if I can but he has a certain pugnacity & seems to have picked up a disrespect for his seniors from your works.

Get into print & I'll punch your head.

Yours as ever,
H.G.

Love to Charlotte

90 / To H.G. Wells

Ayot St Lawrence,
Welwyn, Herts.
28th July 1929

[ALS: Illinois]

My dear H.G.

Yes; but, quite seriously, you must not, after the *Outline of History*, which was essentially your work, appear in another Outline as the mere amanuensis of the neo-Darwinians and mechanists. A very little alteration will save the situation as far as the complete book is concerned, because when it comes down to tin tacks it is with the mechanism of biology that it must concern itself. But the conception of the universe into which it fits must be that of Leonardo & Goethe, of Butler, Shaw & Wells: in short, the comprehensive men, and not that of the microscope men and the vivisectors and the Natural Selectionists. They are a perfectly distinct species, to which you do not belong. They will use you as what they call (with abysmal contempt) a Popularizer and, as such, a best seller; but as to letting you call your soul your own, or admitting that such a thing exists, they would die first; for oddly enough they are all fanatics, though their creed, if they were capable of anything so comprehensive as a creed, recognizes no movement of the mind except in the direction of least physical resistance, which is the negation of fanaticism.

All you need do is to change *The Body Is A Machine* into *The Body As a Machine* (one letter only), to cut out the obsolete stuff about Spontaneous Generation and Acquired Habits, and to make a preamble explaining that for the moment Life, though it is the fundamental subject of biology, must be taken for granted whilst you set forth its observed phenomena, and creation must be studied as variation, mutation (accidental or contrived by breeders) without reference to the problem of its origin and essence.

This will leave your hands free when you come finally to the great question of God, which you cannot finally avoid. You will have to show that though he was crucified under Darwin and Huxley and buried in Belfast by Tyndall he rose again and sat at the right hand of Wells, who announced his arrival as a new discovery. You will have to straighten this out by showing that though Jehovah & Co. are dead, and were never in fact alive, they must be regarded not as corpses to be buried and done with but as discarded hypotheses which have left a blank that must be filled before the universe becomes thinkable. Natural Selection does not fill it: Creative Evolution does – well enough to go on with, at any rate.

Ever
G.B.S.

91 / To G. Bernard Shaw

Easton Glebe
Dunmow
30th July 1929

[ALS: BL 50552 f 53]

My *dear* G.B.S.!

How can you associate names like mine & Leonardo's with freakish creatures like Butler, Goethe (that metameric skull of his!) & yourself. You talk about biology like a bright girl at a dinner party. Read the *Science of Life* humbly & attentively. Pray that God of yours to chasten & enlighten you – & he will vanish as he answers your prayers.

Yours ever,
H.G.

92 / To H.G. Wells

4 Whitehall Court, London SW1
31st July 1929

[ALS: Illinois]

This letter-card is without the usual salutation. 'Nobodaddy' is one of Shaw's many borrowings from William Blake, 'Nobody's daddy' being the world's false God.

Bless you, the bright girls at the dinner parties have all read Back to Methuselah. Hence their brightness. I wish Huxley would brighten himself up with the same belladonna.

My substitute for Nobodaddy is an obvious urge towards Omnipotence and Omniscience. This is the motive of evolution; but it involves the instinct of self-preservation (Safety First) which produces a great deal of adaptation to environment even on the part of the individuals who take the greatest risks under the pressure of the urge. An *exclusive* study of this adaptation is the mark of the naturalist (as we call him): example, Darwin.

Have you anything against that? The Science of Life is so far only a Study of Adaptation. You must come to your title finally. Of course we neither of us know two-pennorth about it, but if we cannot hold our tongues we *must* have a hypothesis.

G.B.S.

93 / To H.G. Wells

4 Whitehall Court, London SW1
2nd August 1929

[ALS: Illinois]

Wells's response to the previous letter seems to have vanished; the nature of its contents may be deduced from the one by Shaw that follows.

My dear H.G.

The reason why you must find a substitute for Nobodaddy is that a work on the Science of Life which shirked the question of the difference between a live body and a dead one would be Hamlet with Hamlet left out.

Also a book with H.G.W. on the cover must be up to date and a bit over. We are now in the thick of a sort of religious war between the Neo-Darwinists and the Neo-Vitalists – the Materialists and the Mentalists. Butler has come to his own so completely that he is almost forgotten among the men who are piling up the technically scientific evidence for his case. Even a Materialist is no longer one who denies that life is anything more than a series of reflexes and chemical reactions: he is an agnostic who is convinced that when the explanation (çi-devant Nobodaddy) is discovered it will be simply a missing material or physical ingredient, and that its activity is entirely purposeless. You could not, even if you were a Materialist, ignore this situation and go back to that from which love extricated Mr. Lewisham. You must write as a contemporary of Joad, not of Jowett. You must bring Huxley up to date, which will, I admit, be a stiff job.

Goethe cannot be called metameric all by himself; but Goethe, G.B.S. & H.G.W. are metameric: they are different men but made of the same peculiar elements. Goethe's side is your side: Weismann's side is Huxley's. The obvious urge is blatantly obvious in the lot: in fact in respect of it all five are metameric. But it has not got Weismann and Huxley far enough.

Facts mean nothing by themselves. All the people at present crowding the Strand are facts. Nobody can possibly know the facts. Naturalists *collect* a few. Men of genius *select* a fewer few, and lo! a drama or a hypothesis. Genius is a sense of values and significances (the same thing). Without this sense facts are useless mentally. With it a Goethe can do more with ten facts than an encyclopedia compiler with ten thousand. The number of facts that you and I don't know is so stupendous that our ignorance is practically infinite and consequently equal. The facts that we are conscious of exist in our minds simply as opinions of them. The phrase 'rather express an opinion than learn a fact' has consequently no meaning.

Study your own mind. You will not doubt the urge then.

ever
G.B.S.

C.E.M. **Joad** (1891–1953) was a philosopher, lecturer, and writer. Among his books are *Shaw* (1949), a study of Shaw's philosophy, and *Shaw and Society* (1953), an anthology of pieces by and about Shaw on which Joad was working at the time of his death. Benjamin **Jowett** (1817–93) was famous as classical scholar, educator, and liberal 'Broad Church' Anglican clergyman.

94 / To H.G. Wells

4 Whitehall Court, London SW1
21st February 1930

[TLS: Illinois]

Wells planned to follow The Science of Life *with a comparable volume dealing with socio-economic development and principles. Eventually it was published as* The Work, Wealth and Happiness of Mankind *(1931). He was markedly less fortunate in his choice of collaborators for this book, and the result was a period of stressful litigation, the story of which is told by his biographers, and by himself in two pamphlets:* The Problem of the Troublesome Collaborator *and* Settlement of the Trouble Between Mr. Wells and Mr. Thring. *The collaborator in question was Hugh P. Vowles, whom Wells found not to be doing suitable work and therefore not to be retained to complete his contracted work, nor to be paid for the unfinished portion; none the less Wells was prepared to find a face-saving formula for dealing with Vowles (and eventually paid him the full amount due under the contract). Vowles, however, sought the support of The Society of Authors through its secretary, G. Herbert Thring (1859–1941), in bringing a lawsuit for breach of contract against Wells. Thring wrote Wells a letter that made him as angry with Thring as he was with Vowles. He wrote Thring an intemperate, almost certainly libellous letter. Since Thring was just being retired from the secretaryship (after thirty-seven years) much against his will, the Society's Committee of Management was doubly involved. As a former eminent member of that committee, prominent in the society for many years, and Wells's friend, Shaw found himself brought near the centre of the storm.*

My dear H.G.

This will end in our having to get up a subscription for Thring. You know, don't you – or do you? – that the unhappy man is down and out? We have superannuated him (he dates from the days of Walter Besant) without giving him a sufficient pension or having ever paid him enough to enable him to save. He has been domestically unlucky too; but I need not put all that on paper.

Two years ago or so we took on a gentleman named Roberts to assist him and be trained to succeed him; and this succession has now occurred, Thring being retained as 'consulting secretary' at £200 a year: the best the Society can do for him officially by way of pension.

A Mr Williamson of the Authors Club here has been sounding me about a subscription; but Lord Gorell has rather sat on this for the moment; and it is in abeyance until T. actually retires.

I enclose a letter which I have received from T. himself, which is rather pathetic, as he does not seem to see that 37 years is a reason *for* superannuation, not against it, and that his difficulty in finding employment is simply that he is too old. Of course he has no notion of why, with his start in life, he has not earned £20,000 a year as a family solicitor. The reason is given in your letter. But as we have had him cheap, and he has been devoted to the Society, incorruptible, and hard working, we cannot leave him in the soup merely because his method of taking up cases includes fixing his teeth in the calves of both parties.

Ever
G.B.S.

PS Tear up T's letter.

[*Enclosure*]

11 Gower Street
14th February 1930

Dear Mr. Shaw

No doubt you saw in the January *Author* a note to the effect that I had been superannuated and that I leave the Society's office on March 1st. I am still retained as 'Consulting Secretary' on a salary.

I am very upset as I had no reason to think while I was physically & mentally sound that I should be asked at three months notice to leave an office that I have held for 37 years.

In the matter of salary the Comtee have treated me very fairly, but they have a veto on whatever work I take up.

As it [will be] impossible for me with my present financial responsibilities to make both ends meet I am now on the look out for something to do that will bring me in an assured income. I hope therefore that you will excuse me for writing you to enquire whether you would allow me to refer to you. Your name is a valuable one to conjure with, and I may be sadly in need of such backing.

However, I have not left the office yet.

I have had two refusals from very likely sources and my difficulty lies in the fact that the market for my special knowledge is very restricted and lies to a great extent with the enemy, i.e. Publishers & Managers.

I have endeavoured during my term here to safeguard the Authors.

Believe me
Sincerely
Herbert Thring

Sir Walter **Besant** (1836–1901), novelist, was founder of the Society of Authors (1884) and had worked especially for the improvement of copyright laws. Denys Kilham **Roberts** (1903–76) succeeded Thring and was secretary until 1963. Lord **Gorell** (1884–1963) was now Chairman of the Society. ***The Author*** was (and is) the journal of the Society of Authors.

95 / To H.G. Wells

4 Whitehall Court (130) London SW1
12th March 1930

[ALS: Illinois]

The original is written in pencil. Attached to it is a draft resolution prepared by Shaw for submission to the Council of the Society of Authors, the governing body of the society, to which the Committee of Management was answerable.

Unfortunately Wells's letters to Shaw dealing with his quarrel with Vowles and Thring seem not to have survived. Almost certainly Wells and Shaw conferred directly or by telephone as well as in writing. Shaw's letters that follow give sufficient indication of the course of events. It appears that Wells had suggested to Shaw that there be a vote of censure, although the precise object and nature of it is uncertain.

My dear H.G.

To rout the foe we must build a bridge for his retreat. This for two reasons. 1. If we attempt a direct vote of censure our supporters on the C. of M. will be forced to stand by their ship and vote against us. 2. If we carried it the Committee would be obliged to resign; and as we are not ready with a salvage crew we should have wrecked the Society.

If we begin recriminations we are lost. Let them begin them, and leave the dignified attitude to us. They cannot oppose our resolutions without taking sides with Vowles, nor accept them without dropping him.

Gorell writes that Galsworthy has made them give Thring £500 a year instead of £200; so he no longer needs your commiseration.

By this post I am sending my draft resolutions to Birrell. I shall not be sorry if the Committee proposes another chairman, as he could do more fighting at the bar than on the bench.

We shall be lunching at home tomorrow (Thursday) at 1:30. If you care to join us, ring up early so that Charlotte may order accordingly. It is possible that Ervine and his Nora may turn up; but we shan't know that until morning.

ever
G.B.S.

PS It looks as if Vowles is overdoing it heavily. All the more reason for leaving it to him to make the running.

Draft Resolution for S. of A. Council
– Vowles v Wells –

That the meeting of the Council of the S. of A., having in view the information supplied to the Committee of Management, the Society's solicitors, and Mr. H.G. Wells, is of the opinion that:

A. As no principle concerning the general interests of our membership, or the profession of literature, is at stake in the matter, the funds of the Society cannot properly be expended in taking it into court; nor should the Society's solicitors, as such, be instructed to act on behalf of either party as against the other.

B. Legal advice on the matter, including counsel's opinion, having been procured by the Society, should be placed impartially at the disposal of both parties; and Mr. Vowles having been advised as to his claim, Mr. Wells should be advised equally as to his answer.

C. The Committee of Management should do its utmost to persuade and help the parties to settle their difference without litigation; but if its efforts fail the Society should withdraw from the case in such terms as to leave it clear that neither party is entitled to go into court as supported by it.

and

D. That the attention of the Society's solicitors should be called to the anomalous situations which must arise if, in the event of litigation occurring between members of the Society, its legal advisers accept instructions from either party before the matter has passed entirely out of the Society's hands.

To be moved by:
Seconded [by]:

John **Galsworthy** (1867–1933) was a novelist, playwright, and essayist – one of the best-known men of letters of his time, winner of the Nobel Prize for Literature in 1932. Augustine **Birrell** (1850–1933), barrister, educator, politician, and author, was a prominent member of the Society of Authors. John St John Greer **Ervine** (1883–1971), Irish dramatist and critic, 'knew G.B.S. intimately for more than forty years,' as he says in the foreword to the biography that he wrote: *Bernard Shaw: His Life Work and Friends* (1956).

96 / To H.G. Wells

4 Whitehall Court SW1
14th March 1930

[ALS: Illinois]

My Dear H.G.

Your costs are implied in resolution B. The merits of the case (which involve the dossier) will come up on C, and cannot be kept out of A.

Gorell says that 'a very great principle *is* at stake on A; and C presents great difficulties.' But he gives no lead as to what the principle is.

I wish I could have met him; but I have had four rehearsals in the three days, and could not manage it.

You must be content with victory without blood and humiliation of the vanquished. The case against the C. of M. is, I think, a fightable one on the point of its handling of this particular incident; but if you say that the C. of M. is useless, dangerous, & ought to be abolished, and that Thring was and is malicious and corrupt, all the members who have served on the Committee, including myself, must throw you over, as no such anathema can be sustained. As for your suggestion of employing an unsuccessful author as secretary (no successful one would touch it) it is crude insanity. He would be worse than ten Thrings.

Birrell approves the resolutions as covering all that we can hope to carry. Of course there may be amendments and a compromise – possibly a dropping of D; but unless we can carry them substantially we shall be defeated.

A good deal depends on the attendance of councillors who are not on the C. of M.

Be a good Christian, and not a splenetic Briton. Leave vengeance to smaller men.

tired out – late at night
G.B.S.

97 / To H.G. Wells Ayot St Lawrence, Welwyn, Herts.
16th March 1930

[ALS: Illinois]

What 'side issues' Wells had proposed raising and how he proposed them are unknown.

My dear H.G.

NO. It will be hard enough to keep them from running off on side issues without raising them ourselves. Besides, they could reply to 1 by asking why you waited until now to object to the Murray partnership; to

2 by pointing out that putting the names of solicitors & bankers on company note paper is common form and that you yourself are similarly advertised, and 3 – see my last letter.

We have the Webbs down here this week end; and I am on duty.

In haste, consequently
G.B.S.

98 / To H.G. Wells

4 Whitehall Court, London SW1
17th March 1930

[TLS (holograph PS): Illinois]

This letter was addressed to Wells at 13 Hanover Terrace, Regent's Park, which was to be his principal and eventually sole London address for the remainder of his life.

My dear H.G.

Miss Patch, struggling with your plausible but really most illegible handwriting over the phone, has conveyed to me enough of your letter to enable me to summarize it as 'I will be drowned and nobody shall save me'. If you persist in repeating your Fabian tactic of forcing the Council into the position of voting either for the disruption of the Society and the throwing over of the old gang or flat against you, you will also repeat your amazing feat of not getting a single vote in a meeting in which the balance of popularity was heavily on your side. You may make what proposals you please later on for the reconstruction of the Society or the immolation of its executive personnel; but your immediate business is with the Society-cum-Vowles versus Wells. That must be stopped; and it will not be stopped but inflamed if you push it aside and take a vote on whether 11 Gower Street is to fall like the Bastille or not. Do give yourself a chance.

If you ask to be allowed to make a statement instead of speaking to a resolution, you will at once be met by a counter demand for a statement from Vowles, who wont be present. It will not seem fair to hear one party informally without hearing the other as well. If I succeed in getting in my resolutions as the motion before the meeting, I can say things on your behalf that you cannot decently say on your own; and then you can speak to the resolutions like anyone else, or ask to be allowed to make a personal explanation if you like. By appearing as a defender of the executive on the general disparagement I can call it to account on the particular charge much more effectively.

This is all I can say until I have your letter in my hand tomorrow morning.

In haste – close on post time
G.B.S.

PS If Vowles & Thring & Modley should be in attendance so much the better: we cannot complain of Vowles *ex parte* & then object to face him. Besides, I have hopes that he will prove even a worse client than you, and hang himself.

Blanche **Patch** was Shaw's secretary from June 1920 until his death. **11 Gower Street** was the address of the Society of Authors.

99 / To H.G. Wells

4 Whitehall Court, London SW1
19th March 1930

[APCS: Illinois]

This card was sent to Wells's Westminster address. The succeeding card suggests that he was dividing his time between London and Easton Glebe. There had been a meeting of the Society of Authors at which the Vowles-Thring-Wells affair had been dealt with, presumably through the resolution drafted by Shaw. The council named a committee comprising (Sir J.M.) Barrie, Gorell, and Birrell to select an arbitrator for the dispute. They proposed Sir Donald MacLean (1864–1932), a solicitor and prominent Liberal parliamentarian, and on 1 April the Society's solicitor reported that MacLean had consented to act.

On the whole, considering the appalling muddle into which authors always get, I think we did as well as was possible. There was no defence; and our resolution was carried *nem con.* Hawkins did the job very well; and if Barrie only had the faintest notion of the order of public meeting he would be quite a good chairman. Gorell was in a worse hole than he knew (all the Committee were); but he is all right: I should have chosen him myself for the triumvirate. You were really very generous.

G.B.S.

100 / To H.G. Wells

4 Whitehall Court
28th March 1930

[TLS: Illinois]

The 'yellow book' was presumably The Problem of the Troublesome Collaborator, *which Wells began circulating at about this time. (The MacKenzies say it 'was sent to all members of the Society.'* The Time Traveller, *p. 362). Shaw must have had advance information of the appointment of Sir Donald McLean.*

My dear H.G.

I have just caught a glimpse of a yellow book. Take care not to circulate it until Sir Donald makes his award. Until then the matter is *sub judice* and cannot without scandal be commented on.

Do not give any cause for reproach to Thring, who is much more pugnacious than you, and wants very much to take an action for defamation. Be careful to let him do all the defamation henceforth. An action is a frightful nuisance, and means a heavy loss to anyone whose time is of considerable value, even if he wins.

ever
G.B.S.

101 / To H.G. Wells

Ayot St Lawrence, Welwyn, Herts.
1st April 1930

[APCS: Illinois]

Your card dated the 30th must have been late for the post at Easton, as it did not reach me until this morning.

And you did not turn up yesterday.

Kilham Roberts tells me that Sir Donald Maclean has been appointed arbitrator.

I am duplicating this to St. Ermin's

G.B.S.

Kilham Roberts was now secretary of the Society of Authors.

102 / To G. Bernard Shaw

614 St Ermin's
8th April 1930

[TLS and enclosure / BL 50552 ff 55–6]

Evidently Shaw continued to press Wells to settle sensibly the Thring problem. The 'campaign' and 'writ' to which Wells here refers concern the actions of Vowles outlined in the headnote to Shaw's letter of 21 February. Lucienne Southgate was Wells's secretary before Marjorie Craig assumed that role, and probably for some time afterward.

Dear Sir

Mr. H.G. Wells asks me to send you the enclosed copy of a letter he has today sent to Mr. Thring.

Yours faithfully
Lucienne Southgate
Secretary to Mr. H.G. Wells

[*Enclosure*]
Dear Mr. Thring

Mr Shaw tells me that you have been to him and that you have complained of the appeal I was obliged to make to my fellow authors against the campaign of annoyance which culminated in the writ the Society has now withdrawn. It has now been made clear that neither you nor the Committee of Management are to be held responsible for that ill-advised campaign which has wasted so much of my time and disarranged my work for the past six months. Apparently it just happened without anyone intending it. In so far as I have held you responsible for that ill-advised campaign I now exonerate you altogether and I am quite prepared to believe that you acted under instructions and regret the irritation, trouble and expense that campaign inflicted upon me. And further Shaw says you find in some passages of my appeal imputations upon your integrity – your 'commercial integrity' is the phrase he used. There you are mistaken. I have never doubted the entire honesty of your actions and motives and if there is any particular phrase or turn of expression you find objectionable I shall be most happy to withdraw it and replace it by some other form of words that will satisfy you. My action has been defensive throughout and I have not and I never have had the slightest desire to injure you. Until I found I could get no consideration in any other way I refrained from discussing this affair with any but the members of the Committee of Management and my appeal after my return to London was restricted to less than two hundred members and it was made as a private and confidential communication. It would be quite easy to follow that up with a brief note explaining your entire freedom from responsibility and admitting my error in fixing any part of the blame on you.

I suppose it is impossible for you to come and have a private talk with me? Perhaps I am not quite the man you suppose me to be and I too may have imagined things. We are neither of us very young men and it seems to me rather stupid to fill any part of the time still before us in bitterness and mutual injuries.

Very sincerely yours
H.G. Wells

PS You need not treat this letter as a private one if now or at any time it seems expedient to show it to anyone. I withdraw unreservedly anything I may have said or done that might shake or seem to shake your credit in the world of affairs.

103 / To G. Bernard Shaw Easton Glebe
[*n.d.*]

[TLS: BL 50552 ff 57–8]

*The MacKenzies date this letter 23 April. Thring refused to accept as sufficient the apology proffered by Wells in the preceding letter. When Shaw attempted to persuade him to do so, he replied, 'I am going to have a proper apology from Wells. His letter is written as if I had been attacking him and he was kindly granting pardon ... Wells is trying to make me the scapegoat, whereas I did nothing except on the direct instructions of the committee, as you from your service on the Com. will appreciate' (*The Time Traveller, *p. 363). Shaw may have prompted Wells to try again; at all events he did so. On his letter as sent to Thring Wells wrote, 'I wish you would take this letter to Shaw or any other impartial friend.'*

Dear Shaw

Enclosed explains itself. Damn the man!

Yours ever
H.G.W.

[*Enclosure*]
Dear Mr. Thring

I do not feel that I can with justice to you leave our correspondence in the case of Vowles v. Wells where it stands at the present. As you know, I feel that I was inconsiderately treated in that matter; and I have expressed my feelings without much regard for yours. You have allowed yourself the same latitude, very naturally. The letters in which we have described each other's conduct would not help us if we employed them as testimonials.

As I cannot think that your activities will end with your retirement from the secretaryship of the Society of Authors, and it is therefore possible that things I have written might prejudice you in quarters where the unceremonious terms on which we stand with one another in the Society are not understood, I had better now put explicitly on record my unreserved withdrawal of anything in my letters which could possibly shake your credit in your pursuit of fresh responsibilities and trusts.

The Society of Authors owed its existence – and may I say its persistence? – to you and the late Sir Walter Besant; and you have sacrificed to it a legal career that had many tempting possibilities. I know no one who seriously questions your entire integrity: certainly I do not, though I reserve the right to relieve my feeling whenever in your championship of those less fortunate members of Society whom you regard as victims of oppression you treat me as if I were a notorious crook. I am as far from holding that opinion of you as I am sure you are of seriously holding it of me; and if you can suggest any better form than this letter of making our reciprocal esteem clear, by all means let me know.

You need not feel obliged to treat this as private should its publication at any time be expedient for you.

faithfully

104 / To H.G. Wells The Palace Hotel Buxton, 25th May 1930

[APCS: Illinois]

Shaw's role in the Vowles-Thring-Wells affair had now ended – evidently with a note from Wells to which the following is a response. The affair itself eventually ended without litigation, but not without a settlement costing Wells a considerable sum. The most coherent and fairest brief account is to be found in MacKenzie, The Time Traveller. *The minutes of the Society of Authors show that the society was involved at least until October.*

Same here, most affectionately.

We came here at Easter for a brief holiday; but after a few days Charlotte went up to 103° with tonsilitis, conjunctivitis, rash, and desquamation (you can diagnose in one word), and very nearly died on me. She is touchingly apologetic for having allowed herself to be dragged back from the gates which she had approached so becomingly at her age, but rather pleased, too, at the obvious sincerity of the drag. However, she has been out in the car every day for a week past; and we return home (to Ayot) on Wednesday. I did not tell her what was the matter with her until it was virtually over; and she was tremendously bucked at having fought off so serious an enemy. Do not tell anyone: I have told only a few people who *had* to be told.

G.B.S.

Charlotte's illness was scarlatina, or scarlet fever.

105 / To H.G. Wells Ayot St Lawrence, Welwyn, Herts. 8th June 1930

[APCS: Illinois]

Evidently Wells had read a news item about an airship accident and had connected the victim with Henry Lowenfeld (1859–1931) who in December 1897 had proposed to Shaw that Arms and the Man *be made a comic opera* (CL, *Vol. 1, p. 825). Wells's note of enquiry to Shaw has not been found. Shaw's card was sent to Lou Pidou, where Wells had rejoined Odette Keun.*

I dont know. My man was a sort of bucket shop Napoleon, always offering me £150 for the continental rights of *Arms & The Man*, and rather liking to be laughed at on a Bonapartist footing. This was after 1894. I lost sight of him before he built the Apollo theatre. I took him to be as old as myself, possibly older; but he might have been any age from 17 to 50 as far as appearance went. He had a strong foreign accent, and had *not* the Manners & Tone of Good Society in London.

As the notices of the man who fell out of the airship said nothing about the Apollo theatre, and suggested a man in the prime of life, it did not occur to me to identify him with my Napoleon, who would have been close on 70 at least, and whose connexion with the theatre would have been a talking point for the Press. Without positive evidence to the contrary you had better assume that they were not the same.

G.B.S.

The **Apollo** Theatre opened in February 1901 – with a musical.

106 / To H.G. Wells 4 Whitehall Court, London SW1
25th July 1930

[APCS: Illinois]

Wells had just sold Easton Glebe. Also, he was giving up his flat in St Ermin's Street (to which however this card was addressed) and had taken one in Chiltern Court, on Baker Street.

It is Lady Cynthia Mosley (Zimmy) who is collecting for Madame Krassin. I sent her £10. She has a definite program to finance for the lady and her daughters.

G.B.S.

Keep me posted as to your new addresses. I see Easton is sold; and then there is Baker St.

Lady Cynthia **Mosley** (d. 1933) was the wife of Sir Oswald Mosley (1896–1980), Labour politician who in 1932 founded the British Union of Fascists. Madame **Krassin** was the widow of Leonid Crassin (1870–1926) who was Soviet trade representative in Great Britain (1920–3). He died in London 24 November 1926, leaving his wife and family in financial straits.

107 / To H.G. Wells 4 Whitehall Court, London SW1
30th October 1930

[APCS: Illinois]

The card has a note in Wells's hand: 'Get him on the telephone for me.' The occasion in question may have been connected with the visit to London of Moura Budberg, who was planning to settle there. *See p. 182.*

Friday is off as far as Charlotte is concerned. She had a fall in Hanover St. yesterday, and cracked her shoulder and her pelvis. Fortunately the bones are not displaced; the hip joint is uninjured; and she has nothing to do but lie up and mend herself. But she will not be out and about for some weeks.

I will turn up unless I hear to the contrary. Do I dress? or shall we pretend to be Bohemians? It is all the same to me.

G.B.S.

108 / To H.G. Wells Ayot St Lawrence, Welwyn, Herts.
11th February 1931

[APCS: Illinois]

An appeal had been made for financial help to be given to Rosamund, daughter of the Fabian Hubert Bland. She had married Clifford Sharp (1883–1935), editor of The New Statesman *until its amalgamation with* The Nation. *He had become a hopeless alcoholic.*

Same here, precisely, twenty pounds and all. So she now has forty to go on with. I sent on her letter to Desmond MacCarthy, who will stir up the New Statesman people about it. Hubert bequeathed John's professional education to me; but I doubt if his practice is yet remunerative enough to enable him to take on Rosamund. Oh these widows and orphans!

G.B.S.

Desmond **MacCarthy** (1877–1952), author and editor, is best known for his dramatic criticisms. Shaw had financed the medical education of **John** Bland.

109 / To H.G. Wells R.M.S. Warwick Castle one day out of Capetown
19th March 1932

[ALS: Cornell]

The Shaws sailed from Southampton, 21 December 1931, for a tour of South Africa, a tour that was interrupted by a car accident in which Charlotte was injured so that she had to be hospitalized; and they remained for a month in Knysna, Cape Province, while she recuperated. Wells's 'new encyclopedia,' The Work, Wealth, and Happiness of Mankind, *had just been published.*

My dear H.G.

The Cape Fabian Society has just presented me with a copy of your new Encyclopedia in gratitude for a great platform display of mine by which they netted £160: unheard-of wealth for them.

Having had it only for a few hours I have only sampled it to the extent of looking up half a dozen of the index references and browsing round about them. I therefore dont know whether you have dealt with a phenomenon of which I have been very conscious for some years past.

Compare Dickens and Thackeray with Wells and Shaw, and Fielding with Chesterton. All of them are troubled by social abuses and regard comedy, *alias* the chastening of morals by ridicule, as part of their business. But the moderns have tried to do what Dickens, Thack., and Fielding never dreamt of. They have deliberately tried to produce something like the Bible, the *Koran*, the works of Aristotle, or the Institutes of Calvin: that is, to lay down the law in religion, economics, history and philosophy for the following generations. This is the intention of my 'metabiological' Creative Evolution, and my Communistic politics, with my essays on education, medicine & criminology. It is the intention of your series of Outlines. Chesterton's Romanism and his Distributive League are evidently the ruins of a scheme which was hopelessly muddled by Belloc, but which would probably not have matured anyhow because intellectual activity has always been practised by Chesterton as a sport, with the odd result that he is now dreadfully in earnest about beliefs that are intellectually impossible. So we must, alas! cut him out of the new phenomenon.

Now as between us it seems to me that though I am fully conscious of what you are doing, you are hardly at all conscious that I am doing it too. I watch your high tidemarks carefully, and begin where you leave off. When the obsolete purblind stuff which you call your education blocks your path I carefully remove it. But it never occurs to you that you ought to take my proceedings seriously as part of a Shavian natural philosophy on exactly the same footing as the Wellsian natural philosophy. I am careful not to present the Shavian philosophy as alternative to and competing with the Wellsian philosophy. We are the world's family solicitors; and we should be partners. We should pool our results and adopt each other's work on this point or that. When you convict me of a superstition I abandon it. When I convict you of one, you gravely explain to the public that there is a screw loose in me.

H.G.: there isnt. When I venture to say that a thing is so, it is so. But you have to get what I say exactly, and not substitute the nearest thing in your own stock, and reject that. For instance you have in your dustbin a superstition called equal pay. You have another even more villainous superstition, or rather habit of thought, which is, that the ability to acquire capital is identical with the ability to administer it competently. And you accuse me, in a work which will have an enormous circulation, of advocating equal pay for all work, and an equal share in the administration and control of capital for everybody. You put this down and print it without ever pausing to reflect that as this is the vulgarest Jack Cade folly, Shaw, not being Jack Cade, couldn't really have said it. You cheerfully and confidently embrace the solution that I *am* Jack Cade.

Let me set this right for you. You see that the point on which the Capitalist paper Utopia has broken down grotesquely and hopelessly is Distribution.

Now, first, clear your mind of that Bromley inheritance: the notion that distribution is simply an arrangement of pay for work. The point at which distribution is supremely important is distribution among babies. Get a baby to work and be paid for it if you can.

I will not pretend that you really believe that Midas is an ideal Treasury official or Chancellor of the Exchequer. Such a belief would be an impossible extension of Jack Cadeism to a theory that all mayors who made their money in the nail and saucepan business are, before God, equally capable of the Higher Clissoldism. There is no natural association whatever between the possession of an income and the ability to spend or invest it wisely: rather is it probable that the selfish singleness of aim that makes Fascination Fledgby rich will impoverish the community if it leaves the control of his riches in his hands instead of surtaxing him and transferring the spoils to a Clissoldian Treasury.

My thesis is that a really fundamental consideration of the problem of Distribution will entirely dissociate it from payments for work or rewards of virtue, and will lead to equality of distribution by the reduction to absurdity or impossibility of every alternative. I have, in the I.W.'s G.S. worked the thesis out carefully and exhaustively and, so far, unanswerably. And you reject my demonstration with the commonplaces of a retired colonel in Cheltenham or Knysna C.P.S.A. and add, as a Wellsian coruscation, that I have the ideas of Jack Cade because my mother was addicted to singing. *Really,* H.G. – !!!

It is not quite as bad as the Science of Life, in which Huxley went back on his own brainiest essays in psychology, and you atavised to neo-Darwinism by denying that there is any difference between a dead body and a live one, and that only a drivelling humanitarian like Shaw could allege that there not only is a difference, but that it is the whole problem of biology.

I won't inflict another page on you; but we must pull together; for we are both in the same boat. What would you think of me if every successive work of mine contained an attack on your intellectual credit? And this not out of malice, but sheer inattention and carelessness, with complete goodwill all the time. I wish that idiot Pavlov (not unrepentant, they told me, in Russia) would devise some nice laboratory experiment to establish a Be Careful reflex in response to the word Shaw.

The bugle sounds for lunch.

ever
G.B.S.

PS I smashed Charlotte up so frightfully by shooting miraculously off the road when I was driving, and charging with the loud pedal hard down over hedge and ditch and bunker and hillside for a hectic seventy five yards that she was in bed for a month, and then got up apparently better than ever.

Gilbert Keith **Chesterton** (1874–1936), journalist, essayist, novelist, prolific man of letters, shared a warm friendship with Shaw throughout his writing career. In his short introduction to *George Bernard Shaw* (1910), he remarked, 'I am the only person who understands him, and I do not agree with him.' Chesterton – familiarly 'G.K.' – was tempted towards socialism as a solution to social ills, but feared the consequences of excessive governmental interference in individual lives. He concluded that there must be developed an economy of small holdings, and in 1926 led in the formation of The Distributist League for the furthering of that cause. By then he had been converted to Roman Catholicism (1922). Joseph Hilaire Pierre **Belloc** (1870–1953) was a close friend of Chesterton and a lifelong Roman Catholic. He was, like Chesterton, an editor and man of letters. Jack **Cade** (d. 1450) was leader of a fifteenth-century rebellion based in Kent. In Dickens's *Our Mutual Friend*, **Fascination Fledgeby** is the unscrupulous upstart who conceals, behind the persona of a man of superficial social grace, the fact that he is a grasping money-lender and bill-broker doing business under the name of Pubsey & Co. **I.W.'s G.S.** refers to The Intelligent Woman's Guide to [*World Capitalism and*] Socialism. **C.P.S.A.** is Cape Province South Africa. Ivan Petrovich **Pavlov** (1849–1936), Russian physiologist and experimental psychologist, discovered the conditioned reflex through his experiments on animals – hence supporting a mechanistic theory of human behaviour.

110 / To H.G. Wells

4 Whitehall Court, London SW1
3rd December 1932

[ANS: Illinois]

In South Africa while Charlotte was recuperating Shaw wrote The Adventures of the Black Girl in Her Search for God. *An advance copy was sent to Wells.*

Dear H.G.

This won't be published until the 5th.

Only half a crown. Books have been ridiculously dear of late. This is my notion of a new departure. 25,000 sold to the booksellers already. Dont bother to acknowledge: I never do.

GBS

111 / To G. Bernard Shaw

47 Chiltern Court, Clarence Gate NW1
12th December 1932

[ALS: Illinois]

Dear G.B.S.

I found your book irritating & delightful. Did I write to thank you for it? Anyhow I thank you again although I am writing of another matter.

Is Signora Matteotti being persecuted or is she not? If she is, you (& I) ought to be able to call the dogs off her. Sylvia Pankhurst is trying to publish a protest that will only exacerbate things further. Cant something thorough be done through Grandi?

Yours ever
H.G.

Signora **Matteotti** was the widow of the Italian Socialist Giacomo Matteotti (1885–1924), whose murder by Fascists precipitated the crisis that carried Mussolini to dictatorial power. Sylvia **Pankhurst** (1882–1960), radical and feminist, was critical of Mussolini's regime. Count Dino **Grandi** was Italian ambassador to Great Britain.

112 / To G. Bernard Shaw London NW1
14th December 1932

[APCS: BL 50552 f 60]

The book in question is The Adventures of the Black Girl in Her Search for God, *in which Pavloff figures as the 'old myop.' It was illustrated by John Farleigh.*

Warmest thanks for the cellophane covered book with its pretty illustrations. Either I must say thank you & no more or else I must write you a large volume. How *wicked* you are about Pavloff! My love to Mrs. G.B.S.

Affectionately,
H.G.

113 / To G. Bernard Shaw 47 Chiltern Court, Clarence Gate NW1
20th July 1934

[ALS: BL 50552 f 61]

Shaw's plays The Six of Calais *and* Androcles and the Lion *ran on a double bill at the open-air theatre in Regent's Park in July 1934.*

Dear G.B.S.

I took the Davidson family to see the *Six of Calais* last night. And old friend Androcles. How young we keep! They say we repeat ourselves but the truth is we just keep up to form & are as good as ever. Bless you.

H.G.

My love to Charlotte. I'm flying to Moscow tomorrow – on the chance of seeing Stalin.

The identity of the **Davidson family** has not been established.

114 / To G. Bernard Shaw 47 Chiltern Court, Clarence Gate NW1
30th October 1934

[ALS: BL 50552 f 62]

Wells went to Moscow, had a three-hour interview with Stalin, toured a variety of Soviet institutions, talked with officials – and was disappointed and depressed by what he saw and heard. He had agreed to give Kingsley Martin, editor of The New Statesman and Nation, *the right to publish his interview with Stalin. Martin invited Shaw (among others) to comment and Wells to comment in turn on Shaw. The following is Wells's initial, personal response.*

Dear G.B.S.

Kingsley Martin has just sent me a pull of your stuff for the *New Statesman.* You have a sister soul in Odette Keun, who has been writing about me in *Time & Tide.* You two ought to get together before it is too late. Bless you.

H.G.

Wells's long affair with Odette **Keun** ended in his outright refusal to marry her. The result was a slashing attack on him in her book *I Discover the English* (1934) and a series of articles that appeared in the London magazine *Time and Tide.*

115 / To H.G. Wells 4 Whitehall Court (130) London SW1
[*n.d.*]

[TLS: Illinois]

Wells's reply being dated November 6, this letter must have been written a day or two earlier. Even while travelling in the Soviet Union Wells was writing the concluding chapters of his two-volume Experiment in Autobiography, *to be published later in the year. He began the 'Envoy' with a reference to writing 'in a friendly and restful house beside a little lake in Esthonia.' In the final chapter of the book –* The Idea of a Planned World *– he reviewed and reflected on his expe-*

rience with the Fabian Society three decades earlier, referring to his having 'antagonized Shaw and Beatrice Webb, for example, by my ill-aimed aggressiveness.' On 8 October Shaw had reviewed the serialized first volume of Experiment, *together with Dean Inge's* Vale, *as published in the* Daily Mail. *He had not then read Wells's account of Fabian matters, which came later.*

Dearest H.G.

What have I done to God that he should plague me with you in this fashion? I seem to spend my life rescuing the victims of your outrageous onslaughts and seeming to remonstrate with you and make fun of you whilst I have to boost you subtly all the time.

When I wrote the Inge-Wells review I had read nothing but the scraps in the Daily Herald; so of course it was not a review at all but a flagrant blurb to stimulate sales. I refused to review the second volume because I had fired my shot and did not want to spoil it by making the stage mistake of trying to repeat a successful effect.

Besides, the second volume of an autobiography is not good game for a friendly reviewer. A child knows what happens to it; and people tell it the truth about itself, or at least about its effect on them, quite brutally. It knows every corner of its little back yard of a world. And by the time it is old enough to write an autobiography its people are dead. Consequently the worst autobiography is interesting and moving in the preadult stages; and the best loses terribly in intensity and reality afterwards.

This is not merely or even chiefly because the truth affects too many living persons (some of them vindictively litigious) to be printable. It is mainly because the adult does not know the world into which he enters, and nobody ever tells him the truth or shews his hand to him dispassionately. Once, when a breakdown of my car held me up in Nancy for fifteen days I read Rousseau's Confessions in the original from end to end. There were heaven knows how many volumes. I might have saved myself the trouble for all I can remember of his routine after he became a notorious philosopher and Madame de Warens a super-fatted wreck in the distance both of time and space. Goethe as a child and youth is interesting; but he bores himself so frightfully later on that he tails off into long accounts of people he came across who are now forgotten.

You keep up the interest for me because your sketches in the Goethe manner are of people whom I have known, and incidents in which I have played a part. But they confirm what I have just said. When you burst into the Fabian Society and played Old Harry there, you did not know where you were or where we were. WE (the old gang) were hard at work bringing a magnificent revolutionary conception down to tin tacks and gas and water municipalism, to black and white Bills, to Webbian 'devices'. We were exploiting our piffling congregation, which we well knew could never exceed (as it never did) two thousand harmless middle class people who did not go to church and practised birth control, to 'permeate' the Opposition-local-Associations and foist Newcastle programs and the like on the parties and newspapers. And you, trying to drag us back – forward, as you saw it – to the magnificent dream which had had its day long before you dreamed it, were disgusted with such trifling and with Pease's shabby little office. Nothing but a senseless discord could come of such a misunderstanding.

You are still wrong about our origins. The little group of Rosminian philosophers formed by Davidson was led out of dreams of Perfectionist colonies in Brazil by the hard common sense of Bland, whose section became the F.S. and was spied out in the London chaos by me. I had already spied out in the same chaos an unassuming figure named Sidney Webb. I have a genius for casting plays; and I picked him as my leading man and forced my acquaintance on him. I had discovered Olivier through Henry George and the Land Reform Union. I made them join the Fabian, where they immediately took the practical lead out of the hands of Bland and his Blackheath group, whom they would have driven out of the Society but for my determination to keep Bland in it, as he had a valuable point of view which we were apt to forget, and was *au fond* on the right side in spite of his being very trying as a censorious libertine. He had a long struggle with poverty, living at times on the half guinea a week that the Weekly Despatch paid her [*Bland's wife*] for poems, some of which were inspired by ME. But at last I was offered a weekly feuilleton job at £5 a week (I think); and I managed to persuade the editor that Bland was the heavenborn man he wanted. It turned out that I was right; for Bland never looked back from that moment, and held his own as 'Hubert', champion feuilletonist and breadwinner, until he died.

You think that when you came along you antagonized me; but you are wildly wrong. As leaders neither you nor Webb looked the part as well as, for example, Hyndman (why didn't you describe Hyndman?); but I did my best to keep you in the Society. My nearest to a real quarrel with the Webbs was when I forced them to recognize that Ann Veronica and you had the upper hand of them because they could not expose you without discrediting the London School of Economics by a sexual scandal. Bland was savagely furious with you because you tried to shake the resistance of Rosamund by citing the example of her parents. A debate between you and Bland would have been a butchery: one with Webb would have been very painful. I was the obvious alternative; but they mistrusted me deeply (and quite rightly) because they knew that I was a Wellsite as far as it was possible for anyone to be a Wellsite in the face of your wild behavior. There was no fear of not defeating you: you were sure to defeat yourself hopelessly every time you opened your mouth or put pen to paper. But you could be let off too easily; and I forced myself on the Executive Committee as its champion only by explicit pledges that I would be unsparing in my exaction of a complete and uncompromising surrender. What I did not say was that I should also exact from you a pledge that you would not leave the Society if the vote went against you.

So you see the story cannot be told; but there has never been any antagonism to you on my part, because, mere natural liking apart, I am free from your besetting fault of ridiculously underrating your contemporaries. From Marx and Webb to Stalin, your gibes are amazing in their triviality: in fact you are very like Marx in this respect. However, I would not have you other than you are. All the idols are the better for having an occasional brick shied at them.

O.K. has missed her chance: she should have written a funny description of H.G. in bed. She has an amazing command of English and is clever, but not clever enough to avoid exhibiting herself as a child crying for the moon and a deeply resentful abandonnée. I am defeating the well meant but mistaken efforts of Lady R. to bring us together.

I must stop this babble: the village post goes at six thirty; but of course I have not said half enough about the book.

GBS

Louise de **Warens** (1699–1762) was a well-to-do Frenchwoman who was the first patroness of Jean-Jacques Rousseau (1712–78), when he was a lad of sixteen. They were lovers for a time. Shaw's mention of **Newcastle programs** derives from a series of proposed social reforms drawn up by the Fabian Society for adoption by the Liberal Party as its election platform in 1892. Collectively they became known as the 'Newcastle Program.' (See Pease's *History* for an amusing account provided by Shaw.)

The **Rosminians** were the Brethren of Charity, a group founded in Italy by Antonio Rosmini-Serbati (1797–1855) that deeply influenced Thomas **Davidson** (1840–1900) in founding the Fellowship of the New Life – some members of which became the originators of the Fabian Society. Henry **George** (1839–97), American economist and social reformer, developed the 'single tax' theory, maintaining that since land and natural resources essentially 'belong' to society as a whole, virtually all taxation should be directed at economic rent. He expounded the theory in *Progress and Poverty* (1879), and preached it widely (Shaw heard him lecture in London in 1882). The **Land Reform Union** was a British association formed for propagating his ideas. The poems that were sold as a partial solution to Bland's **long struggle with poverty** were those of his wife Edith Nesbit (1858–1924). She became better known for the children's stories that she wrote under the pen name 'E. Nesbit.' In the early Fabian days she was for a time in love with GBS. **Lady** Rhondda (1883–1958) was the editor of *Time and Tide* and a prominent feminist.

116 / To G. Bernard Shaw

47 Chiltern Court, Clarence Gate NW1
6th November 1934

[APC: BL 50552 f 63]

It's no good G.B.S., these private disclaimers of public detraction. You get together with the *Time & Tide* lot & collaborate. That's your corner.

H.G.

117 / To H.G. Wells

4 Whitehall Court, London SW1
27th November 1934

[ALS: Illinois]

The publication in The New Statesman and Nation *of Wells's interview with Stalin and Shaw's comment led to a lively debate in that journal that drew in, among others, the economist Maynard Keynes, who came in on Wells's side. Kingsley Martin then proposed publishing the correspondence in the form of a pamphlet. After some bickering and slanging by Shaw and Wells, the pamphlet, entitled* Stalin-Wells Talk, *was published in December, with cartoons by David Low. Martin gives an account of the affair in his* Editor *(1968).*

Dear H.G.

G.B.S., who is expiating his sins in bed at the moment, asks me to write to you about the publishing of this Statesman Controversy – the Wells-Stalin thing.

Mr. Kingsley Martin says you & Maynard Keynes want it published. Is he telling you that G.B.S. wants it published? He is very anxious to get it through & may be playing you off one against another.

I don't want it published. I have deprecated & deplored the whole thing. G.B.S. tells me to say *he* doesn't want it published, but will leave the decision to you & Maynard Keynes.

G.B.S. is ill now – of overwork & a bad cold – nothing really serious.

Our love. I wish we met oftener!

Yours ever
C.F. Shaw

118 / To Charlotte F. Shaw [*No address*]
28th November 1934

[TLS: Illinois]

Dear Charlotte,

It was charming of you to write but it puts me in a quandary. G.B.S.'s wicked little onslaught on me (which really hurt me very much) has been quoted all over the U.S.A., Russia and the communist press. I think the proposed pamphlet with everything in it squares the account and I think G.B.S. ought to take his medicine.

All the same I hate doing anything contrariwise to you.

Yours ever,
H.G.

I'm overworked too and rotten. But I think I can cut off to Sicily for a fortnight or three weeks over Christmas.

119 / To H.G. Wells

4 Whitehall Court, London SW1
28th November 1934

[ALS: Illinois]

Dear H.G.

It is very nice of you to say you dont want to do anything contrariwise to me – but dont let it put you 'in a quandary'. Whatever you want about the matter I want you to do. And G.B.S. has left it to you & M.K., hasn't he. He wrote the same to Mr. Kingsley Martin.

G.B.S. has been really ill – but is better. I hope you will get away soon & have a happy time in Sicily.

Always yours
C.F. Shaw

120 / To H.G. Wells

4 Whitehall Court, London SW1
[*n.d., but clearly same day as preceding*]

[ALS: Illinois]

About an hour after my own little note was sent, G.B.S.'s nurse brought me this & said he wanted me to send it to you.

Goodnight
Bless you.
C.F.S.

[*The enclosure referred to in Charlotte's note comprised three pages of brief notes in Shaw's handwriting, unusually large, signed with his initials and dated 28/11/34.*]

Clissold − Marx = Louis Napoleon in 1834.

L.N. − Austerlitz = Hitler.

Clissoldism − Marxism = Fascism.

Fascism's trump card is its promise to save us from the horrors of Communism as seen in starving enslaved Russia.

Stalin's Russia is blowing that gaff.

When the gaff is blown and the Fascist Corporations find that they can't control the national capital without owning, the situation will clear; and then we shall see whose god is the Lord.

The Stalin-Wells Report presented itself as H.G. in one of his transports of idiocy, teaching his grandmother to milk ducks.

G.B.S. had to come to the rescue of British appreciation of Stalin. On the scale of the situation H.G.'s feelings dont matter, nor do those of G.B.S., which are altogether partial to H.G. Only, H.G. wont use his brains except when he is writing impersonally.

G.B.S. as the thing stands, comes out on top because he has used the opportunity to say several important things. G.B.S. wants to come out on top of the situation; but he does not want to come out on top of H.G. But as H.G. refuses to take the situation seriously, G.B.S. would like to write H.G's part for him. H.G. would then come off with glory.

But when all possible has been done the fact will remain that the Russian interview came to nothing, and is really not worth publishing.

All H.G.'s mistakes have come from underrating his man. It is bad enough to underrate Marx and Stalin; but he has no excuse at all for underrating ME.

I am the Big Noise.

GBS
In bed tired
28/11/34

Louis Napoleon (1808–73), nephew of the Emperor Napoleon I (Napoleon Bonaparte, 1769–1821), began in 1836 the career of self-aggrandizement that culminated in his establishing the Third Empire of France, with himself at its head (1852–70). Challenging the rising strength of Germany, he was defeated by the Prussians, deposed, and exiled to England. He had begun that career with an attempted coup – as **Hitler** began with an attempted coup. The Battle of **Austerlitz** (2 December 1805) had carried Napoleon I to the height of his power. The meaning of Shaw's algebraic formulation is not entirely clear except in its conclusion: that only the adoption of Marxism – which in 1934 for GBS meant Stalinism – would save from **Fascism** the world that Wells's hero William **Clissold** envisaged.

121 / To H.G. Wells

Marine Hotel, Durban
18th May 1935

[ANS: Illinois]

Through much of the winter of 1934/5 the Shaws, Wells, and the Webbs were all plagued with health problems, more or less related to the fact that they were all growing old. The evident gap in the correspondence reflects this fact, although the business of the New Statesman *pamphlet doubtless cooled the relationship for a time.*

Eventually the Shaws sailed for South Africa on 21 March and were away for almost three months. This was the period of celebrations of King George V's jubilee, and on 15 May The Natal Witness *published an interview with Shaw in the course of which the subject of royal honours was discussed – including the failure of various writers to receive them. 'H.G. Wells' fame is international,' said Shaw at one point, 'and would bear any official dignity worthily; but Wells is a professed Republican and not even a very civil one, to say nothing of his contempt for the game of convention. He is a great writer and has proved himself a good son, a good brother, a good father, a good friend, full of all sorts of virtues, but he is not a loyal subject to the crown.'*

Shaw sent a copy of the published interview to Wells, with one of his compliments cards.

If this tribute to your overlooked domestic virtues does not reconcile us publicly, nothing will.

We shall be back, D.V., in the middle of June.

G.B.S.

122 / To G. Bernard Shaw Tredegar Park, Newport, Monmouthshire
1st July 1936

[ALS: BL 50552 f 64]

The volume containing The Simpleton of the Unexpected Isles, The Six of Calais, *and* The Millionairess, *together with their prefaces, in the Standard Edition of Shaw's works, was published in March 1936.*

My dear Shaw,

I've read the three new Plays and Prefaces with the same mixture of irritation & admiration that has been my normal response to you for years. How you go on! God grant me in spite of my drinking & meat-eating & whoring the same vitality.

You go on, less & less propitiatory to the public & more & more yourself. Bless you.

H.G.

123 / To H.G. Wells

4 Whitehall Court, London SW1
13th May 1938

[ALS: Illinois]

The identity of the hotel referred to here is unknown, the letter being on the Whitehall Court stationery. Both the Shaws were unwell, and Charlotte may have advocated her standard treatment: change and a rest. In any case, three weeks after the date of this note GBS collapsed in London and was found to be suffering from pernicious anaemia, an illness that lasted for months. Charlotte's note indicates that their friendship with Wells had by no means ended.

Dear H.G.

How very, *very* nice of you to remember my little plaint & to take the trouble to write & tell me about this hotel. I am quite touched by the thoughtful kindness of it – & G.B.S. is quite pleased! – we are both so loth to get a move on & so inclined just to stay put.

We both enjoyed our lunch with you & are hoping to get you to come here – also the Baroness – one day soon.

Yours affectionately
C.F. Shaw

Wells had first met **Baroness** Moura Budberg in 1914 when, as Marie von Benckendorff, she had served as a guide for him and Gip in Russia. Subsequently she had been secretary to Gorki. Her long-lasting love affair with Wells was the cause of at least one of his quarrels with Rebecca West and contributed to the break-up of his affair with Odette Keun. When she moved to London he hoped to marry her, but she declined.

124 / To H.G. Wells

4 Whitehall Court, London SW1
9th October 1938

[TLS: Texas]

Shaw had received a copy of Wells's Apropos of Dolores, *'a savage recapitulation of his life with Odette Keun,' as Norman and Jeanne MacKenzie describe it in* The Time Traveller. *The prefatory note began with the customary disclaimer: 'Every character and every event in this novel is fictitious, and any coincidence with the name or conduct or circumstance of any living person is unintentional ... The story is told in the first person but the voice is the voice of an invented personality – however lifelike and self-conscious it may seem. Never will the author proceed against his publisher for libel.'*

My dear H.G.

I have read Dolores and consider the first sentence of the prefatory note the most thundering lie ever penned by a great writer.

I have collided with her on more than one of her avatars; and I KNOW.

Still, what are we to do when we use them as models? They are bearable on paper.

as ever
G. Bernard Shaw

125 / To G. Bernard Shaw 13 Hanover Terrace, Regent's Park NW1
[*n.d.*]

[Photographic reproduction of holograph, published in *H.G. Wells A Pictorial Biography* by Frank Wells, 1977. Present location unknown.]

It is impossible to date this letter precisely. Wells moved to Hanover Terrace in the autumn of 1931. The letter may refer to Shaw's illness of 1938. It was a long illness, Shaw 'scoffing at doctors' and insisting that he was curing himself, before he finally agreed to be seen by a pathologist. On the other hand, Shaw was in London throughout that period, and Wells's reference to 'the house' suggests Ayot rather than Whitehall Court.

You are masochist – there is no other word for it. Still you must have your way. For goodness sake keep quiet for a bit & dont go stomping all over the house on your crutches. Everything is going well here & I get better & better & better.

Bless you.
H.G.

126 / To H.G. Wells 4 Whitehall Court (130) London SW1
7th December 1939

[TLS: Illinois]

The last four sentences of this letter were handwritten by Shaw. Wells's new book The New World Order *was appearing in serial form in* The Fortnightly.

My dear H.G.

There are one or two things that I want to impress on you. As a rule I have nothing to say because our minds jump together so much that we have both said it already. All the same there are a few out-lying things that I know and you dont, or the other way about.

I have been reading the Fortnightly Review, and find you saying there that Capitalism is a chaos without a theory. This is a most dangerous hole in your case. It is by its theoretical strength on paper that Capitalism has convinced men as able and benevolent as De Quincey, Austin, and Macaulay that it is inevitable, irresistible, and on the whole, beneficial. From Turgot and the Physiocrats to Malthus and Ricardo it was built up on paper until it collapsed into Socialism in the hands of John Stuart Mill and Sidney Webb and was violently smashed into abhorrence by Karl Marx. But it is still orthodox at the universities. To Asquith and Inge, for example, it was, most mischievously, the alpha and omega of political science. There are a good many Socialists who would succumb to it if they understood it. If 'human nature' were as unchangeable as Capitalist theory assumes it to be (instead of being the most easily changeable thing in the world) it would be, with a few alleviations, as good a system as men are capable of. Never say again that Capitalism is an intellectual chaos.

Next, you must get clear about the class war. When Shelley wrote 'ye are many: they are few' he made a dangerous mistake. Every increase of the Marxian Mehrwerth (rent, interests and profits) by Capitalism creates a parasitic proletariat as well as enriching the proprietariat. The domestic retainers, the employees of the sport and luxury trades, and the fashionable professional men, are all dependent on the specifically capitalist incomes and will vote for them and fight for them. The unemployed young men on the dole (a new class) are purchasable by the highest bidders, who will, like Satan, find mischief still for idle hands to do; and your calling attention to them is a real contribution. But though the class war is not the simple confrontation of the few rich with the many poor that Shelley sang about, it is there all the same all the time. The Spanish war was a class war; and anybody who calculates the chances of the present war without taking the class war factor into account will be badly out in the result.

We owe our present Government to British snobbery, which has been terrifically reinforced by votes for women.

It is no use remonstrating with you about Marx. You are subject to attacks of what the Elizabethans called 'the spleen' in which there is no holding you. It spoiled your first instalment in The Fortnightly (the second is first rate). You can say, in their due proportion, plenty of unpleasant things about Marx. He was quarrelsomely jealous about his reputation and authority; he pretended to be a mathematician and wasnt, to be an economist and knew no more of scientific economics than a horse; and his dialectic is for English purposes, and even for Germans now that Hegel is forgotten, obstructive junk. But who cares? Newton made outrageous mistakes; but Einstein speaks of him with profound respect. You are like myself, a pamphleteer: well, read the Communist manifesto and ask who but Marx has ever produced such a pamphlet. The first volume of Capital (all I ever read of it) changed the mind of Europe: a thing we two have been trying to do all our lives, whereas Marx has Russia and National Socialist Germany to show for it. He found Liberal Europe optimist, vainglorious, and Gladstonian: he left it convicted of every crime and abjectly apologetic. Before Marx your Time Machine would have been impossible and unintelligible. The difference between you and Dickens is the difference between pre-Marx and post-Marx. The difference between my first four novels, which I trust you have never read, and my subsequent work, is Marx. His blunders are nothing: his big generalizations have never been shaken. When you disparage him as a shallow third rate Jew – a monstrous ingratitude – you shake all confidence in your judgement and temper when it is most important that confidence in you should be rocklike. And remember that I who am blowing you up for this am the man who as editor and part planner of Fabian Essays, made a point of getting them through as a British book in which there was not a single reference to Marx. You can quite well ignore Marx in your propaganda; but if you must drag him in, do it good-naturedly and with at least an air of doing him justice.

And that's all, I think, for the present. Except this. I think that in telling our stick-in-the-muds that they will wreck civilization with their wars, you flatter them. Englishmen who belong to the oligarchy like to think of themselves as like the Templar in Ivanhoe: 'bold bad men'. Better debunk them by measuring them on the astronomical scale and shewing their empires as ripples made on the ocean of history by a flight of minnows from a pike.

I am sending you the two latest plays. We – Charlotte and I – are very old and muddled now, and are always late or wrong or both with things; otherwise you should have had the books sooner.

Dont bother to answer all this: you can let fly when next we meet. I think we should meet oftener if it were not that we are afraid of boring people. We are ten years older than you; and when that sort of thing gets into the eighties it becomes serious. I took care to resign my chairmanship at the B.B.C. and all platform work at 80, before I became intolerable. My naked weight has gone down to 10 stone, and remains fixed at that figure immoveably. But I have got over my bout of pernicious anaemia, which anyhow did not affect my head. Charlotte has had two horrible months of excruciating lumbago; but now she is out of pain and mending satisfactorily. I was greatly pleased by your tribute to Chesterton, especially coming as it did on top of Inge's dig at him. Inge loathes Chesterton – says he crucified Christ head downward. The truth is that G.K.C. was a marvellous boy: he never grew up and was the real Peter Pan *de nos jours.*

G. Bernard Shaw

Thomas **De Quincey** began the study of economics 'with wonder and curiosity' in 1818, and in the following years wrote several essays on the subject, the best known being the book-length *The Logic of Political Economy*, 1944. John **Austin** (1790–1859) was an English jurist whose lectures were published in 1832 as *The Province of Jurisprudence Defined.* In *The Intelligent Woman's Guide* Shaw named him and **Macaulay** as two of 'the more clear-headed converts of the theory of Capitalism.' Anne Robert Jacques **Turgot** (1727–81) was a French economist and administrator who adopted the physiocrats' theory of free trade and generally laissez-faire economics. The line 'Ye are many – they are few' is the final line of Shelley's *The Mask of Anarchy* (written 1819, published 1832). The **Templar** in Scott's *Ivanhoe* is Sir Brian de Bois Guilbert.

Shaw's **two latest plays** were *Geneva* and *In Good King Charles's Golden Days.* Charlotte's **excruciating lumbago** may have been mending, but it was the beginning of the painful illness from which she died, less than three years later. In part 2 of the serialization of his book (*Fortnightly*, December 1939), Wells referred to G.K. Chesterton as 'one of the loveliest characters I have ever known.'

127

[ALS: Delaware]

In Wells's copy of In Good King Charles's Golden Days *Shaw wrote the following note. James Jeans (1877–1946) and Sir Arthur Eddington (1882–1944) were well-known physicists.*

Dear H.G.

The figures on page 24 are wrong: I added the Leap Years instead of deducting them.

Jeans did the logarythms for me.

Eddington gasped at the perihelion of Mercury; but as it [is] a sure stage laugh (like Weston super Mare) I could not sacrifice it.

GBS
7th Dec. 1939.

128 / To H.G. Wells

4 Whitehall Court (130) London SW1
23rd February 1940

[APCS: Illinois]

I should get rid of the hostages by excommunicating the whole practice as a barbarous form of mental torture backed by massacre of the innocents.

I should drop the word punishment altogether and argue that organized society must put a price on the privilege of living in it and of living at large in it. Public nuisances should be unvindictively and painlessly liquidated. People who are all right under tutelage (the soldier & habitual criminal type) should be handled accordingly. When the restraint is humane, as it should be, there is no reason for placing a limit on its duration.

Freedom of complaint is essential, but must not include power to dictate the remedy, which would in that case be probably cruel, wicked, and futile. Adult suffrage must be regarded as reduced to absurdity by the enfranchisement of Begonia Brown.

G.B.S.

The final sentence is written along the side of the card. **Begonia Brown** is the Dame of the British Empire in *Geneva.*

129 / To H.G. Wells 4 Whitehall Court (130) London SW1
15th April 1941

[TLS: Illinois]

The postscript is in Shaw's hand. Wells's novel Babes in the Darkling Wood *was published in 1940. Shaw had begun working on* Everybody's Political What's What *in 1940.*

My dear H.G.

I have just finished The Babes, which was impossible until everyone else had finished it first. You are not dead yet (I am unfortunately): there are luminosities and subtleties that are newly born as well as the old Wellsian faculty.

I was specially tickled by your onslaught on brass tacks, because I am trying to write a book with the express object of bringing your Declaration of Rights down to these useful articles. Churchill was absolutely right the other day in his broadcast when he said that if he declared his war aims the united nation behind him would split into fifty irreconcilable factions.

My book is a little list of the things a person ought to understand (no matter what his or her conclusions may be) before being trusted with a vote or put on the panel as eligible for public work of this or that grade.

You are less splenetic than you were. The British spleen that broke out occasionally and upset your valuations is mellowing a bit. This is very noticeable in your description of Stalin. I rate him higher than you do. He was equal to two very big opportunities of going wrong. The first was Socialism in a single country versus Trotsky's world revolution. The second was collective farming versus the moujik. His choice and the success with which he carried it out rank him as the greatest living statesman. Collective farming is the only chance for our agriculture; but we stick helplessly to the moujik and the Kulak. Stalin would not have a dog's chance in a British constituency. He made a favorable impression on me when I met him in 1931. The attentive silence in which he listened to us until we had said everything we had to say and the good humor with which he laughed at us when his turn came (for he did laugh at us) could not have been improved on in point of pleasant manners and grasping of the situation. Lothian's proposal that he should invite Lloyd George to Moscow with a view to his leading the progressive Liberals to the Left of the Labor Party as a Party of scientific Socialism simply amused him, though he cordially invited Ll.G. to come and see for himself. When Lady Astor told him that the Soviet knew nothing about handling children of five years he was outraged. 'In England' he said 'you beat children'. But Nancy went for him like a steamroller and ordered him to send a sensible woman to London to learn the business. The moment he saw that she knew what she was talking about he made a note of her address, and presently dumped not one but half a dozen sensible women on her doorstep. This trifle impressed me; for I thought his noting the address was mere politeness. I, who had heard nothing of Lothian's proposal until he paid it out to Uncle Joe, had nothing to say; but when Astor, who is by temperament a born Communist, gave him assurances that Russia had many friends in England, I asked him whether he had ever heard of Cromwell, and quoted the refrain of the old song

> 'So put your trust in God, my boys;
>   And keep your powder dry',

he knew all about Cromwell, and intimated that at any rate he would keep his powder dry. He was very friendly; and as I was treated all through as if I were Karl Marx risen from the grave, I did not see the rough side of anybody or anything. But there was no attempt to humbug me. They were too full of their achievements to dream of any need for that, especially as they were convinced that Capitalist England was in comparison a Chamber of Horrors.

I was prepared for Finland, as Ireland is the British Finland, and I have said ever since the Treaty that in the event of a world war England would have to re-occupy Ireland militarily, or at least take over the ports, for the duration. Churchill and Roosevelt may still have to do it if the battle of the Atlantic continues to go against us. The only novelty about Finland was the unprecedented fact that Russia took only what she needed instead of taking back the whole place as any other Power would have done.

Talking of Ireland, were you aware that in 1937, when the ports were given back, the ownership of Eire was formally and explicitly transferred to The Most Holy Trinity? I discovered that a month ago. Had you ever heard of it?

I think you and Benedetto Croce are not civil enough to Karl Marx. I have myself pointed out his purely academic mistakes; but as he was unquestionably an epoch making philosopher who changed the mind of the intellectually conscious world, attempts to belittle him fail and belittle their authors.

To balance it I dismiss Pavlof as a supremely damned fool. But he seems to have been as civil to you as Uncle Joe was to me, for which I give him one good mark. His personal resemblance to me I take as an unpardonable liberty. Your difficulty about him is fundamentally due to the fact that you were educated by your schooling, which you carried to its end by becoming a teacher and crammer. My education was entirely aesthetic: I learnt nothing at school, and loathed it. It kept me from becoming a young gangster; but it did this by imprisoning me; and I have never forgiven it. I have at last come definitely to believe that all effective education is aesthetic, and that the Materialistic Mechanistic science which you had to get up for school purposes was all wrong. As an aesthetic worker I claim to be scientifically a biologist and an economist, my laboratory, or rather my observatory being the wide world in which the events are not put-up jobs (see Love and Mr Lewisham) and, barring mere accidents, their cause is always in the future and never in the past. In short I understand why we differ; so there is no harm done, as I am careful to say nothing about it; for the idea must not get about that the Wellsians and Shavians have any differences. They are in fact the same body.

We are quiet here. Up to last November we had a searchlight here with the result that every raid began on us: we have several craters to shew. But I.C.I. took a house here. The searchlight was taken away. Whether the two events were connected I dont know; but since then we have had no bombs. Frank is nearer the viaduct, which is a target; but it is of less importance now that there is an alternative line. We presume you are well, as anything happening to you would be in the papers. I havent been in London for months. *My* imagination is nearly dead; I forget everything in ten minutes; and my weight has fallen to 9 stone; but I keep up a stage effect of being an upstanding old man. I am not unhappy in spite of this senseless war, though I ought to be dead, and am not in the least troubled by that fact.

Always yours
G.B.S.

PS I havnt written a play for nearly two years. I am by no means sure that I shall ever write another.

As the Babes was really an exhaustive letter to me, this is an acknowledgment, and need not be acknowledged, as you must have something better to do.

Read my letter in today's Times. It is not about the war.

Phillip Henry Kerr (1882–1940), Marquess of **Lothian**, was, like Shaw, a member of a group organized by Nancy **Astor** that toured the Soviet Union in 1931. Shaw's reference to **Finland** concerns the 1940 war by which the USSR seized strategic territories belonging to Finland. Benedetto **Croce** (1866–1952) was an Italian philosopher and historian, and a leading opponent of fascism. **I.C.I.** was a large manufacturer of war materials. Shaw's **letter to the *Times***, occupying a full column, was about the reform of English spelling and the alphabet.

130 / To G. Bernard Shaw

13 Hanover Terrace, Regent's Park NW1
18th April 1941

[ALS: Texas]

Presumably Wells had seen the film version of Major Barbara, recently released. His new book was Guide to the New World Order: A Handbook of Constructive Revolution.

My dear G.B.S.

I was going to write to you today – our minds move in sympathy. I saw Major Barbara on Monday and I found it delightful. You have given it fresh definition. Andrew Undershaft might have been better cast with a more subtle face. As it is he seems to be astonished at himself throughout. The house was packed. Moura & I got the last two seats & you could not have had a more responsive audience. They laughed at all the right places. Mostly young people in uniform they were. That old Fabian audience is scattered forevermore. I firmly believe that we are getting the young. We shall rise again sooner than Marx did & for a better reason.

Pavlof was invincibly like you. You will probably be compared by posterity. He talked almost as well. But he wrote damnable prose. I was never educated by any sort of schooling. I left school at thirteen. Afterwards I did biological work at the R.C.S. but the nearest I came to 'Materialistic Mechanistic Science' was a half year in the Physics course at Kensington. It bored me so much that I learnt Latin & German & matriculated while it was going on. It is a pity you never had a sound dose of biology. Still, you do pretty well as you are.

This getting old is tiresome. I dont feel old in my wits but my heart seems to falter & I have phases of brain anemia when I forget names & all that small print stuff. I've written a Guide to the New World Order which Gollancz will publish in a week or so & I am writing a novel. So get on with your play.

My warmest love to Charlotte.

Whatever happens now we have had a pretty good time.

Yours as ever
H.G.

I'm asking my daughter in law to type a copy of this for your convenience in reading.

131 / To H.G. Wells Ayot St Lawrence, Welwyn, Herts.
20th April 1941

[ALS: Illinois]

The signature has been cut away from this letter. The document enclosed with it was typed, with the names of Murray, Shaw, and Wells in capital letters by Shaw at the end. The Bishop of Chichester had written to the Times *on 17 April in support of an appeal made by the Pope denouncing the atrocity of the war. The bishop proposed that the British Government begin with a pledge to refrain from night bombing, 'provided that the German Government will give the same undertaking. If this single limitation were achieved it would at least make a halt in the world's rushing down to ever deeper baseness and confusion.'*

My dear Wells

How would it do to send the enclosed to the Press from the three of us? Churchill has lost his temper (his most dangerous weakness); and the papers I have read are all utterly demoralized. It is a complete rout, and a triumph for Hitler.

Somebody must say something cool, no matter what it is. Besides, I think we are bound to come to the rescue of the Bishop of Chichester.

We three can make an impression that no other combination could, and that we could not make singly.

I am duplicating this to Gilbert Murray.

[*signature cut away*]

[*Enclosure*]

Cui Bono?

Sir,

First, may we make clear that though we are about to propose an arrangement with the Axis, it is not in the nature of an armistice or a statement of war aims or anything else that could be interpreted as a symptom of weakening on the part of the Allies. Nor is it a new departure.

As a precedent we cite the dealings between our postal authorities and those of the enemy by which at last prisoners of war on both sides are receiving letters from home with certainty and regularity in three weeks after their date. This enormous improvement on the pre-existing state of things could not have been effected without negotiations which, if not precisely cordial, were governed by a reciprocal disposition to listen to reason and make a bargain benefiting the belligerents equally.

The postal arrangement must have been explicit; but there are tacit arrangements which might as well be made explicit. There is, for instance, the unwritten agreement not to resort to gas or pathogenic germs, as neither side could gain any advantage from them (they could be home made cheaply to any extent) and both would be intolerably plagued by them. There is the understanding that neither side shall try to exterminate the other by the selected slaughter of its women. There is, in short, no such thing as all in fighting, which would at once reduce the war to absurdity.

But there are other methods of warfare which not only cannot produce a decision but are positively beneficial to the side against which they are directed. The bombardment of cities from the air may be one of them. Its conditions are quite unprecedented. Both victory and defeat are impossible, because the vanquished cannot surrender, and the victor must run for home at 300 miles an hour, pursued by fighters at 400 miles an hour. The recent bombardments of Berlin and London, though quite successful as such, have not produced any military result beyond infuriating the unfortunate inhabitants. Some of them have been killed. If raids could be maintained nightly, and each raid killed 1000 persons, half of them women, it would take over a century to exterminate us, and a century and a half to exterminate the Germans. Meanwhile, as both sides are depending for victory on famine by blockade, the reduction in the number of mouths to be fed would be a relief to us. If the Germans, instead of dropping tens of thousands of bombs on us, had parachuted thousands of live babies, they would have embarrassed us and reduced our food supplies much more effectively. But as we should retaliate in kind, we should solve our evacuation problem at Germany's expense. We apologize for the extravagance of the suggestion; but we hope it will help to raise the question whether if every city in Europe were wiped out the victory which both sides are determined to win would be one step nearer.

As to the specific case [*course?*] which the War Cabinet has been provoked into taking: to wit, the threat to demolish Rome if Athens or Cairo be attacked from the air, it forces us to ask whether Rome does not belong to the culture of the whole world far more than to the little Italian speaking group of Benitos and Beppos who at present are its local custodians. By destroying it we should be spiting the noses to vex the faces of every educated person in the British Commonwealth and in America, to say nothing of the European mainland. We may smash it for the Italians; but who is to give it back to us? No one is a stranger and a foreigner: we all feel when we first go there that we are revisiting the scene of a former existence.

As to the effect of the threat, surely the way to save Athens and Cairo is not to defy Herr Hitler to bombard them, and thus make it a point of honor for him to reply by a shower of bombs on them. He, far from the seven hills, may even echo the late Lord Clanricarde's reply to his Irish tenants 'If you think you can intimidate me by shooting my agent you are very much mistaken'. Athens can be pulverized without touching the Acropolis as easily as Rome without touching the Vatican; but our spiritual ally the Pope can be frightfully inconvenienced by having St.

Peter's and the Vatican stormed by Romans seeking shelter just as in London the Underground was stormed.

That we should in the same breath indignantly deny that our last raid on Berlin was a reprisal, and announce a major reprisal which must have staggered the historical conscience of the world, shews that our heads are not as clear as they might be on this subject. The more we endeavour to think it out the more we find ourselves driven to the conclusion that whatever may be said from the military point of view for our treatment of Bremen, Hamburg and Kiel, there is nothing to be said for the demolition of metropolitan cities as such, and that the Bishop of Chichester's plea for a reconsideration of that policy is entirely justified.

Yours truly
MURRAY
SHAW
WELLS

George Gilbert Aimé **Murray** (1866–1957) was for many years Regius Professor of Greek at Oxford. One of the best-known classical scholars of his time, he was especially famous for his translations of Greek plays and his part in bringing about stage performances of them – an activity that brought him into close association and a lifelong friendship with Shaw. After the First World War he devoted much of his life to the cause of peace and was chairman of the League of Nations Union from 1923 to 1938. Ulick de Burgh, 5th Earl and Marquess of **Clanricarde** (1604–57) was an Irish Roman Catholic royalist who tried to unite the Roman Catholics and Protestants in loyalty to King Charles I. He made peace with Cromwell in 1652.

132 / To G. Bernard Shaw

13 Hanover Terrace
22nd April 1941

[TLS: Illinois]

My dear G.B.S.

No. I will not do anything of the sort. You will keep on assuming that man is a rational being whereas he is nothing of the sort. At present the whole species is mad, that is to say mentally out of adjustment to its environment. We are, as a people, a collection of unteachable dullards at war with an infectious lunatic and his victims. Your letter will not be *read* by half a dozen people. It will be misunderstood. Also I *detest* Rome. I dont care if all the treasures in the world are ground to powder. (This is between ourselves.) I want to see humanity de-cultivated and making a fresh start. Culture is merely the ownership of stale piddle. Mantegna, Brahms, my Tang horse, St. Paul's Cathedral, I rank a little higher than the lavender smelling correspondence of my nicer great-aunts. I'd like to keep them but not if they lead to idolatry.

Bless you
H.G.

133 / To H.G. Wells Ayot St Lawrence, Welwyn, Herts.
23rd April 1941

[ALS: Illinois]

Still, you *do* write Babes and other things and put your name to them (so do I); and I see no reason why you should not put your name to this unless the writing, being senile, is not good enough, in which case you can rewrite it to your taste.

Murray has not replied: he must be away from home. If he agrees, you *must* sign; for if I am forced to go ahead single handed, or even double, it will not have one tenth the weight of the complete trio, not to mention its novelty.

If you dont you will never forgive yourself.

That is how I see it.

G.B.S.

134 / To H.G. Wells Ayot St Lawrence, Welwyn, Herts.
24th April 1941

[ALS: Illinois]

Murray will sign if I omit paragraph 3, page 1, and the last 7½ lines of par. 4, p.1. Also the 7½ lines on p. 2 about the Vatican and the Underground. On those conditions he will sign, with or without you. Of course I will cut as he desires: in fact I should have cut these Shavian touches myself.

Phone or wire me tomorrow on receipt of this to say that I may put your name to it and send it off to The Times. I am quite certain you ought to; and, as you know, I am infallible when I speak *ex cathedra.*

G.B.S.

At the bottom of this letter the word NO is printed and circled, presumably by Wells.

135 / To H.G. Wells

Post Office Telegram
[*Stamped* 'handed in 24 Ap. 41' *and* 'N.W.D.O. 25 Apr.41 N.W.1' (*date of delivery*)]

[Illinois]

CODICOTE HI
WELLS 13 HANOVER SQUARE NW
YOUR LETTER IS GLORIOUS NONSENSE STRIKE OUT LINES 13 TO 21 AND 35 TO 42 ON FIRST PAGE AND 13 TO 17 ON SECOND IN THIS MUCH IMPROVED CONDITION MURRAY WILL SIGN LETTER WHICH MUST GO TO THE TIMES TOMORROW TRUST OUR JUDGMENT AND WIRE THAT I MAY ADD YOUR NAME TO OURS IT WILL MAKE ALL THE DIFFERENCE IN THE WORLD – SHAW

136 / To H.G. Wells

Ayot St Lawrence, Welwyn, Herts.
8th May 1941

[TLS: Illinois]

The signature of this letter has been cut away. On Monday, 28 April, The Times *published the 'Cui Bono?' letter after subjecting it to a good deal of cutting, and substituting the heading 'Bombing of Cities' for Shaw's proposed title. It was published without comment, over the names 'Gilbert Murray' and 'G. Bernard Shaw.' The location of Wells's letter to which Shaw here replies is unknown.*

My dear H.G.

Chiozza Money has suddenly risen from oblivion with a typed circular at the outset of which he quotes you as having advocated the bombing of enemy cities some time ago. I did not know this when I urged you to sign the letter to The Times. I should have urged you all the same (Mr. Britling's second thoughts were best); but I should have mentioned it. Anyhow Churchill's characteristic splutter about Rome was a new departure and a moral mistake; and it did not affect the spear point of the letter, which was that experience had now proved that retaliatory bombing, equally mischievous to both parties, cannot produce either victory or defeat, and as a matter of fact produces the sort of exasperative demoralization that neither of them is aiming at.

Your letter had nothing in it to stop me bothering you; so for the moment I ignored it. It said that as a sane man in a world of lunatics you would not waste your time preaching. But if you have to live with lunatics you have to learn how to manage them; and one of the ways is by writing letters to The Times. That is why I do it, though I go farther than you in doubting whether man can ever succeed as a political animal, and console myself with the reflection that as there is no reason to fear that Evolution has played its last card, mankind may be superseded by a higher species and scrapped as the dinosaurs were scrapped.

Your other point, that man must be decivilized and recivilized from the ground up, is a return to Marx's rival Bakunin, who preached the same doctrine in a very fascinating manner. It was the climax of Nihilism and Anarchism, and had quite a little Party in the Fabian Society until Webb and I extinguished it. Decivilized mankind, being the children of its bourgeois parents, would reach Socialism by the same old road through the valley of dry bones; so that the return to the starting point would be sheer waste of time. Until you get round this objection the question remains where Bakunin left it.

The Times evidently did not like the letter; for it did not allow a correspondence to follow, though it must have had lots of replies. We had a fairly good press, considering. I am sorry I failed to get you into the cart with Murray, as he is an authentic sage and saint from Australia; and his translations not only bring the Greek playwrights to life and light (modern light) again, but have the finest sort of literary beauty. I think Ruskin, Morris, and Murray will be finally classed as saints: a very necessary category.

How will it class us?

[*signature cut off*]

Sir Leo Chiozza **Money** (1870–1944) was an economist who had been a prominent Liberal MP (1906–18). Early in the war Wells had advocated the bombing of Berlin and other Axis cities. **Mr. Britling** was the hero of Wells's largely autobiographical novel of the First World War, *Mr. Britling Sees It Through* (1916). Mikhail **Bakunin** (1814–76) was a militant revolutionary Russian anarchist.

137 / To G. Bernard Shaw 13 Hanover Terrace, Regent's Park NW1
29th July 1941

[ALS: BL 50552 f 67]
GBS's 85th birthday was July 26.

Dear G.B.S.

We are above astronomy & I see no reason for congratulating you for your return to some particular point in the world's orbit. Nevertheless until the autumnal solstice you are 11 (eleven) years older than I am. Then I pull into the seventy-five class & its 10 again. My warmest love to Charlotte and the both of you.

H.G.

138 / To G. Bernard Shaw 13 Hanover Terrace, Regent's Park NW1
28th September 1941

[ALS: BL 50552 f 68]
In 1937 there was first published a small book with the forbiddingly long but sufficiently descriptive title The Birth of Language: Its Place in World Evolution and its Structure in Relation to Space and Time. *It was a study by Professor Richard Albert Wilson (1874–1949), of the University of Saskatchewan. Shaw wrote about it to Beatrice Webb in February 1941: 'Professor Wilson of the University of Sascatchewan [*sic*] in the city of Saskatoon (of which I had never heard) sent me a book called* The Birth of Language, *which was so up-to-date and emancipated from the damnable post-Darwinian Materialism cum Determinism, that I immediately urged Dent to publish a cheap edition, and offered to write a preface. This preface has taken me a goodish while.'* (CL, *Vol. 4, pp. 595–6). The edition with Shaw's preface was published later in that year by Dent for the British Publishers' Guild, with the title* The Miraculous Birth of Language.

My dear G.B.S.

Why didn't you pick up a little biology from me instead of entangling your richly sensitive mind in the spite systems of old Samuel Butler? Your man is a mucky reader. He seems to be totally ignorant of your double Pavloff (and of *Babes in the Darkling Wood*) & to have got his ideas of Behaviourism from that bloke Watson. He sits away there in Saskatoon & probably he doesnt turn over his ideas to a living soul once a year. I am, by the bye, quoting you to the British Association as a great authority on Phonetics. You are.

Bless you. My warmest love to Charlotte.

H.G.

John Broadus **Watson** (1878–1958), professor at Johns Hopkins University, originated the behaviourist school of psychology.

139 / To H.G. Wells

Ayot St Lawrence, Welwyn, Herts.
30th September 1941

[ALS: Illinois]

I am not much of a phonetician; but, to my great astonishment, I find myself eminent as a biologist. But as Marx said of Mill, my eminence is an illusion produced by the flatness of the surrounding country.

I have gone carefully through Pavlov again, and find that I only half realized what a damned fool his Druidical reflex made of him. This reflex, and the anti-God reaction, have reduced biological thought to mischievous imbecility throughout our lifetime. Butler was not spiteful about it: he was *horrified*. His feeling about it was too deep for his mere bad manners – deeper even than his hatred of his father.

G.B.S.

140 / To H.G. Wells

Ayot St Lawrence, Welwyn, Herts.
19th October 1941

[ALS: Illinois]

What elicited this note of advice from GBS to Wells is unknown.

In 1888, in Bath, I read a Fabian Essay to the Economic Section of the B.A. When my turn came, the secretary (Palgrave) told me none too civilly that there was no time for my lecture and that I must either cut it short or, preferably, cut it out and let it be taken as read.

I got up and told the audience what I had just heard. I added that the nature of my paper did not admit of abridgment, and that I should read it just as it stood, and ask the chairman to stop me when my time was exhausted.

I then read the paper at the fullest of full length, and saw and heard no more of poor Pal, who must have soon realized, too late, that it was I who had drawn the big house, and that it would have taken more than his or the chairman's nerve to stop me.

Make a note of this effective counter.

G.B.S.

Sir Robert Harry Inglis **Palgrave** (1827–1919), banker and economist, served for a time as secretary of the Economics Section of the British Association. The paper read by Shaw at Bath on 7 September 1888 was 'The Transition to Social Democracy,' published in the November issue of *Our Corner* and in *Fabian Essays in Socialism* (1889).

141 / To H.G. Wells

Ayot St Lawrence, Welwyn, Herts.
3rd January 1941 [1942]

[TLS: Illinois]

In dating this letter, Shaw overlooked the fact that a new year had begun. While Norman and Jeanne MacKenzie in The Time Traveller *accept Shaw's date, the reply from Wells makes it clear that the year was 1942.*

My dear H.G.

On page 154 Tavistock should be Torrington, as it afterwards becomes. I think Ampthill would be better; for I cannot imagine Tewler living south of the Euston Road in professional literary Bloomsbury.

On page 181 Tannhäuser should be Lohengrin. The Tannhäuser march is a festival one: the wedding march is in Lohengrin.

I read the book bang through very quickly and found it positively rollicking. Perhaps that is because I am on the same subject myself. I am writing a book on the things people should know before they are allowed to have any part in Government except ventilation of grievances. In one of my later plays called Geneva I introduced a female

Tewler named Begonia Brown, illustrating my old remark that Votes For Women was a *reductio ad absurdum* of democracy. Adult Suffrage means the Dictatorship of the Tewlerariat, prostrate before Churchill and Hitler: Horatio Bottomley, Titus Oates and Lord George Gordon being no longer available. Mental oligarchy, self-elected, has produced Stalin, before whom Tewler falls equally prostrate (he can understand a One Man Show); but when Stalin dies we may see again what happened when Henri Quatre and Charles II died. We have to find constitutional forms that will get over this difficulty. Tewler will never be free until he is disfranchized.

What your book needs to complete it is an election at which Tewler has a real choice between a Bottomley and an ordinary cut-and-dried plutocrat. Begonia Brown's political career is a vital part of Geneva. I should have been tempted to make Tewler end as a dictator.

As I am very dotty in my 85th year my book will be only a book of senile ramblings and repetitions (just the thing for Tewler). You must take up the running as to adult suffrage. The snag in the Declaration of Rights is that as all the terms are abstract everybody agrees because they may mean anything: that is, nothing. I am trying to bring it down to tin tacks.

Anyhow the Tewler book amused me, and is very reassuring as to your being still in prime condition.

By the way, why do you and St. John Ervine hate Marx so virulently? 'Lousy Jew' is St. John's kindest word for him. He made a few technical mistakes which dont matter; and he had no legislative or administrative experience; but he lifted the golden lid off hell when Europe was glorying in what it called its prosperity; and it took more than a mere lousy Jew to do that.

This is only a hasty scrawl: forgive it.

The first Mrs. Wells is becoming quite a public character in Kimpton.

GBS

Wells's novel *You Can't Be Too Careful* was published in 1941, its protagonist being Albert **Tewler**, reminiscent of Kipps. The **book** on which Shaw was working was *Everybody's Political What's What* (1944). Lord George **Gordon** (1751–1793), an anti-Catholic conspirator, fomented the Gordon Riots. The deaths of **Henri Quatre** (1553–1610), king of France, and of **Charles II** (1630–85), king of England, were both followed by periods of civic unrest and political dispute, sometimes violent, over the question of succession.

142 / To G. Bernard Shaw 13 Hanover Terrace, Regent's Park NW1
5th January 1942

[ALS: Hofstra]

My dear G.B.S.

If ever you are out of a job & want to turn an honest penny I am always ready to offer you one as proof reader. I'm delighted to hear of your next book. Brains that keep active dont seem to decay but the damned circulation & so forth falters as the years go on. We dont react so well & we have to pause for the lagging stimulus but when we are there we are there – to judge by you as good as ever. How is Charlotte? Please give her my love & greetings for the New Year.

Why does Ervine call Marx a Jew? He was an extremely snobbish Christian who never succeeded in understanding the Trade Union mentality. Engels had ten times his intelligence.

I dont understand your last sentence 'The first Mrs Wells is becoming quite a public character in Kimpton.' The first Mrs Wells, my cousin, died some years ago of insulin poisoning. We were very good friends to the end & saw a lot of each other[.] Is someone personating her or what?

Bless you & Begonia Brown.

H.G.

The parents of Karl **Marx** (1818–83) were Jews who had been converted to Protestant Christianity in Germany. Marx was baptized at the age of six. Wells married his **cousin** Isabel in October 1891 and they were divorced in January 1895. After a break of a few years, in which she remarried, they adopted a friendly relationship and Wells was generous with financial help to her and her second husband, Fowler-Smith. (See *Experiment in Autobiography*, chap. 7.)

143 / To H.G. Wells Ayot St Lawrence, Welwyn, Herts.
16th March 1942

[ALS: Illinois]

Wells's The Outlook for Homo Sapiens *had just been published.*

I was on the point of writing to you about the new Sapiens book when a weekly called The Tribune, which I have never seen, but understand is a Stafford Cripps organ, wrote to me for a review of it, mentioning 1000 words as all they wanted. Of course the book could not be reviewed in less than 10,000, if in that; but I felt I must do it to prevent some young person who regards us as back numbers doing it worse, and proving incapable of interesting readers in himself or anyone else. So I have fired off what I hope will prove a selling notice – not a review but readable gossip about us two. At least that is what I intended; but I am too old to know whether I can still write or not. Having a book of my own on hand I am curious to know whether people will pay eight & sixpence nowadays. I dont know what to charge.

G.B.S.

Sir Stafford **Cripps** (1889–1952) was a corporation lawyer and prominent Labour politician. At the time when Shaw's letter was written he was under expulsion from the Labour party but was serving as lord privy seal and leader of the Commons in the Churchill government. Shaw's **review** appeared in the Tribune on 27 March under the title 'The Testament of Wells.' It is reproduced as part of this collection's 'Afterword' (pp. 216–19).

144 / To G. Bernard Shaw 13 Hanover Terrace, Regent's Park NW1
21st March 1942

[ALS: Hofstra]

After the long break in their friendship following the Fabian Society affair, Wells and the Webbs had gradually resumed more or less friendly relations in the 1930s, in part because of the Shaws. Beatrice did not overcome her distaste for the sexual liberty that Wells exercised, or accept many of his political views, but she admired his imaginative genius and his generous dedication to socialist causes to which she had given her life. Six months before her death in April 1943 she wrote in her diary, 'GBS and H.G. Wells cannot stop writing; they will die with an unfinished book on their desk.'

Dear G.B.S.

I opened my Tribune this morning with bright expectations, but I see they have put you off for a week in order to stimulate their sales. Whatever you write (though I know it will be good) will please me. As we of the old gang grow older we grow more affectionate. I write nice love letters to Beatrice & wonder why it was we were ever antagonists. The Tribune is a threepenny paper that sells for sixpence.

You say you feel old now – partly thats the normal spring depression – but I dont see a quiver in your handwriting – none of that shakiness you get in the later Shakespeare signatures.

About book prices. Put them high I say, because your book will be kept & lent. The shortage of paper (damn that bloody fool Beaverbrook's 'paper chase') prevents large editions & reprints anyhow. People & the libraries will pay 10/6 now just as readily as 7/6. That *Outlook for Homo Sapiens* is already nearly sold out. We shant reprint. The T.B. Club will be selling copies at 5/– or 6/– & very few at that.

My warmest regards to you both. Do you remember a letter you sent me once proposing an exchange of wives? [*See pp. 37–8. What Shaw proposed was not precisely an 'exchange.'*] Anyhow I adore Charlotte.

And am
most affectionately yours
H.G.

The **T.B. Club** was the Times Book Club.

145 / To H.G. Wells

4 Whitehall Court, London SW1
4th August 1943

[ALS: Illinois]

We are up here in town for the first time since the big blitz, and expect to be fixed for a few weeks to give our Ayot staff a holiday.

Charlotte is terribly crippled with her *osteitis deformans*: moving her up was quite an adventure; but it came off successfully and she is happier here, and in her dotty moments asks me when you are coming to see her. At 86 and 87 we are not fit to be seen by anybody; but we must fix up something.

Webb is pretty lonely down at Passfield, reading incessantly but unable to think or write – or so he says.

I dont think the pamphlet was stinted of paper more than was inevitable. I am losing no opportunity of backing Russia. I have a book in the press; but the corrections are costing more than the setting-up through my senile blunderings. I ought to be dead!

G.B.S.

In 1929 Sidney Webb was created Baron **Passfield**. Beatrice declined such recognition and in an entry in her diary – at Ayot St Lawrence on 29 June that year – referred with amusement to 'the episode of "Mrs Sidney Webb," wife of Lord Passfield.' She was similarly amused – but must also have been pleased – when Wells, on her eightieth birthday, wrote of her in the *New Statesman* as 'a Great Lady ... the greatest lady I have ever met.' She died on 30 April 1943; Sidney, who had suffered a partial stroke in 1938, died 13 October 1947. The **pamphlet** referred to was probably Wells's *Crux Ansata. An Indictment of the Roman Catholic Church* (1943).

146 / To G. Bernard Shaw

[*No address*]
7th August 1943

[TLS(c): Illinois]

Wells's handwritten draft of the following letter to Shaw, on plain paper, was presumably transcribed and sent to be typed by Marjorie, who continued to be his secretary. Wells had responded promptly to Shaw's suggestion of a visit. The 'documents' were the two versions (1940 and 1944) of Wells's The Rights of Man. *On the same page as the draft letter to Shaw, Wells drafted a letter to the physician Dr R.D. Lawrence. It would not have been sent to GBS, but is nevertheless appended here.*

Dear G.B.S

I think you will like to see these documents. I will communicate with Lawrence & let you know about him in due course. It was delightful to find you in such good form & Charlotte so much better than I had expected.

Drink.
Yours ever

[*The copy is unsigned, but has Wells's instructions*:
Send Shaw
The *Rights of Man* revised up to date
The *Natural Rights of Man*
I sign]

My Dear Robin

G.B.S. is in London for a few weeks. He's very sprightly but poor Charlotte has some obscure disease of the bones that has shrunken her to a half of her former size. G.B.S. ought to be living on beeftea & alcohol. He has gradually lost his former antagonism to doctors based largely on vivisection & he explains that 'these new doctors' are very different from the old. Would you care to have tea with them one day at Whitehall Court & have an argey-bargey with the old man? He *wants* a doctor & he wants some one who would discuss his health with him. I told him how you never dogmatised with me & discussed everything with me. 'That's the man I want,' he said. Maybe you dont want to be Physician in Ordinary to G.B.S. for his last year or so of life, but I think he'd be grateful if you were. He hates the fear of death; he hates infirmity & he has a sort of insanity about money. You have been warned.

[*Again, the draft carries Wells's directive,* 'I sign.']

147 / To H.G. Wells [*no address*]

12/9/1943

[TLS: Illinois]

Although in her last days Charlotte hallucinated much, sometimes imagining that she and GBS had returned to Ayot, her death occurred at Whitehall Court.

Charlotte died this [*Sunday*] morning at 2:30. You saw what she had become when you last visited us: an old woman bowed and crippled, furrowed and wrinkled, and greatly distressed by hallucinations of crowds in the room, evil persons, and animals. Also by breathlessness, as the osteitis closed on her lungs. She got steadily worse. The prognosis was terrible, ending with double pneumonia.

But on Friday evening a miracle began. Her troubles vanished. Her visions ceased. Her furrows and wrinkles smoothed out. Forty years fell off her like a garment. She had thirty hours of happiness and heaven. Even after her last breath she shed another twenty years, and now lies young and incredibly beautiful. I have to go in and look at her and talk affectionately to her. I did not know I could be so moved.

Do not tell a soul until Thursday when all will be over. I could not stand flowers and letters and a crowd at Golders Green.

G.B.S.

148 / To G. Bernard Shaw 13 Hanover Terrace, Regent's Park NW1
13th September 1943

[ALS]

Wells ignored Shaw's reference to letters to the extent of sending him a very brief note immediately, and another on the following day.

My dear G.B.S.

Life has to end and I am glad dear Charlotte just went to sleep and thought no more about it. Life told me life has to end but you two have had a great time & done some fine things.

yrs ever
H.G.

149 / To G. Bernard Shaw [*no address*]
14th September 1943

[ALS]

My dear Shaw

Thank you for your letter. People who have really lived into our lives never die. Often they influence us more after they are 'dead' than when they are everyday companions. I still think quite often 'Jane wouldnt stand for this' or 'How shall I tell this to Jane?' It is as if she had just gone into another room. I think Charlotte was the sanest, most generous & loveable person I have ever known. I lose her & I grieve because she has gone out of my world for ever. But she will never go out of yours.

You may last a long time yet G.B.S. & there are still many things you can do in this distracted world.

yrsever [*sic*]
H.G.

150 / To G. Bernard Shaw 13 Hanover Terrace, Regent's Park NW1
5th September 1944

[TLS: Texas]

Wells refers to the photograph by Yousuf Karsh of Ottawa, taken in 1944, that became a frontispiece for Everybody's Political What's What. *In accordance with the custom that occasioned the first letter in this volume of correspondence, Wells was among the first to receive a copy of the book. His reference to translation concerns a passage that Shaw calls 'Pavlov's own account' of the method of vivisection, in chapter 23.*

My dear Shaw,

In the interest of artistic photography you must never die. Your wicked old face in the frontispiece is the best piece of camera work you have ever inspired. I'm glad I perused the book and later on I will send you a comment or so on it. You forget my Gip knows Russian fairly well & that the abominable translation into English which is really a school paraphrase, became lucid under this circumstance.

In the meanwhile bless you

yours ever
H.G.

151 / To G. Bernard Shaw

7 Buckland Crescent
London NW3
21st August 1946

[ALS: BL 50552 f 69]

Letter on Wells's Hanover Terrace letterhead, address deleted. Wells died on 13 August 1946. He was cremated at Golders Green three days later. At the ceremony, J.B. Priestley spoke, in a brief eulogy, of Wells's 'passionate loyalty for the whole toiling, contriving, endlessly hopeful family of Mankind.' An obituary written earlier by Shaw for the New York Journal-American *appeared 14 August and was published in the* New Statesman *on the day after the cremation. Unable to attend, Shaw had written a brief message to Gip.*

Dear Shaw:

Very many thanks for your kind postcard – and also for your obituary in the New Statesman which we appreciated. The letters of sympathy and public tributes have been a real help and consolation to us in this distressing time.

Though he had been ill for a long while, H.G. died suddenly. He had been very low, then he seemed to improve and we all thought he was going to rally miraculously (as he had done before) and live to see his 80th birthday. But after being quite bright and cheerful in the morning, and moving round his room and so on, in the afternoon he lay down on his bed to rest, and in a few minutes he had quietly died.

It was sad that you could not be at Golders Green. We will send you a copy of Priestley's address, which was very good, when we get them. Sad also that you did not see him recently. He was 'difficult' about making appointments, and his condition and mood varied very much. The best way was to ring up Marjorie in the morning (my wife and his secretary) and say, 'May I drop in this afternoon?' But it is too late to talk about that.

Thanks again,

Gip Wells

We had to call the cremation 'private' for obvious reasons, but we think that there should be some sort of public ceremony later on – say in late September, when the holiday season is over. We don't quite know at the moment how to get started on this but will write to you again later.

[*The following is the obituary by Shaw.*]

THE MAN I KNEW

So our H.G. is no more. He has written his own epitaph and his own biography, which is, like most autobiographies more candid than any second-hand account of him is likely to be; and I shall not attempt to paraphrase it. But as I knew the man – and he could not have recorded the impression he made on me even if that had been his intention – I record it myself for what it is worth.

H.G. was not a gentleman. Nobody understood better than he what gentry means: his Clissold novel proves this beyond question. But he could not, or would not, act the part. No conventional social station fitted him. His father was a working gardener and professional cricketer. His mother was a housekeeper, and by his own account not a very competent one. The two kept a china shop in Bromley, from the basement of which the infant H.G. contemplated the bootsoles of the inhabitants through a grating in the pavement, and noted that they were mostly worn out. Lower middle class, you will say: a father who in the cricket field was denied the title of Mister, and a mother who was a domestic servant, small shopkeepers both: could anything be more *petit bourgeois*, as Lenin labelled H.G.? His glimpses of high life were gained in his visits to the country house in which his mother was employed; and there he must have been a bit of a pet, though his references to it in later life were anything but grateful. He began to earn his living as a linen draper's shopman, this being in his mother's opinion a high destiny for him. Many years later, when he made his first essay as a public speaker, he kept behind the chairman's table and addressed the audience leaning across it with his fingers splayed on it in a 'What's the next article?' attitude. He rose to be a schoolmaster; graduated as a science student, winning a B.Sc.; and presently, like Dickens and Kipling, left it all behind and found himself a great popular story teller, freed for ever from pecuniary pressure, and with every social circle in the kingdom open to him. Thus he became entirely classless; for though Erbert Wells had become H.G. Wells, Esquire, he never behaved like a gentleman, nor like a shop assistant, nor like a schoolmaster, nor like anyone on earth but himself. And what a charmer he was!

In one category, however, I can place him. He was the most completely spoiled child I have ever known, not excepting even Lord Alfred Douglas, who, having been flogged at Eton, had had to bear criticism at least once, though indeed neither of them could bear it at all. This puzzled people who regarded Wells's youth as one of genius chastened by poverty and obscurity. As a matter of fact it was one of early promotion from the foot of the ladder to the top without a single failure or check. He never missed a meal, never wandered through the streets without a penny in his pocket, never had to wear seedy clothes, never was unemployed, and was always indulged as more or less of an infant prodigy. When he reproached me for being a snob and a ready-made gentleman, I had to tell him that he knew nothing of the horrors of chronic impecuniosity in the progeny of the younger sons of the feudal class who had the pretensions and obligations of gentility without the means of supporting them. Editors had jumped at his stories and publishers at his novels at the first glance: I wrote five massive novels and had to endure nine years of unrelieved failure, before any considerable publisher would venture on mine. It hardened me until my shell was like iron: H.G. was pampered into becoming the most sensitive plant in the literary greenhouse. His readers imagined that this man who understood everything could pardon everything. In fact the faintest shadow of disapproval threw him into transports of vituperative fury in which he could not spare his most devoted friends.

But do not infer from all this that H.G. was an intolerably unamiable person who made enemies of all his friends. One remembers the saying of Whistler's wife: 'If I die, in twelve months Jimmy will not have a friend left in the world.' Douglas could not live in the same house with his wife, though they lived and died on affectionate terms. Yet H.G. had not an enemy on earth. He was so amiable that, though he raged against all of us none of us resented it. There was no malice in his attacks: they were soothed and petted like the screams and tears of a hurt child. He warned his friends that he went on sometimes like that and they must not mind it. When Beatrice Webb, whom he consulted as to his filling some public position, told him frankly but authoritatively that he had not the manners for it, which was true, he caricatured, abused, vilified and lampooned her again and again; but I never heard her speak unkindly of him; and they ended as the best of friends. He filled a couple of columns of the *Daily Chronicle* on one occasion with abuse of me in terms that would have justified me in punching his head; but when we met next day at a sub-committee of the Society of Authors our intercourse was as cordial as before; it never occurred to me that it could be otherwise, though he entered with obvious misgivings as to his reception, which at once gave way to our normally jolly friendliness.

Nothing could abate his likeableness. I once had to lead the case against him in public debate when he joined the Fabian Society and attacked its leaders (ten years older, tougher and more experienced than he), not only challenging their policy but recklessly defaming their characters and imputing disgraceful motives to them. I forced myself on the committee as its spokesman to save him from being slaughtered by sterner hands. That I easily and utterly defeated him was nothing; it was like boxing with a novice who knocked himself out in every exchange; but the Society, though it did not give him a single vote, reproached me for my forensic ruthlessness and gave all its sympathy to H.G. If he had been the most tactful and self-controlled of mortals he would not have been half so well beloved.

H.G. was honest, sober, and industrious: qualifications not always associated with genius. He loved to assemble young people and invent new games for them, or referee the old ones, whistle in hand, as became the son of his father. In an age of masters of the art of conversation like Chesterton, Belloc, and Oscar Wilde, the Prince of Talkers, he was first-rate company without the least air of giving a performance. Nobody was ever sorry to see him.

His place in literature and in the political movement of his day I must leave to another occasion or to other hands. He foresaw the European war, the tank, the plane, and the atomic bomb; and he may be said to have created the ideal home and been the father of the pre-fabricated house. To Fabian Socialist doctrine he could add little; for he was born ten years too late to be in at its birth pangs: the work had been done in the Old Gang of the Society as well as it could be done. Finding himself only a fifth wheel in the Fabian coach he cleared out, but not before he had exposed very effectively the obsolescence and absurdity of our old parish and county divisions as boundaries of local government areas.

There is no end of the things I might say about him had I space or time. What I have said here is only what perhaps no one else would have said.

G.B.S.

152 / To Dr M. Baxter Ayot St Lawrence, Welwyn, Herts.
17th April 1948

[TLS: Cornell]

A memorial service was held at the Royal Institution on 30 October 1946. In the following year, a committee was formed to promote the establishing of a memorial fellowship in Wells's honour. (Dr Baxter was the secretary of that committee.) The idea was regarded by some of Wells's friends as insufficient, by some as inappropriate, and was eventually dropped. Shaw's mention of a mulberry tree is presumably a reference to the famous tree in Cambridge associated with the memory of John Milton.

Dear Dr Baxter,

I think the Wells Committee's suggestions need further consideration.

First, I detest the practice of sending presents to ourselves in the shape of hospital beds and lectureships on the pretext of commemorating the great. A memorial should be a public monument having no further utility whatever, like the Scott monument in Edinburgh. A statue on Primrose Hill, a bust in Hanover Terrace, or even a mulberry tree in Regent's Park, would be a genuine memorial.

But let that pass.

A Wells Fellowship for the promotion of his ideas is recommended: but what were his specific ideas? Those which took any practical form, the division of our absurd local government areas into planned regions, the tank, the radio-active bomb, need no promotion. His declaration of Human Rights was not a step in advance of Jefferson and Tom Paine 175 years ago, and left him in despair. He chalked up many ideas, but ran away from them when anyone proposed to put them into practice. He attacked his best friends at home and abroad furiously, denouncing Fabianism and Marxism, the Webbs and Stalin, recklessly. Finally his spleen made him, though once the most readable and hope inspiring of authors, almost unreadable and very discouraging.

In short, he was a great author and should be commemorated, but the last man on earth to be the subject of propagandist lectureships, or indeed of any permanent organization.

What we need is money, a sculptor, and a site.

G. Bernard Shaw

Afterword

Shaw outlived Wells by four years. He died on 2 November 1950, and his body was cremated at Golders Green four days later. His ashes were mingled with those of Charlotte and scattered in the grounds of the house at Ayot St Lawrence.

What Wells might have written in an obituary notice had he outlived Shaw is for any reader of the correspondence to imagine, as he or she may wish. In 1945 the *London Daily Express*, in a moment of journalistic foresight, invited the two to write obituary articles about each other. Shaw refused, but Wells agreed, and his article entitled 'G.B.S. – A Memoir by H.G. Wells,' appeared on the day after Shaw's death. Its tone is more personal and unrestrained than that of the usual obituary notice. Yet since Shaw had written a comparable piece entitled 'The Testament of Wells,' published in the *Tribune* on 27 March 1942 (see Letter 143), it may interest readers of their letters to read what the two old men had to say about each other after half a century of sparring. (Shaw's 'real' obituary of Wells follows Letter 151 in this collection.) The pieces are published here in the order in which they were written. They need no annotation except to point out a factual error at the beginning of Wells's memoir and a bad guess at the end. As he had noted in *Experiment in Autobiography* (p. 454), the two men first met at the opening of Henry James's *Guy Domville* (5 January 1895), not Wilde's *The Importance of Being Earnest*, a few weeks later. And the greatest part of Shaw's estate was bequeathed to three great public institutions – but not to a National Theatre for either Shakespeare or G.B.S.

The Testament of Wells

The last sixty years have seen the rise of two new sects, the Wellsians and the Shavians, with a large overlap. The overlap may suggest that as our doctrine must be the same, our mental machinery must be the same also. But in fact no two machines for doing the same work could be more different than our respective brains. Ecologically (H.G.'s favourite word) and intellectually I am a seventeenth-century Protestant Irishman using the mental processes and technical craft of Swift and Voltaire, whilst Wells is an intensely English nineteenth-century suburban cockney, thinking anyhow, writing anyhow, and always doing both uncommonly well. The doctrine in my hands is a structure on a basis of dispassionate economic and biological theory: in his it is a furious revolt against unbearable facts and exasperating follies visible as such to his immense vision and intelligence where the ordinary Briton sees nothing wrong but a few cases that are dealt with by the police. He has neither time nor patience for theorising, and probably agrees with that bishop whose diocese I forget, but who said very acutely that I would never reach the Celestial City because I would not venture beyond the limits of a logical map. These differences between us are very fortunate; for our sermons complement instead of repeating one another; you must read us both to become a complete Wellshavian.

When Wells burst on England there were no Wellshavians; but there were Webbshavians, *alias* Fabians, who had the start of him by ten years, and had the advantage of having been caught by the literature of Socialism when they were just the right age for it; that is to say in their mid-twenties, when he was in his teens, too young to take it in to its full depth.

At first the ten years were all to the bad. Wells, throwing himself into the Fabian movement to reform everything that was wrong in the world as well as the economic system, found himself confronted by a disillusioned Old Gang of wily committee men and practised speakers whose policy it was to keep the Fabian Society to the economic point and head off all excursions into religious controversy, party controversy, and sex controversy. Against this policy Wells hurled himself furiously, smashing down its compromises and platform tricks with a one-man artillery barrage of vituperation, reckless of whether he contradicted himself in every second sentence or even in the same sentence. He called for a society of millions of members and an expenditure of hundred of thousands of pounds. It was a glorious episode in the history of the Society; but the Old Gang, with their ten years' experience and hard training, knew the possibilities only to well; and H.G. shook its dust off his feet after kicking up a prodigious cloud of it, leaving the Old Gang in possession.

He never thereafter worked with any existing Society of practising politicians or became a committee man with committee manners, broken-in to accept the greatest common measure of a council of colleagues as the limit to which things could for the moment be carried, and with an eye always on the jury. He would not fit himself into any movement or party, though he raged through them all, playing for his own hand and leaving his mark wherever there was stuff plastic enough to take an impression. Far from keeping an eye on the jury he no sooner took up a question than he forgot everything and everybody else and charged into it, kicking out of his way everyone, friend and foe, who obstructed him for a moment, and always being forgiven and getting away with it. He insulted all his friends and never lost them, and made no enemies except the simpleton whose enmity hallmarks its object as a friend of humanity. He obeyed no rules of conduct except his own, and scattered his invective in all directions as an R.A.F. pilot scatters bombs; but nobody has ever accused him of doing a malicious injury or being capable of it. He is the most ungovernable man of his rank in ability in England; but his fundamentally noble and generous nature keeps his halo undimmed all the time. And he is the best of good company: one of the few writers of whom it can be said that if his conversation could have been reported and all his books destroyed, the gain to his reputation might have been greater than the loss.

Wells, as a very English Englishman, is subject to attacks of a sort of mental gout or Berserkeritis which the Elizabethans called the spleen, the symptoms of which are in war reckless violence and in peace wild vituperation. When he sickens in this way, woe to the individual whom he dislikes and selects as whipping boy for his educational campaigns. Now it happens most unfortunately and quite unaccountably that his pet aversion is Karl Marx. The story of that famous exile is so pitiable that it hardly bears thinking of by any humane person. Marx's first beloved children died of slow starvation, which wrecked his health and shortened his own life. His two youngest daughters committed suicide. His wife was driven almost crazy by domestic worry. And yet he managed to write a book which changed the mind of the world in favour of Wells and nerved Lenin and Stalin to establish a new civilisation, largely Wellsian, in Russia. Yet Wells, when the fit is on him, loses his head and pursues this unhappy great man with a hatred so foreign to his own nature that one has to laugh it off as brain fever. Mention Marx to him and with the ink still wet on his chapters on the Class War and the woes of 'the unpropertied' he will deny that there is any class war or any such thing as a proletariat, both being Marxian lies. He will belittle the Russian revolution and declare that the vital issue between experimenting with Socialism in a single country and waiting for an impossible world revolution was only a wretched personal squabble between Stalin and Trotsky.

Happily, after raving like this for pages and pages, he comes out at last on the perfectly sound ground that it is England's business not only to make the same inevitable revolution in its own way in its own country (Stalinism) but to make an equally successful job of it without any of the mistakes and violences that would have wrecked Bolshevism had not we and the other western powers rallied Russia to its side by senselessly attacking it and making its leaders national conquerors and saviours as well as international Communists. Which is excellent Fabianism.

If H.G. in the next edition of his Testament will stick to his conclusion and drop his vituperation of Marx with a handsome apology, asking himself what would have become of him and of me if we, luckier than Marx, had not chanced to possess a lucrative knack of writing novels and plays, he will, I think, gain in authority and consistency.

There are moments too when our Protestant anti-clerical habits get the better of Wells's Socialism. He is at the top of his form when he shows that the Reformation is still only half finished; but he is a bit hard on the Roman Catholic Church when he blames it alone for the poverty and ignorance that have made civilisation a disease and that none of the churches have been able to cure. It is true that the Roman Catholic Church, in desperation, had made a merit of 'holy poverty' and pleaded that without it we should be without the virtue of charity, whilst the Protestants have on the contrary made a supreme merit of prosperity ('holy riches'). But both persuasions are equally helpless against the economic consequences of private property. Without an economic Reformation none of the attempts to realise the ideal of a Catholic Church, which has never yet existed in Rome or Geneva or Moscow or anywhere else, will succeed. Meanwhile the Ulster slogan 'To Hell with the Pope' is only a red herring across the trail of Socialism.

I suppose I must honestly conclude by warning readers that my opinion of any work by Wells is so prejudiced in his favour by my personal liking for him that I do not myself know how much it is worth. Anyhow, his books have to be read, and no merely read about.

27th March 1942

G.B.S. – A Memoir by H.G. Wells

I have known G.B.S. intimately since I was for a brief interval dramatic critic – probably the worst dramatic critic who ever criticized – for Harry Cust's Pall Mall Gazette half a century ago. I found myself leaving the theatre side by side in the same direction with a long, lean, red-haired, unconventionally dressed individual whom I knew by sight and name already as the critic of Frank Harris's Saturday Review. I accosted him and we walked up to our respective quarters in Regent's Park together. It was a Wilde play we had seen – 'The Importance of Being Earnest'; and I found everything I had thought out and prepared beforehand entirely unsuitable for the occasion. I had to write something before the pillar box at the corner was cleared at 1 A.M. and send it in a scarlet envelop to the Pall Mall Gazette. I asked him frankly what he thought of the show, and why it was extravagantly not what I had expected from Oscar.

He responded magnificently with a dissertation on the contemporary comedy of manners, pithy, sound, shrewd and convincing, so that by the time I sat down to write I already knew something of the business I had in hand.

That was not Shaw's only contribution to my education. Later on he taught me how to listen to music by insisting that I get a pianola, that even-fingered gorilla, so that I knew the shape and intention of anything I was going to hear beforehand, and could listen unencumbered by structural complications.

But between the dramatic criticism and the pianola there was a long interval, and we had come to a very close friendly antagonism, and endless bickering of essentially antagonistic natures. I was a biologist first and foremost, and Shaw had a physiological disgust at vital activities. He rebelled against them. He detected an element of cruelty, to which I am blind, in sexual matters. This repulsion was mixed up with a passionate hatred of vivisection, so that he would and did misrepresent the work of Pavlov – to whom he had a very strong personal resemblance, bright blue eyes instead of bright brown – quite recklessly. Underlying it all was an impulse to opposition and provocation which was I think fundamental in his made-up.

He got his excitement by rousing a fury of antagonism and then overcoming and defeating it. At that game, which covered a large part of his life, he was unsurpassable.

And now for his most estranging fault. He was ruled by a naked, unqualified, ego-centered, devouring vanity, such as one rarely meets in life. And I found myself asking: Was this egotistical vanity something innate, or did it creep into an essentially combatant nature and take possession of it? Apparently he could not think of any other human being, and particularly any outstanding and famous human being, without immediately referring it directly to himself. And even more manifest was his impulse to establish a dominant relationship to it. 'Shakespeare' is manifestly a synthesis of a group of collaborators, one of whom in particular had a turn for happy language and poetic creations, but Shaw fell into the trap that identifies the author of 'Coriolanus' with the poet of the 'Midsummer Night's Dream,' and found in the collective result a formidable rival who had to be mastered and superseded.

One method of his self-assertion was portraiture. The number of pictures, busts and portraits that encumbered Shaw's establishment was extraordinary. I used to imagine some great convulsion of nature making a new Herculaneum of London. As one art treasure was disinterred after another, the world would come to believe that for a time London was populated entirely by a race of men with a strong physical likeness to the early Etruscans – men with potato noses and a flamboyant bearing.

That was one method of self-assertion peculiar to Shaw. Another, more general, has been practised since Homo sapiens began his career, and that is to inflict pain. Shaw let himself do that to me, in spite of the protests of that most lovable of women, his wife.

I was suddenly recalled to England, which I had just left, by an urgent message from my sons. An operation by Bland Sutton some years before had failed to remove a superficial irritant growth completely, and my wife was suffering from secondary cancer which would end inevitably in her death in six months. I had always expected to die before my wife, and the shock I got was terrific. On the return boat to England, fearing the chance enquiries of friends who might be aboard, I took refuge in a private cabin and there I blubbered like a baby. But this event released a queer accumulation of impulses in Shaw. He was impelled to write that this was all stuff and nonsense on the part of my wife and imply that she would be much to blame if she died. There was no such thing as cancer, and so forth, and so on.

This foolish bit of ruthlessness came to hand, and with it came a letter from Charlotte Shaw, his wife. I was not to mind what he had said, wrote Charlotte. I must not let it hurt either him or myself. He had to do these things. She tried to prevent them, and that was more and more her role as life went on. She had married this perplexing being in a passion of admiration. Her money made the production of his plays good business so that he was speedily independent of her, and she found she had launched that incalculable, lopsided enfant terrible, a man of genius, upon the world.

Dear Charlotte! Her last days were embittered by a distorting disease of the bones which involved deafness and that isolation from the world which deafness can bring. Shaw wept bitterly when she died; he went about London weeping. Most of us older people who have known love know that irreparable sorrow for endless wasted opportunities for kindness and for stupid moments of petty irritation. It might all have been so much better. Shaw drank that cup to the dregs – and then seemed to forget about it. That is the way with us aging men. In the decay of our minds the later acquisitions go first. The Shaw who has just died was the Shaw of twenty years ago. The later Shaw has wept itself away. After his culminating outburst of grief he relapsed to earlier and more flattering associations. But I had no desire to see him now that Charlotte had gone, and after one encounter I avoided him.

His is one of those minds to which money is real and not merely a counter in a game, and I shall not be surprised to find that he has devised his very considerable accumulations to a 'National Theatre' that will glorify * * * Shakespeare-Shaw?

[*written in 1945*]

Table of Correspondents

Unless otherwise noted the letters were written by Bernard Shaw and H.G. Wells

Index

(Since the names of Shaw and Wells appear on most pages of the volume, they are included in the index only where specific works are mentioned.)

www.ingramcontent.com/pod-product-compliance
Lightning Source LLC
Chambersburg PA
CBHW061025120726
47910CB00006B/2101